THE BIG BOOK
of
CHRISTMAS PLAYS

The
Big Book
of Christmas
Plays

21 modern and traditional one-act
plays for the celebration of Christmas

Edited by
Sylvia E. Kamerman

Publishers   PLAYS, INC.   *Boston*

CAUTION

Library of Congress Cataloging-in-Publication Data

The Big Book of Christmas Plays / edited by Sylvia E. Kamerman.
   p. cm.
  Summary: Twenty-one, royalty-free plays about Christmas for ages from elementary through high school. Includes both modern and classic plays.
  ISBN 0-8238-0288-4 : $16.95
  1. Christmas plays. 2. One act plays. 3. Children's plays.
[1. Christmas—Drama. 2. Plays.] I. Kamerman, Sylvia E.
PN6120.C5C5143   1988
808.82′41—dc19   88-15691
                                           CIP
                                           AC

Manufactured in the United States of America

Contents

Junior and Senior High

RED CARPET CHRISTMAS   *Helen Louise Miller*   3

VIDEO CHRISTMAS   *Earl J. Dias*   26

CHRISTMAS EVE LETTER
     Mildred Hark and Noel McQueen   41

A TREE TO TRIM   *Aileen Fisher*   59

CHRISTMAS COAST TO COAST   *Lewy Olfson*   80

A CHRISTMAS PROMISE   *Helen Louise Miller*   99

A STAR IN THE WINDOW
     Mildred Hark and Noel McQueen   118

Middle and Lower Grades

HAPPY CHRISTMAS TO ALL   *Jeannette Covert Nolan*   137

WHATEVER HAPPENED TO GOOD OLD
     EBENEZER SCROOGE?   *Bill Majeski*   151

SANTA CLAUS IS TWINS   *Anne Coulter Martens*   169

THE NORTH POLE COMPUTER CAPER   *Frank V. Priore*   186

WE INTERRUPT THIS PROGRAM . . .   *Claire Boiko*   200

LONG LIVE CHRISTMAS   *Islay Benson*   213

RANDY THE RED-HORNED RAINMOOSE   *Rick Kilcup*   228
CHRISTMAS AT THE CRATCHITS   *Deborah Newman*   240

Puppet Play

SANTA'S MAGIC HAT   *Jane Foster Thornton*   253

Curtain Raiser

THE CHRISTMAS DOUBTERS   *Charles Baker*   265

Christmas Classics

A CHRISTMAS CAROL   *Charles Dickens*   277
    Adapted by *Adele Thane*
SHERLOCK HOLMES' CHRISTMAS GOOSE
    Sir Arthur Conan Doyle   298
    Adapted by *Paul T. Nolan*
LITTLE COSETTE AND FATHER CHRISTMAS
    Victor Hugo   313
    Adapted from *Les Misérables*, by *Adele Thane*
A MERRY CHRISTMAS   *Louisa May Alcott*   332
    Adapted for round-the-table reading, from
    Little Women, by *Walter Hackett*

THE BIG BOOK
of
CHRISTMAS PLAYS

Junior and Senior High

Red Carpet Christmas

by Helen Louise Miller

Christmas is no time for feuding! Old-fashioned Yuletide spirit and a surprising discovery bring two families together again . . .

Characters

MARCIA HITCHCOCK, *16*
ANITA PAGE, *Marcia's friend*
PAM HITCHCOCK, *14*
MRS. ETHEL HITCHCOCK
MR. HENRY HITCHCOCK
BILLY HITCHCOCK, *12*
BESSIE, *the maid*
TONY CORELLI, *18*
JIMMY HALE
MAGGIE
COUNT CORELLI
GINA CORELLI, *12*

TIME: *The afternoon of the day before Christmas.*
SETTING: *The living room of the Hitchcock family. In addition to the usual living-room furnishings, there are Christmas decorations in evidence, as well as a televi-*

sion set. A large window is right.

AT RISE: MARCIA *is kneeling on sofa, looking out of window through binoculars.* ANITA *is beside her.*

ANITA (*Excitedly*): Can you see him, Marcia? Can you see Tony?

MARCIA: I'm not quite sure, but there's somebody in the living room.

ANITA: Is it Tony?

MARCIA: I think so. Yes, I'm almost positive. I can see the back of his neck and one ear.

ANITA (*Grabbing binoculars*): Let me look! Let me look!

MARCIA: Stop shoving. You'll get him out of focus. Now he's leaning over. He seems to be moving a piece of furniture. I wish he'd come closer.

ANITA: I'll concentrate. (*Shuts her eyes tightly*) Closer, closer, closer! (*Opens eyes and leans over* MARCIA's *shoulder*) Is he coming any nearer?

MARCIA: A little. He's stopping at the table . . . now . . . now . . . oh, Anita! He's coming toward the window. He's . . . oh, my goodness! He's looking right over here, right at our house. (*Scrambles off sofa and ducks behind curtain*) Do you think he saw me?

ANITA: Of course not. The house is too far away. (*Snatching binoculars*) I simply *must* see him! (*Pause*) Wow! He's adorable! Oops! Don't do it! Don't do it! Don't you dare do it!

MARCIA: What? What is he doing?

Anita (*With exaggerated sigh of relief*): It's all right now, but for a minute I almost had heart failure. I thought he was going to pull down the shade.

MARCIA: You've had the binoculars long enough. Let me look.

ANITA (*Holding onto binoculars*): Just a few seconds more, Marcia, please. You can look at him all afternoon after I've gone. Ummm! He has that European look — tall, blond, and romantic looking.

MARCIA: That's funny. I remember Tony as having dark hair.

ANITA: Well, his hair is blond now, and he has a marvelous tan — that real Riviera look.

MARCIA: Let me see.

ANITA: Uh-oh! Sorry! He just walked out.

MARCIA: Now I've missed him again. I've been watching for three days, and I've never once had a good look at him.

ANITA: I don't see why you don't ask him over for your Christmas party tonight. After all, you were once engaged to him.

MARCIA: Engaged to him! What are you talking about?

ANITA: You told me so yourself. He gave you a ring and everything.

MARCIA: Oh, Anita, you idiot! That was ten years ago when he was eight and I was six. The ring came out of a Crackerjack box.

ANITA: But you promised to wait for each other. And I'll bet you still have the ring.

MARCIA (*Crossly*): What if I do? It was only a silly game we played the last summer he was here visiting his grandmother Briggs. He's never been back since she died.

ANITA: But the whole family's here now. (*Digs clipping out of purse*) Did you see this write-up in the Sunday paper? (*Reads*) "Countess Corelli and family to winter in Bakersville. After a twenty-year absence in Italy, the former Margaret Briggs will re-open her family home in time for Christmas."

MARCIA: I didn't see that one. Is Tony's picture there? (*Looks at clipping*)

ANITA: No, just the Count, the Countess, and Gina. What are they like?

MARCIA: I've never seen any of them. Tony used to visit his grandmother by himself. Gina is younger — closer to Pam's and Billy's age.

ANITA: But your mother knows the Countess. Didn't they grow up together?

MARCIA: Sure. They used to be very close friends. Mother still calls her Maggie Briggs. But there was some sort of quarrel, and Mother never heard from her after she married the Count and went off to Italy. In fact, I don't think Mom's too pleased that they've come back here to live.

ANITA: I think it's great. Imagine living right next door to a Count and a Countess.

MARCIA: It's stretching a point to say we live right next door. There's a big garden between the Corelli house and ours.

ANITA: But they're still your nearest neighbors. Oh, Marcia, why don't you ask the whole family to your Open House? That would be the neighborly thing to do.

MARCIA: I told you Mother doesn't want to be that neighborly. She's already told us she doesn't want us pushing ourselves in. She's afraid people will think we were being friendly to them just because they're rich.

ANITA: But that's ridiculous! Tony is an old friend. What harm would there be in asking him? Besides, you do need an extra man.

MARCIA: But he's been here three whole days and hasn't called or dropped in. He probably doesn't even remember us.

ANITA: Well, you should certainly be able to think of some way to meet him. (*Handing binoculars to* MARCIA) Here. Take the binoculars. I promised to meet

Jimmy about four. Anything you want me to pick up downtown?

MARCIA: It would be a help if you could pick up a man to fill in for Bob Lucas. What a time for him to get tonsillitis!

ANITA: I'll see if Jimmy can think of someone. He knows everybody.

MARCIA: Thanks a lot. See you tonight. (*As* ANITA *exits left,* MARCIA *takes binoculars and resumes her lookout post*) Too bad. The room is still empty. I wonder when he'll be back. (PAM *enters right with plate of cookies, one of which she is eating.*)

PAM: At it again, are you? You'd better not let Mom catch you snooping on the new neighbors.

MARCIA: I am *not* snooping, Pamela Hitchcock.

PAM: Then I will. (*Offering cookies*) Here, have some of Bessie's hermits while I try to spot Gina. I want to see if she looks happier. When I saw her this morning after breakfast she seemed to be crying. (*Takes binoculars*)

MARCIA: Why would a girl who has everything want to cry?

PAM: Don't ask me. Hey, who's been fooling with these binoculars? I can't see a thing.

MARCIA: There's nothing to see. (*Puts cookie plate on coffee table*) Everybody's out.

PAM: I like to look at the room. Did you ever see such gorgeous decorations and such beautiful furniture?

MARCIA: I didn't notice.

PAM: That's because you're too busy looking for Tony.

MARCIA: I haven't seen him, except for one, teeny-weeny glimpse.

PAM: I sure wish Mom would invite the whole family over for Open House tonight, but I guess it's just as well. This house is so shabby!

MARCIA: What a thing to say! I like our house just the way it is.

PAM: Oh, sure, but compared to the Corelli house, it's nothing. They must have done the whole place over. They've taken up that ugly old carpeting, and they have the most gorgeous Oriental rugs.

MARCIA: Mom's been talking about getting a new rug in here.

PAM: You ought to see their draperies.

MARCIA: Now who's snooping.

PAM: *I* didn't say it was snooping. That's just what Mother calls it. To me it's just like watching a play — in fact, it's better than television. We actually know the people, and we like to see everything they're doing.

MARCIA (*Clapping her hand to her head*): Television! Oh, no! I forgot to call the repair shop! Dad told me to call right after breakfast. I hope it's not too late. (*Goes to phone and dials*)

PAM: Dad will be furious if he can't see his Christmas programs tonight. Hey, sis, come and look. Somebody's going into the Corelli house.

MARCIA: Oh, dear! The line is busy. (*Running to window*) Who? Where? Let me see. (*As girls pass binoculars back and forth,* MRS. HITCHCOCK *enters from center entrance.*)

MRS. HITCHCOCK: Marcia! Pam! Put those binoculars down this minute! I will not have you spying on the Corellis.

PAM: But, Mother, they're so fascinating, and it's so exciting, living so close to royalty.

MRS. HITCHCOCK: Royalty, my foot! In Italy everyone has a title. As far as I'm concerned, Maggie Briggs is no more royalty than we are.

MARCIA: Maggie Briggs! Oh, Mother, she's the Countess Margarita now.

MRS. HITCHCOCK: She was just plain Maggie Briggs when I knew her. Now put those binoculars down and get away from that window. Marcia, you go help Bessie with the punch and sandwiches for the party.

MARCIA: I have to call the TV repair shop first, Mother.

MRS. HITCHCOCK: Good heavens! Haven't you done that yet?

MARCIA: The line was busy. I'll try again. (*Goes to phone and dials*)

MRS. HITCHCOCK: And you, Pam, you can polish the silver tray. Bessie has so much extra work to do, making Christmas cookies besides everything else.

PAM: Oh, Mother! Do I have to?

MRS. HITCHCOCK: You most certainly do.

PAM: But she's giving them away to the whole town. She even baked a fresh batch this morning. Can't you stop her?

MRS. HITCHCOCK: That new batch was for our party. I wouldn't have the heart to stop her, even if I could. Bessie's Christmas cookies are a tradition in this town.

PAM: Maybe that's why they named it Bakersville.

MRS. HITCHCOCK: Don't try to be funny, Pam. You know how much those cookies mean to Bessie. She sends them to neighbors the way other people send Christmas cards. Now get moving.

PAM: What about Billy? What's he doing to help get ready for the party?

MRS. HITCHCOCK: Your brother did his share this morning. Now it's your turn. Get busy! (*Shoos PAM offstage. PAM exits.*)

MARCIA (*At phone*): Oh, I see. Well, I can understand that you are rushed, but couldn't you possibly? . . . That would be fine. We certainly would appreciate it. . . . Thank you. Goodbye. (*Hangs up*)

MRS. HITCHCOCK: Any luck?

MARCIA: Mr. Young said his men are working over at the Corellis, putting in two new sets.

MRS. HITCHCOCK: The Corellis! Sometimes I wish they had stayed in Europe! They've done nothing but upset this household ever since they came back.

MARCIA: But, Mother, it isn't actually their fault. They haven't really done anything. It's just that . . . well, they're so important, and glamorous . . . and it's exciting to have them as neighbors.

MRS. HITCHCOCK: We're not exactly neighbors just because there are no houses between the old Briggs mansion and 925 Hilltop Road. And, furthermore, I don't want you wasting any more time gawking at the Corelli family with those binoculars. I'm going to take them upstairs and put them under lock and key.

MARCIA: Oh, Mother, don't you understand? I'm dying to see Tony.

MRS. HITCHCOCK: If he stays here all winter and goes to public high school, you'll see him every day.

MARCIA: But I want to see him now, tonight. Oh, Mother, please, couldn't I ask him to the party to fill in for Bob Lucas?

MRS. HITCHCOCK: Forget it, Marcia. If Tony wants to see you, he knows where you live. He certainly never had any trouble finding his way over here when he was a little boy.

MARCIA: And you always liked him then. I don't see why you object to him now.

MRS. HITCHCOCK: Of course, I liked him. He was a nice child, and I have no doubt he's grown into a nice young man. But I am not going to have you falling all over anyone just because his name is Corelli. Now please hurry, dear. Bessie needs your help.

MARCIA (*With resignation*): O.K., Mom. I'll go fix the punch and sandwiches. (*Turning at door*) You can tell Dad Mr. Young said he'd send one of the men over from the Corellis to fix the TV set if they finish before five. (*Exits*)

MRS. HITCHCOCK (*To herself*): They have some nerve! We've been good customers of theirs for years, but who cares with the Corellis in town? I'll bet Maggie figures the whole town will come flocking just because she has a title and some money. I'd love to see what she's done with that old house. (*Picks up binoculars and looks around guiltily*) For two cents, I'd take a peek myself . . . (*Gets into position on sofa*) That front parlor used to be a regular mausoleum, but now I suppose . . . (*Lifts binoculars to her eyes, as* MR. HITCHCOCK *enters left with several packages.*)

MR. HITCHCOCK (*As he drops his parcels on chair*): I think I've got everything on the list. Ethel! What are you doing?

MRS. HITCHCOCK (*Startled and embarrassed*): Henry! You scared me to death! I didn't hear you come in.

MR. HITCHCOCK: Don't tell me you've succumbed to the family weakness of Corelli-watching!

MRS. HITCHCOCK: Not quite. I admit I was close. But don't you dare tell the children!

MR. HITCHCOCK: What's the big attraction? Every time I come in, somebody's glued to those binoculars.

MRS. HITCHCOCK: I know, Henry. It's terrible, simply terrible. But between you and me — and I'll be furious if you tell anyone — I'm dying to see Maggie Briggs.

MR. HITCHCOCK: It seems only yesterday I heard you swear that you never wanted to see Maggie Briggs as long as you lived.

MRS. HITCHCOCK (*Ruefully*): I know — that was the time she didn't show up at my Christmas Eve party, remember?

MR. HITCHCOCK: How could I forget? That was the night we announced our engagement. You said you'd never forgive her.

MRS. HITCHCOCK: But I did . . . or I almost did. In spite of everything I always loved Maggie. I guess I still do.

MR. HITCHCOCK: Then why don't you let bygones be bygones and invite the whole family over tonight?

MRS. HITCHCOCK: Henry! We couldn't possibly!

MR. HITCHCOCK: Why not?

MRS. HITCHCOCK: Because . . . well, in the first place, Maggie's a countess now. They have their own friends. The society pages of the papers have been full of their coming back to Bakersville and moving into the Briggs mansion. And anyhow, this house . . . this room —

MR. HITCHCOCK: What's the matter with this house and this room?

MRS. HITCHCOCK: Oh, it's fine, Henry, and I love every bit of it. But . . . well, actually, it's shabby. Look at this rug, for instance.

MR. HITCHCOCK: I'm looking at it.

MRS. HITCHCOCK: Don't you see how worn it's getting? Oh, I know this sounds snobbish and silly, but I just can't see ourselves entertaining the Corellis. . . . And besides . . .

MR. HITCHCOCK: And besides, you're still mad at Maggie.

MRS. HITCHCOCK: I guess I am. I never could figure out why she did such a nasty thing. She was my best friend!

MR. HITCHCOCK: As I remember the story, she always claimed you never invited her.

MRS. HITCHCOCK: But I *did* invite her. I even wrote her a special little note and told her what I had never told another living soul.

MR. HITCHCOCK: Not even me?

MRS. HITCHCOCK (*Shaking her head in mock exasperation*): You already knew what I wrote her.

MR. HITCHCOCK: I did?

MRS. HITCHCOCK (*Smiling affectionately*): I wrote to tell her we were engaged. Don't you remember? We were going to keep it a secret, but I always told Maggie everything. I took the note over to her house early one morning and slipped it under the door.

MR. HITCHCOCK: I still think it's about time you forgot that schoolgirl quarrel and had the Corellis over here. I understand the Count's pretty fast on the tennis court.

MRS. HITCHCOCK: You're as bad as Marcia and Pam. You seem to think we can go barging in on the Corellis as if . . . as if —

MR. HITCHCOCK: As if they were our neighbors, which is exactly what they are.

MRS. HITCHCOCK: But they're no ordinary neighbors, Henry. Besides, Tony has been ignoring Marcia. He's been here three days and hasn't come near her. And anyhow, I don't want the children getting big ideas about cars and clothes and fancy furniture and . . .

MR. HITCHCOCK: Seems to me you've been getting some of those big ideas yourself. After all, you don't seem to think our living-room rug is socially acceptable.

MRS. HITCHCOCK: But that's different, Henry. You know yourself we've been talking about replacing this rug for years. (BILLY *enters left, carrying a strip of red carpet in a roll over his shoulder.*)

BILLY: Hi, Mom. Hi, Dad. Look what I've got.

MRS. HITCHCOCK: What on earth is that?

BILLY: It's a strip of hall carpet. It'll be great for the club-house the gang's fixing up. (*Drops rug onto floor, but does not unroll it.*)

MR. HITCHCOCK: Where did you get it?

BILLY: I bought it for twenty-five cents from Eddie Murphy. Mrs. Corelli asked him to haul their trash away this morning. Want to see it?

MRS. HITCHCOCK: I most certainly do not want to see it. And you can just take it out and put it in our trash, Billy Hitchcock. I will not have any of the Corellis' castoffs in this house.

BILLY: Oh, come on, Mom. It's a perfectly good strip of carpet.

MR. HITCHCOCK: Better take it out to the garage, son. Your mother is anti-Corelli right now.

BILLY: What's the problem, Mom? I've been thinking of inviting Gina to the New Year's Eve dance.

MR. HITCHCOCK: Aren't you a little ahead of yourself? After all, we haven't met any of the family yet.

BILLY: Speak for yourself, Dad. The Countess and I are already on pretty good terms. She's nice, Mom. You'd like her.

MRS. HITCHCOCK: Oh, really! And just when and where did you meet the Countess?

BILLY: In her kitchen this morning, when I went over to borrow the sugar.

MRS. HITCHCOCK: Borrow the sugar? What did you do that for?

BILLY: Bessie. You know how she's always running out of things in the middle of her cookie-baking.

MRS. HITCHCOCK: Good heavens! What will they think of us?

BILLY: They'll think we ran out of sugar. What else?

(*Moves to television set*) Anything good on television?

MRS. HITCHCOCK: It hasn't been fixed yet. (*Acidly*) Mr. Young's men are busy installing two new color TVs for the Corellis.

BILLY: That's what we ought to have — two new sets instead of this antique. And besides, this one never works well.

MRS. HITCHCOCK: If it's not repaired soon, I'll miss my favorite Christmas programs!

BILLY: There's a little TV repair shop down on Ninth Street we could try. Maybe if we drove down there, we could bring a technician back with us.

MR. HITCHCOCK: I know the place you mean. Come on, Billy. I'll drive, and you can run in. We'll never find a place to park. (MR. HITCHCOCK *and* BILLY *exit left.*)

MRS. HITCHCOCK: This is too much! Dragging that old carpet in here, and actually running over there to borrow sugar. I certainly have a few things to say to Bessie. (*Calling*) Bessie, Bessie, where are you? I want to talk to you.

MARCIA (*Entering, right*): I can't find Bessie anywhere, Mother, and we don't have enough bread. I've used it all up. If you'll finish the punch, I'll go to the supermarket for the bread.

MRS. HITCHCOCK: No, I'll go. You might as well finish the punch, now that you've started. What do you suppose has become of Bessie?

MARCIA: Who knows? Nobody can keep track of her at Christmastime!

MRS. HITCHCOCK: I hope Bessie isn't up to something. Christmas seems to go to her head. But I suppose it's all right. She's helped us for so long, she's really part of the family. Well, I'll run along to the store. (MARCIA *and* MRS. HITCHCOCK *exit right. After a short*

pause, BESSIE *and* TONY CORELLI *enter from left.* BES-
SIE *carries a dress over her arm.*)

BESSIE: Come in, Tony, and make yourself at home.

TONY: It's wonderful to be back again, in this house, I
mean. Ours is such a complete madhouse. Mother all
upset, Gina homesick, Dad wandering around like a
lost sheep, and now Carlotta in hysterics over the new
electric stove — that was the last straw.

BESSIE: Don't worry, Tony. Everything will be all right.
I'll just run up to my room and fix this dress of Gina's.
And then, if we can't get that stove of yours to work,
I'll do your turkey over here.

TONY: I don't know what we'd do without you, Bessie.
It's so good of you to go to all this trouble.

BESSIE: Trouble? Don't be silly! I'm always glad to help
out — especially neighbors.

TONY: When we lived in Italy, Carlotta was the one who
helped everyone out.

BESSIE: Poor thing! It must be confusing when you're
working in a strange country. Maybe she never cooked
on an electric stove. But I'll have Carlotta fixed up in
no time. Just wait and see.

TONY (*Looking around room*): Gee, nothing's changed a
bit. Same furniture, same rug, even the same old television set. (*Walks over to it*) Remember how you used
to drag Marcia and me away from it when it was time
for supper?

BESSIE: I sure do. You never did know when to go home.

TONY (*Adjusting television set*): Is . . . is Marcia here?

BESSIE: Sure. She's supposed to be in the kitchen making
the refreshments for tonight. (*Calling*) Marcia, Marcia,
somebody here to see you. (*To* TONY) I'll just run upstairs and fix the dress. (BESSIE *exits center.*)

MARCIA (*Offstage*): Bessie, is that you? I've been waiting for you. I can't tell if this punch is too sweet or too sour. (*Enters left with glass of punch*) I want you to taste it. (*Sees* TONY *at TV set*) Oh, I thought Bessie was here. Did she let you in?

TONY: Yes . . . that is . . . well . . . we came in together.

MARCIA: Well, I'm glad you got here in time. I hope you can fix this stupid TV set. (*Sets down glass of punch*)

TONY (*Blankly*): Fix it?

MARCIA: Don't look at me like that! I know the set is old, but it's worth fixing. The picture jumps a lot and the sound fades out every now and then. Hey, where are your tools? Don't tell me you didn't bring them!

TONY: Well, you see . . . I —

MARCIA: Don't apologize. Just see what you can do. I'll bring you anything you need from my father's workshop. Shall I turn on the set?

TONY (*Clearing his throat*): I — I guess I should see where it's plugged in.

MARCIA: Back here. We'll have to move it out from the wall.

TONY: Let me do that. (*As they move set forward, he gets a coughing spell.*)

MARCIA: My goodness, you have a terrible cough.

TONY (*Choking and sputtering*): Yes! I know. I guess it's the climate. (MARCIA *runs to table for glass of punch.*)

MARCIA: Here, take a sip of this. (*As* TONY *drinks, his cough subsides.*) Drink all of it. The fruit juice will be good for you.

TONY: Thanks. This is delicious. Much better than cough medicine. What is it?

MARCIA: Just some fruit punch. Do you think it's sweet enough?

TONY: Perfect.

MARCIA: Maybe you'd better sit down for a few minutes till you catch your breath.

TONY: Thanks, I will. (*Sits*)

MARCIA (*Offering him plate of cookies*): Here, have some cookies.

TONY: Thanks. I didn't have much lunch.

MARCIA: I guess Mr. Young keeps you repairmen jumping this time of year. And then when people like the Corellis want two sets installed on the day before Christmas! Well, some people just have no consideration, that's all. (*As* TONY *chokes again*) Be careful of those cookies or you'll start coughing again. Let me get you some more punch.

TONY (*Rising*): No, no, thank you. I'm all right. I'll take a look at that set now and see what I can do. (*Moves set farther from wall and squats down behind it as* ANITA *and* JIMMY *enter left.*)

ANITA: Marcia! We have good news.

MARCIA: Hi, Anita. Hi, Jimmy. Help yourselves to the cookies.

JIMMY: Thanks, Marcia. Is this a sample of what we're getting tonight?

ANITA: Don't start stuffing yourself before you tell her the news.

JIMMY: I found an extra man for you, although I still don't see why you can't get that wonderful Tony Anita keeps raving about. I sure would like to see that guy.

ANITA: Maybe you can. (*Using binoculars*) Maybe he's over there now. (*Looking*) Hey, there he is. Look, Jimmy.

JIMMY: Where? Where? I don't see him.

ANITA: Right there by the window. He's moving a chair or something. Oh, Jimmy, don't you think he's the greatest-looking guy you ever saw? (TONY *raises his head above the television set and then ducks back.*)

JIMMY: I still don't see him.

ANITA: How can you miss him? He's the only person in the room.

JIMMY: But that's not Tony Corelli!

ANITA: It most certainly is! And he's a real Count!

JIMMY: That's no Count! That's Gus Flanders. He works for an interior decorator.

ANITA: It can't be!

MARCIA: Are you sure?

JIMMY: If you don't believe me, you can ask him yourself. He's the guy I invited to your party tonight.

ANITA: I can't believe it!

MARCIA: I *knew* Tony had dark hair.

ANITA: And I admired his Riviera tan!

JIMMY: Riviera? Gus has never been out of Bakersville except to the next town on holidays and weekends.

MARCIA: Then I've never seen the real Tony at all.

TONY (*Stepping forward*): I think your set will work now, miss. Shall I turn it on?

MARCIA: You startled me! I forgot you were there. This is the television repairman Mr. Young sent us. (*To TONY*) I'm sorry I don't know your name.

TONY: Just call me Mr. Fix-It!

MARCIA: These are my friends, Anita Page and Jimmy Hale.

TONY (*Beaming with mock courtesy*): Charmed, I'm sure. (*To MARCIA*) If you have any further trouble, just call Mr. Young. (BESSIE *enters, carrying dress on hanger.*)

BESSIE: I'm all set. The dress is ready to wear, and I've got some aspirin for Carlotta. We'll have her back on her feet in no time. (*To MARCIA*) Isn't it wonderful to see Tony again?

ALL: Tony!

MARCIA: Oh, no! It can't be!

ANITA: Not Tony Corelli!

JIMMY: But he's the repairman!

TONY: Not a very efficient one, I'm afraid. I didn't even bring my tool kit. But I managed to get it going.

MARCIA: Oh, Tony, I'm so embarrassed.

BESSIE: Don't tell me you didn't recognize Tony!

MARCIA: But he's changed so much, Bessie.

TONY: So have you. No braces on your teeth — no more pigtails.

BESSIE: I have to go next door. (*To* MARCIA) Their maid, Carlotta, is having hysterics over the new electric stove. Poor thing, she can't get the hang of it. I'm going over to see what I can do. Tell your mother I'll be back in plenty of time to start supper. (*Exits*)

ANITA: And we'd better go, too. I'm sure you and Tony have lots to talk about. It was good to meet you, Tony. Let's go, Jimmy.

JIMMY (*Shaking hands with* TONY): Tony, maybe I'll see you tonight after all.

ANITA: Jimmy, you're not in charge of invitations for this party.

JIMMY: I know, but something tells me Tony will be at the party tonight. See you all later! (JIMMY *and* ANITA *exit left.*)

MARCIA: Oh, Tony, I'm so ashamed. I wanted to call you, but, well . . . I guess I was waiting for you to call me.

TONY: Marcia, I'd have been over here long ago, but the doctor has had me in bed ever since we got here. The sudden change of climate gave me a bad case of bronchitis. This is the first day I've been out of the house.

MRS. HITCHCOCK (*Calling from offstage*): Marcia, where are you? Is Bessie back yet?

MARCIA: Oh, Mother, come and see who's here. (*As* MRS. HITCHCOCK *enters*) Look, Mother! It's Tony!

TONY (*Shaking hands with* MRS. HITCHCOCK): It's good to see you again, Mrs. Hitchcock.

MARCIA: Oh, Mother, he's been sick in bed, and I thought he was the television repairman, and he saw us using those binoculars, and . . . oh, Mother, the whole thing is impossible!

MRS. HITCHCOCK: I must say it's impossible for me to understand what you're talking about, but I'm certainly glad to see you, Tony. How's your family?

TONY: Terrible! We all have colds, Mother's upset, Gina is homesick, and Bessie's over at our house now trying to explain electricity to Carlotta.

MRS. HITCHCOCK: Oh, dear! I'm sorry to hear that. Is there anything we can do? (MR. HITCHCOCK *and* BILLY *enter left*)

BILLY: I'm sure I could fix it, Dad. Just let me try.

MR. HITCHCOCK: Do you want me to have to buy a whole new set?

MARCIA: Don't worry, Dad. The set has been fixed.

TONY: I think it will be O.K. now, Mr. Hitchcock.

MR. HITCHCOCK (*Beaming*): That's fine, young man. What do I owe you?

TONY: I've already been paid in punch and cookies, Mr. Hitchcock.

MARCIA: Dad, this is our neighbor, Tony Corelli.

MR. HITCHCOCK: Not that little kid who was always breaking our hedge on his way over here!

TONY: Glad to see you again, sir. (*They shake hands.*)

MRS. HITCHCOCK: And this is our son, Billy.

BILLY (*Shaking hands with* TONY): Glad to meet you, Tony. I've sure heard a lot about you.

MARCIA: Billy!

BILLY: Well, it's the truth. I'll bet if Marcia had known you were coming, she'd have spread out the red carpet for sure!

MRS. HITCHCOCK: Billy! That's enough.

MR. HITCHCOCK: Speaking of carpets reminds me. I thought your mother told you to take that (*Pointing to rolled-up carpet*) out to the garage.

BILLY: Will do. (*Shoulders roll of carpet*) Excuse me, Tony. (*As he brushes past* TONY, *he drops the carpet which unrolls at his feet.*) Oops! I didn't mean to drop it, Mom.

TONY: That looks familiar.

BILLY: It should. It came out of your house. (PAM *enters left in a dither of excitement.*)

PAM: Marcia! Mother! Guess who is coming down our walk this very minute. You'll die when I tell you.

MRS. HITCHCOCK: I hope not, dear. At least not until I've had the chance to introduce you to Tony. Tony, this is my younger daughter, Pam.

PAM: Tony? Tony Corelli?

TONY: That's right.

PAM: Why, I just looked out the window and saw your mother and father —

MRS. HITCHCOCK (*Breaking in*): Maggie? Coming here?

PAM: And she's bringing Gina.

BILLY: Gina? If she's coming, we need the red carpet for sure! (MAGGIE CORELLI *runs in, followed by* GINA *and* COUNT.)

MAGGIE: Ethel! How are you? Merry Christmas!

MRS. HITCHCOCK (*Embracing her*): Oh, Maggie! I'm so glad to see you! Why, Maggie Briggs, I believe you're crying.

MAGGIE: Look who's talking! So are you!

MRS. HITCHCOCK (*Wiping her eyes*): Come, I want you to meet my family.

MAGGIE: But I know them — every single one! Henry, of course . . . (*Shakes hands with* MR. HITCHCOCK) And this must be Marcia, and Billy, and little Pam. (*They greet each other.*)

TONY: And this is my Dad, and my sister, Gina.

BILLY: I'm certainly glad to see you, Gina.

COUNT CORELLI: This is a pleasure. Indeed, I think my wife and children would not have survived Christmas without calling on you.

GINA: I've been so lonely!

MAGGIE: Poor Gina, she's been terribly homesick. But all of us, all of us are lonely, especially because it's Christmastime. We felt as if we didn't have a friend in the world until Bessie came over and brought the cookies. Oh, Ethel, I just had to come over and tell you what it meant to me, having you send those cookies over to me! (BESSIE *enters.*)

MRS. HITCHCOCK: Oh, Maggie, it's all Bessie's doing.

MAGGIE (*Putting her arm around* BESSIE): And this blessed Bessie! She's brought Carlotta to her senses, and showed her how to work all the American gadgets, from the electric stove right down to the electric can opener.

BESSIE: Right now she's like a kid with a lot of new toys. When I left, she was opening cans right and left! Hey, where did that red carpet come from?

GINA: It looks like our old hall carpet.

BILLY: That's just what it is. I almost forgot — I was supposed to get it out of here. (*As he starts to roll it, he finds a note.*) Say, what's this thing stuck underneath? (*Stands*) It looks like an old letter. I can hardly make out the writing, but I think it's addressed to Maggie Briggs.

MAGGIE: To me? Let me see it. (*The others crowd around as* MAGGIE *opens it and reads.*) "Dear Maggie, I couldn't go to sleep without telling you my wonderful, wonderful news . . ."

MRS. HITCHCOCK: Maggie! That's the note I wrote — the invitation I slipped under your front door twenty years ago.

MAGGIE: Only you must have slipped it under the hall carpet instead, and it's been lying there all these years! Oh, Ethel, weren't we foolish to be upset over a little thing like that?

MRS. HITCHCOCK: We certainly were, Maggie. It was all a stupid mistake. But what better time than Christmas to make up our little differences? Let's forget it, and concentrate on having a good time!

BILLY: Give me a hand, Dad, and we'll get this carpet out of here.

MR. HITCHCOCK: No, Billy! I want that red carpet to stay right where it is!

BESSIE: Not right in the middle of the living room floor!

MRS. HITCHCOCK: It looks beautiful there! A red carpet's just right for Christmas and the guests of honor at our Open House tonight. (*With a curtsy*) Countess Margarita! Count Corelli, will you do us the honor?

COUNT CORELLI (*Bowing*): We will be delighted.

MAGGIE (*Throwing her arms around* MRS. HITCHCOCK): Oh, Ethel, you silly thing! We'll be thrilled to come.

TONY: Too bad you already have that extra man for tonight, Marcia.

MARCIA: Oh, Tony, please come. You too, Gina.

TONY: I wouldn't miss it.

GINA: I never thought I'd be going to a party tonight.

PAM: I guarantee you won't be lonely after tonight, Gina.

BILLY: Pam's right, Gina. There are lots of kids our age in the neighborhood, and I've invited them all to the party.

BESSIE: You know, I always did like a red carpet. There's something so warm and friendly about it. Too bad it's gone out of style.

MRS. HITCHCOCK: Gone out of style! Why, Bessie, it's the height of fashion. The Hitchcocks and the Corellis are just about to celebrate their first Red Carpet Christmas! (*Curtain*)

THE END

Video Christmas

by Earl J. Dias

The Carsons share their family Christmas with the television audience. . . .

Characters

MRS. CARSON
FLORENCE HAMMOND, *TV director*
SAM BURKE, *TV technician*
BETH CARSON, *16*
MR. CARSON
GRANDMA CARSON
TOM CARSON, *17*
CAROLERS, *extras*

SCENE 1

TIME: *Early afternoon of December 24th.*
SETTING: *Living room, with fireplace, right, on which five Christmas stockings are hung. Door, center, leads to front porch; door, left, leads to another room. Christmas tree is to one side. Furnishings include couch, several chairs, table, etc. Telephone is on table.*

AT RISE: MRS. CARSON *and* FLORENCE HAMMOND *are seated on couch.* SAM BURKE *stands center, talking animatedly.*

SAM: So, you see, Mrs. Carson, you really don't have a thing to worry about. When the program is ready to begin, Florence Hammond, our program director, will give the signal. We'll have a camera near the fireplace, and another one near the door.

MRS. CARSON: I have to admit, I am a bit nervous, and so are my husband and the children. After all, it's our first time on TV.

FLORENCE *(Rising)*: Think nothing of it, Mrs. Carson. Even Bill Cosby made his TV debut once, and look where he is now.

MRS. CARSON: How did you choose us for this "Family to Family" Christmas Eve program?

SAM: The network wanted to find a typical American family—one that kept Christmas Eve as traditionally as possible. Your husband's friend, Joe Batson, is a writer on one of our series, and he suggested your family.

FLORENCE: Besides, yours really is a typical American family, Mrs. Carson. You and your husband work, You're both active in community affairs, and you have two teenage children. And having your husband's mother here for Christmas—well, that's the icing on the cake. (BETH *enters.*)

BETH *(Exasperated)*: Mother, my dress still hasn't arrived. It was supposed to be delivered today.

MRS. CARSON: Well, Beth, this is the Christmas rush.

BETH: If I can't wear that dress tonight, I'll just die. Besides, I wanted to wear it tomorrow night, too. I'm going out with Bob Sutherland.

FLORENCE *(Rising):* Beth, don't worry. I'm sure everything will work out. Come on, Sam. We still have lots to do at the studio before tonight.

SAM (*To* MRS. CARSON): Tonight's show starts at ten sharp. A couple of cameramen will come by later this afternoon to set up their equipment. Florence and I will be here at about 8:00 to go over everything before the show airs.

FLORENCE (*Going to door*): Now, remember—everything is planned to the minute: Mr. Carson will read from "A Christmas Carol," you'll all take the gifts out of your stockings, then there'll be a little chit-chat about what Christmas means to all of you. It'll run like clockwork.

SAM: There's one more thing. The prop department will be bringing over a pile of packages—for atmosphere. They'll be empty boxes, gift-wrapped. Just put them under the tree.

MRS. CARSON: Fine. (*Nervously*) I hope I remember everything.

FLORENCE: I'm sure you will, Mrs. Carson. (*Squeezes* MRS. CARSON's *hand*) Now, don't be nervous. We'll see you later. (*She and* SAM *exit.*)

MRS. CARSON (*To* BETH): Beth, where's your father?

BETH: He's next door, talking to Mr. Faber.

MRS. CARSON: Arguing is probably more like it. There ought to be a law against lawyers living next door to each other.

BETH: Apparently, they'll be at each other in court next Tuesday. Mr. Faber's the prosecutor in that case Dad's defending—Holm vs. Jackson.

MRS. CARSON (*Surprised*): I didn't know that! (*Frowning*) I'm afraid your father won't exactly be overflowing with the Christmas spirit if he and Ralph Faber are discussing *that* case. (MR. CARSON *enters.*)

MR. CARSON (*Angrily*): Our next-door neighbor is not what I'd call the most engaging specimen of humanity. He must have learned his law through a correspondence course!

BETH *(Giggling):* Oh, Dad, that's not true!

MRS. CARSON: Now, Jerome, calm down.

MR. CARSON: Don't worry. I'll have him begging for mercy in court next Tuesday

MRS. CARSON: Then why not forget about it till then?

MR. CARSON: How can I? You don't have to listen to his inane arguments.

MRS. CARSON: You *love* listening to his arguments—just so you can prove them invalid. I'm surprised you're not still battling with him right now.

MR. CARSON: I would be, but Ralph claims he isn't feeling well. He says he has a peculiar pain in his stomach.

MRS. CARSON: I hope it's nothing serious.

MR. CARSON: Probably just his bad temper. *(Goes down left and stops suddenly)* What happened to my chair? This is a new one.

MRS. CARSON: Florence Hammond thought that your chair was too shabby-looking for the TV program tonight.

BETH: We moved it into the den, Dad.

MR. CARSON: Is nothing sacred? Not even a man's favorite chair that has been with him for years? (GRANDMA *enters.*)

GRANDMA: What's bothering you, son?

MR. CARSON: Oh, hello, Mother. My chair is missing, and then there's that stubborn Ralph Faber next door.

GRANDMA *(Chuckling):* Every time I visit for Christmas, it's the same old story with you and Ralph Faber.

MRS. CARSON *(Exasperated):* And this is supposed to be the season of good will.

GRANDMA *(Vivaciously):* I'll tell you one thing. This TV program tonight is the best thing that's happened to me since I sailed around the Cape of Good Hope—mostly because it will make Dottie Preston turn green with envy. Wait until she sees me on her television screen!

She's always bragging about her family and her ancestors.

MRS. CARSON: Well, I think it's nice that she's so proud of her family.

MR. CARSON *(Looking at watch):* I think I'll go upstairs and do some work on Tuesday's brief. I have a couple of surprises for Ralph! *(Exits)*

BETH *(Agitatedly):* Mom, what am I going to wear if my dress doesn't come?

MRS. CARSON: Beth, you have loads of clothes. I'm sure you have something else you can wear.

BETH *(Stubbornly):* But I don't! If the dress doesn't come this afternoon, I just won't appear on the show at all. *(Others ignore her.)*

GRANDMA: I'm going to start getting ready for tonight. You never know when a famous Hollywood agent might be watching local TV for a new star! *(Exits)*

MRS. CARSON *(Shaking her head):* To think the network people selected us as a typical American family. If we're typical, heaven help the nation! (TOM *enters, carrying an armload of Christmas packages.*)

BETH: Where did all the packages come from, Tom?

TOM: I found them on the front doorstep, but there aren't any tags on them.

MRS. CARSON: They must be the empty packages that the television people said they would be sending over. We're supposed to put them under the tree for atmosphere.

TOM *(Putting boxes under tree):* Wouldn't you know those TV people would bring a bunch of fake presents?

MRS. CARSON: Tom, what's wrong with you? Why are you so grouchy?

TOM: I'm not grouchy. *(Sighs)* It's just this program tonight.

BETH: Don't you want to be a TV star with fan letters

from thousands of girls?

TOM: I'm interested in only one girl.

BETH *(Sarcastically):* Simpering Sally Blake—the one who pretends she's as fragile as a lily.

TOM *(Sitting up; angrily):* Knock it off, Beth. You're just jealous of Sally.

BETH: Oh, please! Give me a break, Tom.

TOM: Mom, I'm taking Sally to the Christmas Eve dance tonight. Since I'm the chairman of the dance committee, I'm supposed to crown the Queen. But because of this dumb TV show, I'll have to leave the dance early, and somebody else will probably get to crown the Queen.

BETH: Poor Tom. He'll have to tear himself away from fragile Sally. *(Takes handkerchief from pocket and pretends to weep)* Love stinks!

TOM: You're too much, Beth. *(Archly)* You know, you'll have offers after tonight's show, too. *(Cuttingly)* Without the benefit of your new dress, they'll be begging you to star on "Lifestyles of the Dull and Dumpy."

BETH *(Advancing on* TOM): Don't look now, Mom. I'm about to do damage to your only son.

MRS. CARSON *(Angrily):* You two stop your bickering, this minute! *(To* TOM) Tom, why don't you bring Sally here from the dance? She might enjoy watching all the filming.

TOM: I don't think she'd be interested.

MRS. CARSON: Well, you won't know unless you ask. *(To* TOM *and* BETH) By the way, Mrs. Morrow phoned me this morning. She wants you both to join her carolers between six and seven.

TOM *(Rising; sarcastically):* How jolly!

BETH *(Sighing):* Mrs. Morrow is just loaded with great ideas.

MRS. CARSON: I think caroling on Christmas Eve is a

lovely custom. So—can I tell Mrs. Morrow you'll join her group?

BETH: Really, Mom, with all we have to do about this TV show, I don't see how we can waste time on foolish things like carol singing.

MRS. CARSON: Foolish? I hardly think that singing Christmas carols on Christmas Eve is foolish. You've always gone caroling in the past.

TOM: But, Mom, things aren't normal this year. After all, if you're chairman of a dance committee, you can't spend an hour singing carols. First things first.

MRS. CARSON: Mrs. Morrow will be so disappointed.

BETH: I'm sure she'll understand our problem, Mom. Besides, she can get plenty of kids to sing. They're not all going to be on TV tonight.

MRS. CARSON: I'm beginning to think they're lucky. I'm just not very excited about tonight. Everyone in the family seems so out of sorts today.

BETH (Softening): Oh, Mom, we don't mean to be. It's just that problems seem to be piling up right now.

TOM: That's for sure.

MRS. CARSON: It seems to me that both of you are making your own problems. (MR. CARSON enters.)

MR. CARSON (Worriedly): I just saw an ambulance pull up outside of Ralph Faber's. I'm going over to see what's the matter.

MRS. CARSON: Be sure to ask if there's anything we can do.

MR. CARSON: I'll see you later. (Exits)

TOM: I'd better phone Sally and find out what color dress she's wearing tonight. I want to be sure the corsage I'm getting her will be all right. (Exits)

BETH: If Tom ever gets off that phone, I'm going to call about my dress. (She exits. GRANDMA enters, looks toward *fireplace mantel. She crosses quickly to fireplace, examines large, ornate Christmas card displayed on mantel. Angrily)* Why is Dottie Preston's Christmas card set up so prominently? They'll be able to see it on TV.

MRS. CARSON: That was Ms. Hammond's idea. She looked at all our cards, and she thought that Dottie's was the most suitable. They're planning on taking a close-up shot of it.

GRANDMA: What? That'll make Dottie as proud as a peacock! I wish those TV people wouldn't stick their noses into other people's business. *(Comes to center; chuckling)* I wonder if it would be all right if I just said a few words of greeting to Dottie Preston over the air— something that would really needle her.

MRS. CARSON: Oh, Grandma, I don't think that would be quite right.

GRANDMA: Nonsense. Anything's right that can get that conceited Dottie Preston riled up. *(Goes to left)* Yes! I'm going to write a little speech right now. *(Exits)*

MRS. CARSON: Typical American family? Yes, I suppose we are. Mother, father, son, daughter, grandmother— but is that enough? No, there should be something else. If we're typical, then where's our Christmas spirit? All this television business has driven it out of the house. *(Sighs heavily)* I only hope we can find it again. *(Curtain)*

* * * * *

SCENE 2

TIME: *About seven o'clock; the same day.*
SETTING: *The same. There are TV cameras in the room.*

AT RISE: BETH *is hanging ornaments on Christmas tree.* TOM *is pacing back and forth.* MRS. CARSON *is sitting on couch, and* GRANDMA *is sitting in chair down left.*

MRS. CARSON: Tom, I wish you'd relax. You're making me nervous.

TOM *(Still pacing):* Well, I have to get to the dance by eight-thirty. *(Looks at his watch)* It's nearly seven already. If the TV people don't come soon, I won't be able to stay for the rehearsal. *(Sits on couch)*

BETH: You think you have problems. What about me? No new dress. *(Looking down at her dress)* I look awful.

TOM: If you say so.

MRS. CARSON: Beth, you look fine. There's not a thing wrong with that dress.

GRANDMA *(Chuckling):* I called Dottie Preston this afternoon and told her not to miss the program tonight. "Oh," she said, cool as an iceberg, "I'll be watching." Is she ever due for a surprise!

BETH: What do you mean, Grandma?

MRS. CARSON *(Disapprovingly):* Grandma has written a little speech—composed only for Dottie Preston's ears.

GRANDMA *(Chuckling):* Her ears will be ringing tonight. (MR. CARSON *enters.)*

MRS. CARSON: Any more news on Ralph, Jerome?

MR. CARSON: I just called the hospital. Ralph had appendicitis, all right. An acute case.

OTHERS *(Ad lib):* Oh, no. That's too bad. Is he O.K.? *(Etc.)*

MR. CARSON: They operated on him, and he's fine, but he'll be in the hospital for a couple of days.

GRANDMA: That's a real shame.

TOM: Imagine having to spend Christmas in the hospital.

MRS. CARSON: It makes you realize just how fortunate you are, doesn't it?

BETH *(Thoughtfully):* It really does.

MR. CARSON *(Shaking his head):* Poor Ralph. I hope our little sparring match this afternoon didn't bring on his attack.

MRS. CARSON: Of course it didn't, Jerome. But I do think it would be nice if you and Ralph could have a nice, friendly relationship, instead of arguing with each other all the time. *(Doorbell rings. BETH goes to door, opens it, and returns with small package.)*

BETH: It's for you, Grandma.

GRANDMA *(Surprised):* For me?

TOM: Maybe you have a secret admirer, Grandma. *(GRANDMA opens package, takes out corsage.)*

GRANDMA: What a beautiful corsage!

BETH: Who sent it, Grandma?

GRANDMA *(Looking at card):* Well, I'll be! It's from Dottie Preston. *(Reading)* "With best wishes for tonight. Warmly, Dottie." *(GRANDMA looks thoughtful, as BETH pins the corsage on GRANDMA's shoulder.)*

MRS. CARSON: What a thoughtful thing for Dottie to do! *(Voices of CAROLERS singing "Silent Night" are heard outside.)*

TOM: That must be Mrs. Morrow's group.

MRS. CARSON: A group you and Beth should be with. *(BETH and TOM look sheepish.)*

GRANDMA: Caroling is such a lovely custom.

MRS. CARSON: It certainly is. Listen. *(CAROLERS complete "Silent Night," then go on to another song, which fades.)*

BETH: That was beautiful.

MR. CARSON: Those old carols do something to you. They make you stop and realize just what Christmas is all about.

TOM: They really do. For the first time, I think I'm beginning to feel the real Christmas spirit.

MR. CARSON: I know . . . and with what's happened to

poor Ralph—well, it makes a man want to stop and count his blessings.

BETH: You're right, Dad.

MRS. CARSON *(Smiling):* I'm glad to see this family on the right track again. If you must know, up to now, I've been dreadfully disappointed in all of you. Everything I've heard around here today has made me wonder just what kind of job I've done in bringing up my family.

BETH *(Sincerely):* You've done a good job, Mom. There isn't a better mother in the world.

TOM *(Enthusiastically):* Count me in on that.

MRS. CARSON: I'm not so sure. Our family has been selected for this program because we are supposed to be typical Americans who keep Christmas for all the good, old-fashioned reasons—good will and kindness toward others. But you've all been wrapped up in your own problems today—not one of you has given thought to anyone else. You, Beth, have thought of nothing but that new dress. And Tom, for you the program is just an inconvenience that might detract from your role at the dance and your desire to impress Sally. Jerome, the only thing that interested you was your argument with Ralph. It took Ralph's illness to make you see the light. And, Grandma, all this Christmas seems to mean to you is the glorious opportunity to impress your friendly enemy, Dottie Preston.

BETH *(Contritely):* I'm sorry, Mom.

MR. CARSON: I guess I have behaved pretty badly.

GRANDMA: I'm just a foolish old woman, Margaret.

TOM: I feel awful, Mom.

MRS. CARSON: You should. You and Beth refused to devote even an hour to singing carols.

BETH: Mom's right. We are selfish. *(She goes to* TOM.) Tom, I'm sorry I said those things about Sally. She's not really a drip.

TOM: That's O.K. Beth, and I'm sorry too. You'll be the star of tonight's show, even if you wear overalls.

MRS. CARSON *(Softening and smiling):* That's more like it. Now, just try to keep up this Christmas spirit. Otherwise, the program tonight will be just a mockery. (GRANDMA *rises and goes to fireplace. From her pocket, she takes piece of paper, which she begins to tear into pieces and throw into fireplace.)*

BETH: What are you doing, Grandma?

GRANDMA: Tearing up something I never should have written.

MRS. CARSON: Your special message to Dottie Preston?

GRANDMA *(Returning):* Yes, there's no reason for me to hurt her feelings. She brags about her ancestors because she's a lonely old woman, with nothing else to be proud of. *(Shaking her head)* I'm ashamed of myself. She's a good friend.

BETH: You know, all of a sudden it really seems like Christmas. (FLORENCE HAMMOND *and* SAM BURKE *appear in doorway. The family does not yet see them.* BETH *goes to* MRS. CARSON *and kisses her.)* Merry Christmas, Mother. (BETH *then kisses* MR. CARSON, GRANDMA, *and* TOM.)

SAM *(Coming to center):* This is a heartwarming sight. Joe Batson knew what he was talking about when he recommended you folks as the typical American family. When you enter this house, the Christmas spirit seems to be everywhere.

FLORENCE *(Crossing center):* Merry Christmas, everybody!

ALL: Merry Christmas!

SAM: I'm sorry we have to burst in on you so early. I know it's not much after seven, but we have to be sure of all of the technicalities. *(He points to TV cameras.)* Oh, good. I see the cameras are all set up.

FLORENCE: Now everyone, just try to relax, and pretend the cameras aren't there. Throughout the program, I'll be motioning to you, showing you where to stand and sit. Just watch me, and follow my cues. You'll all be fine!

MR. CARSON: What part of "A Christmas Carol" do you want me to read?

FLORENCE: Christmas dinner at Bob Cratchit's would be best, I think.

OTHERS *(Ad lib):* Yes, that's always been my favorite part. Good idea. *(Etc.)*

FLORENCE: O.K. Right now we should do a quick rehearsal. I'd like all of you to stand by the fireplace. *(Others rise and go to fireplace.)* That camera *(Points to camera)* will pan in on the scene, and then you'll take down your stockings. You don't need to do that now; we'll wait till we're on the air. Now, Mr. and Mrs. Carson, you stand in the middle.

GRANDMA: Where would you like me?

FLORENCE: Right next to Mr. Carson. Beth and Tom, you stand at either end. *(They line up as directed.)* How does it look to you, Sam?

SAM: The way Christmas was meant to be.

FLORENCE: After you take down your stockings, I'm going to ask each of you the same question: What does Christmas mean to you? (FLORENCE *looks toward Christmas tree.)* Oh, Sam. Would you hand that big red package to Mrs. Carson? (SAM *goes to tree and lifts up large red box.)*

SAM: You mean this one?

FLORENCE: That's it. We'll want a close-up of it—it looks so Christmasy—and a close-up of the card on the mantel, too.

SAM *(Jiggling box):* I think there's something in here.

FLORENCE: There shouldn't be. I just asked the prop department for some large empty boxes.

MRS. CARSON: It was with the other props you brought in, wasn't it, Tom?

TOM: Yes, they were all on the front porch. (BETH *goes to look closely at box.*)

BETH *(Excitedly):* But, Tom! Didn't you notice the label on it? It's my dress! (BETH *quickly opens box and pulls out dress.*) It's wonderful!

TOM: I'm sorry, Beth. I didn't realize . . .

BETH *(Magnanimously):* It's O.K., Tom, don't worry about it. All that matters is that the dress is here in time for tonight's show—and my date tomorrow.

SAM: That's the true Christmas spirit, Beth.

FLORENCE: I'm glad you'll be able to wear it on the program, Beth. It's really lovely . . . Now, if you'll all line up again, we'll get to that question: What does Christmas mean to you?

BETH: Do we actually have to make speeches?

FLORENCE: Not speeches, Beth. Just something that comes to mind. *(Phone rings.)*

TOM: I'll get it. *(Crosses to phone, answers it)* Hello . . . Hi, Paul, how are you? . . . What? . . . No kidding! . . . That's perfect. It solves all my problems. Sure . . . Thanks, Paul. 'Bye. *(Hangs up; excitedly)* Hey, listen to this! Paul's bringing a TV to the dance tonight so that everyone can watch the show. And they're not going to crown the Queen until the show's over, so I'll be able to get back to the dance in time. Isn't that great?

OTHERS *(Ad lib):* That's wonderful, Tom. Great! Good news. *(Etc.* TOM *returns to his place before fireplace.)*

FLORENCE: Shall we get started? How about you, Mrs. Carson? What does Christmas mean to you?

MRS. CARSON: Well—I—*(She motions to the whole fam-*

ily.) I suppose that Christmas to me is epitomized in this little scene. It means having my family around me, it means sharing with them the good things in life, and, above all, it means giving some thought to others less fortunate than ourselves.

FLORENCE: That's lovely, Mrs. Carson . . . . Mr. Carson?

MR. CARSON: I can't improve on what my wife has said. Christmas is being together. It's happiness and good will.

GRANDMA: I'm an old lady, and I've spent many Christmases away from home. But Christmas isn't where you are, it's what you are. *(Gestures)* It's here—in your heart.

FLORENCE: Tom?

TOM: It's difficult to put into words how I really feel. Christmas is Mom and Dad and Beth and Grandma. It's receiving presents, but more than that, it's the fun and the warmth you feel when you give a present. It's just a happy, giving feeling all over.

BETH: Tom's right. That's it. A happy, giving feeling all over.

FLORENCE: How did it sound, Sam?

SAM *(Enthusiastically):* It sounded great. We've picked the right family, all right.

FLORENCE: I have a feeling tonight's program will be really special. Now, Mr. Carson, try reading from "A Christmas Carol." (MR. CARSON *picks up book from table and sits on sofa. Others take chairs.)*

GRANDMA: This is going to be the happiest and merriest Christmas ever! *(Others nod in agreement as* MR. CARSON *begins reading from the book. As he reads,* SAM *and* FLORENCE *exchange happy smiles. Curtain)*

THE END

Christmas Eve Letter

by Mildred Hark and Noel McQueen

Will Virginia get the answer she hopes for? . . .

Characters

IRENE STEVENS, *12*
BOB STEVENS, *14*
NORMA STEVENS, *15*
VIRGINIA STEVENS, *7*
CONNIE STEVENS }
HENRY STEVENS } *their parents*
MR. JOHNSON
CAROLERS

TIME: *Christmas Eve.*
SETTING: *The Stevens living room. A large Christmas tree is up left, with a stepladder and box of decorations on chair near it; mantel decorated with Christmas greens and cards is up center; up right is window. Diagonally up right is a sofa, behind which is a small table with packages visible above back of sofa. Down-*

41

*stage right is a large easy chair, table and telephone.
Exit right leads out; exit left to rest of house.*

AT RISE: BOB *is standing on stepladder, fastening ornament high on tree.* IRENE *is taking small Santa Claus
from box of decorations.*

IRENE (*Handing Santa to* BOB): Here's the Santa Claus,
Bob. We mustn't forget him.

BOB: I should say not. . . . He's getting a little dusty
looking, though, Irene.

IRENE: Well, no wonder, we've had him since we were
little.

BOB: I know—he needs a new suit. (*Hangs Santa on tree*)

IRENE: Dad gave it to you when you woke up late one
Christmas morning and cried and cried because you
missed Santa.

BOB: I was afraid he was stuck in the chimney, and I
didn't want Dad to light the fire. The Santa ornament
finally made me stop crying, I remember.

IRENE (*Standing back and looking up at tree*): Oh, Bob,
the tree looks beautiful! (*Rummages through box
again*) Oh, look. Here are the Christmas angels Ginny
made last year. Where will you put them?

BOB: I don't know. Where is Ginny, anyhow?

IRENE (*Dropping angels on chair*): I don't know. (*Calls
left*) Ginny! Ginny, where are you? (*After a short
pause,* GINNY *enters left.*)

GINNY (*Softly*): Here I am, Irene. Why did you call me?

IRENE: I was just wondering where you were . . . (*Staring
at her*) Ginny, don't you feel well?

GINNY: I'm all right. I was just playing. . . .

BOB: I'll bet you were watching Mom make the Christmas pies.

IRENE (*Sniffing*): Oh, Bob, don't they smell good? I hope
Mom serves them tonight when we get back from caroling.

BOB: So do I.

GINNY: Has the mailman come, Irene?

IRENE: Why, he came this morning. There's a whole stack of Christmas cards on the mantel.

GINNY: I know, but I think he'll come again. The day before Christmas Eve he might make an extra delivery. I wish I'd get a letter.

IRENE: A letter? From whom? *(She picks up the angels again and goes over to mantel.)* Ginny, where shall we put your Christmas angels—on the mantel here? *(She sets them along the middle of the mantel.)*

GINNY *(Starting off left; sadly):* I don't care, Irene. Anywhere is all right. *(Exits)*

IRENE: But, Ginny—Bob, what in the world is the matter with Ginny? She's acting so strangely.

BOB *(Crossing to tree and rearranging tinsel):* I thought so, too. She was so quiet.

IRENE: She's always been more excited than anyone about Christmas, and that's saying a lot in this house! You don't suppose she's sick, do you?

BOB: I'm sure she's all right. You know Ginny—she's probably up to something and can't think about anything else at the moment. Probably a surprise for Mom and Dad or—(NORMA *enters right, her arms full of packages.)*

NORMA: Hi!

IRENE: Norma! Just in time. *(She runs to NORMA and helps her put packages on easy chair. NORMA takes off her hat and coat and tosses them on sofa.)*

BOB: Did you get that tie for Dad?

NORMA: Yes, and the prettiest necklace for Mom.

IRENE: And the doll for Ginny that we saw the other day?

NORMA: Yes, I'm glad it was still there. Mom said we had so many things for Ginny already, but this is so cute. *(She opens box.)* Look, Bob. *(He looks in box.)*

BOB: That's great.

NORMA *(Opening smaller package):* And here's Mom's necklace.

MRS. STEVENS *(From offstage; calling):* Irene, Bob—is the tree done?

NORMA *(Calling):* Mother, don't come in right now. *(Shows* IRENE *necklace)*

IRENE *(Whispering):* How beautiful, Norma! Mom will love it. (NORMA *puts necklace in box, then back into bag, and takes out package of "icicles.")*

NORMA: And here are the icicles for the tree.

BOB *(Taking package):* Great. I thought we needed more. *(Opens box and starts putting them on tree)*

NORMA *(Calling off):* You can come in now, Mom. (MRS. STEVENS *enters, smiling.)*

MRS. STEVENS *(Cheerfully):* Oh, I can, can I? What's going on here? *(Looking at tree)* The tree is beautiful!

BOB: Of course. That's because every year we get new ornaments and decorations.

IRENE: Now if it would only snow, everything would be perfect. Did it look like snow when you were outside, Norma?

NORMA: Not at all—the sky was bright and clear.

IRENE: Oh, dear. I *do* want a white Christmas.

BOB: Well, there's no time to dream of a white Christmas—there are too many things to do.

IRENE: Yes, we didn't hang the mistletoe yet, Mom—

MRS. STEVENS: Your father can do that when he comes home. I wish he'd hurry—he's missing half the fun. I just took the pies out of the oven and put a sprig of holly on each one—

BOB: They smell terrific. I've got a good mind to sample one.

MRS. STEVENS: Don't you dare! And the puddings are

mixed, but I still have to make the stuffing for the turkey.

NORMA: And there are presents to wrap—

MRS. STEVENS: I won't get to that until late tonight. I do hope your father's new slippers fit. After all these years, I never seem to be sure I'm getting the right size.

IRENE: I wish I could think of something besides ties and socks and slippers for Dad.

MRS. STEVENS: But your father would be lost if he didn't get a new pair of slippers for Christmas. Besides, I bought him a real surprise this year. He's always wanted a red dressing gown—*(Goes over to chair)* Hm-m-m, I see someone's been shopping.

NORMA *(Standing in front of her):* Uh-uh—mustn't touch. Secrets. But you can look at this—I got Ginny's doll. *(She opens the box.)*

MRS. STEVENS: That's lovely! What a beautiful face.

IRENE: Mom, have you seen Ginny?

MRS. STEVENS: No, dear, not lately. I thought she'd be helping you with the tree.

BOB: She was in here for a few minutes. She acted kind of funny, Mom.

MRS. STEVENS: Funny?

IRENE: You don't think she's sick, do you?

MRS. STEVENS: Oh, I hope not. She gets so overexcited about things—

BOB: No, it wasn't that, Mom. She was just very quiet.

MRS. STEVENS *(Relieved):* Well, then, she's probably in her room, figuring out some unusual way to wrap her packages. You know how she likes to make each one different. But I'll go see. I have to go upstairs anyhow. *(Exits left)*

NORMA: We'd better start wrapping our gifts, if we're going caroling tonight. *(Going to table behind sofa)* Is this all the Christmas paper we have?

BOB: No, there'a a whole lot more and some ribbon on the dining room table. *(Exits.* IRENE *goes to window right.)*

NORMA *(Starting to wrap package):* What are you doing, Irene?

IRENE: Looking to see if it's snowing. (BOB *enters with paper and balls of ribbon.)*

BOB: Here you are. *(Drops them on sofa)*

IRENE: Say, does anyone remember where we hid the rest of Mom's presents?

NORMA: Sure I do. Wouldn't it be funny if we forgot some year?

BOB: Remember when we all hid our presents in the same closet? What a mix-up! *(They laugh.)*

MR. STEVENS *(From offstage):* Hello, everyone! Is the coast clear?

IRENE: It's Dad! (MR. STEVENS *enters, carrying a small table, covered with brown paper, and lots of packages.)*

MR. STEVENS *(Whispering):* Your mother isn't in here, is she?

BOB: No, but, Dad—what in the world . . .

MR. STEVENS *(Putting table down):* It's for your mother—the kind she's been wanting for years. The finest mahogany with a hand-rubbed finish.

IRENE: Oh, Dad! She'll love it.

MR. STEVENS: Where can I hide it?

IRENE: Maybe we could put it in the hall closet.

MR. STEVENS: The hall closet is full of packages. And, besides, your mother would notice it there right away.

BOB: I have an idea, Dad. Look—*(Goes to back of sofa)* Mom put this old table behind the sofa so it wouldn't show so much. We can put the new one next to it—

MR. STEVENS: I don't know. Your mother would see . . .

BOB: Not if we pile a lot of stuff on both of them. We can put a piece of paper on the top to protect it. Then if we cover it with presents and paper and ribbon, Mom will think it's part of the old table.

MR. STEVENS: Well, let's try it. *(They set new table behind sofa and* BOB *starts to cut off brown paper.* GINNY *enters.)*

GINNY: Daddy—

MR. STEVENS *(Picking her up):* Virginia! How's my little girl? All full of Christmas, I bet. *(He puts her down and turns to table.* NORMA *is moving packages, pulls out newspaper stuck between boxes.)*

NORMA: What's in all these packages, Dad?

MR. STEVENS *(Taking them from her):* Never you mind— I'll take care of them. *(Picking up newspaper)* And my newspaper. *(Puts packages on sofa and newspaper on table near easy chair. Hands* NORMA *one package)* Here, you can have this one.

NORMA: What is it?

MR. STEVENS: Icicles. *(They all laugh.)*

IRENE: More icicles!

MR. STEVENS: Well, we never seem to have enough.

BOB *(Uncovering table):* Here it is, folks! Solid mahogany!

NORMA: Oh, Dad, it's beautiful.

IRENE: Look at the finish—

MR. STEVENS *(To* GINNY): It's for your mother, Ginny. *(She nods, seriously.)*

BOB *(Carrying table behind sofa):* See, Dad, this will be perfect. *(Puts it next to other table, and covers it with Christmas paper.)* This paper will protect it. Now give me some things to put on it. *(Girls hand* BOB *paper, ribbon, and packages.)*

IRENE: Mother will never notice it.

NORMA: The more we put on it the better off we'll be.

MR. STEVENS *(Worried):* But the top might get scratched.

IRENE *(Continuing to put packages on top):* It's as safe as can be. These things are light anyhow.

MRS. STEVENS *(From offstage; calling):* Henry, is that you?

MR. STEVENS *(To children):* Quick—get away from the table. She's coming! (MRS. STEVENS *enters.)*

MRS. STEVENS: Henry, I thought I heard your voice.

MR. STEVENS *(Crossing to kiss her):* Connie, my dear.

BOB: Hey, Dad, you can't kiss Mom yet—the mistletoe isn't up. *(He picks up sprig of mistletoe from table and grins.)*

MR. STEVENS *(Taking it):* Oh, I can't, can't I? *(Holds mistletoe over* MRS. STEVENS'*s head and kisses her again.)* Just for that, I'll do it again. *(They all laugh.)*

MRS. STEVENS: I'm glad you're home, Henry—*(Doorbell rings.)* Now, who can that be?

NORMA: Someone delivering presents early?

MRS. STEVENS: I'll go see. *(She exits.)*

GINNY *(Eagerly):* Maybe it's the mailman.

MR. STEVENS: Now, what are you expecting, Virginia? (BOB *has opened the new box of icicles and is putting them on tree.)*

BOB: Never too many icicles, I always say.

IRENE: Did it look like snow when you came in, Dad?

NORMA *(Shaking head):* Irene and her snow.

IRENE: What did it say in the paper? Did you read the weather, Dad?

MR. STEVENS: I haven't read the paper yet.

BOB *(Laughing):* Well, it *must* be Christmas if Dad hasn't read his paper.

IRENE *(Picking up newspaper and reading):* Snow tonight and tomorrow.

MR. STEVENS: Well, if *The Chronicle* says snow, it will

probably snow. (IRENE *goes to window.* MRS. STEVENS *enters with packages and cards.*)

IRENE: But it doesn't look a bit like it.

MRS. STEVENS: That was the mailman. *(Sifting through envelopes)* More cards—and a package, too.

GINNY: Was there—anything for me?

MRS. STEVENS *(Opening letter):* No, dear. *(Reading)* Mr. and Mrs. Henry Stevens—Mr. and Mrs. Henry Stevens and family—Henry, I haven't had time to look through half of these beautiful cards.

MR. STEVENS: We'll look through them tonight.

BOB *(Taking package from her):* Here, Mom, I'll put that back here. *(Puts it on new table)*

MR. STEVENS: Be careful, Bob.

MRS. STEVENS: What's that, Henry?

MR. STEVENS: Er—nothing.

GINNY *(Persistently):* Are you sure there wasn't a letter for me, Mother?

MRS. STEVENS *(Stacking cards on mantel):* Now, Virginia, who in the world are you expecting a letter from? Of course there will be something for you in those packages from Aunt Sophie and Cousin Emily, but we'll save those to open tomorrow, when we open the things that Santa Claus brings. (GINNY *bursts into tears.*)

GINNY: Oh, Mother—*(Turns and starts to exit)*

MRS. STEVENS: Ginny, darling, what's the matter?

GINNY: Nothing, Mother.

MR. STEVENS: Ginny, aren't you feeling well?

IRENE: We thought you were acting funny before. What's wrong? (MRS. STEVENS *leads* GINNY *to sofa and sits with her arm around her)*

MRS. STEVENS: Now, tell me, darling—do you have a stomach ache? A sore throat?

GINNY *(Sniffling):* No, I'm not sick, Mother.

MR. STEVENS: I think you might be catching a cold. *(Leaning over and taking hold of her chin)* Say ah-h-h, Virginia.

GINNY *(Opening her mouth):* Ah-h-h.

MR. STEVENS *(Looking, then standing up):* It doesn't look a bit inflamed.

MRS. STEVENS *(Holding hand to* GINNY'*s forehead):* And she doesn't feel hot.

MR. STEVENS: Connie, I think we'd better call the doctor just the same. (MRS. STEVENS *nods.*)

GINNY: Oh, Mother, please—(MR. STEVENS *starts toward phone.*)

MR. STEVENS: What's Dr. Brown's telephone number, Connie? (GINNY *rises and runs to* MR. STEVENS.)

GINNY: Please don't call Dr. Brown. I'm not sick.

MR. STEVENS: But, honey, why would you be crying on Christmas Eve unless you were sick?

GINNY: It isn't because I don't feel well that I'm crying. It's because—*(She stops.)*

MR. STEVENS: What is it?

GINNY: Because there isn't any Santa Claus! *(She runs off left.)*

NORMA: So that's it.

IRENE: Some of the other kids at school must have been talking to her.

BOB: What do you suppose the letter had to do with it? Do you suppose she wrote a letter to Santa Claus?

IRENE: Probably to the North Pole, and when she didn't get an answer—*(Sighs)*

MR. STEVENS: This will ruin her whole Christmas!

IRENE: And ours, too. If Ginny's unhappy, I can't enjoy things.

MRS. STEVENS: We'll just have to hope we can think of the right things to say to her. *(Doorbell rings.)*

BOB: Who could that be?

MRS. STEVENS: Will you get it, Henry? I'll go up and talk to Ginny. *(She exits left, as* MR. STEVENS *exits right.)*

BOB: I feel so bad.

IRENE: So do I.

NORMA: It'll be harder on Ginny than anyone else. She's so sensitive and things mean so much to her. (MR. STEVENS *enters with* BILL JOHNSON, *who carries large package.)*

MR. STEVENS: Come on in, Bill. Children, say hello to Mr. Johnson.

ALL *(Ad lib):* Hi, Mr. Johnson. Merry Christmas! *(Etc.)*

MR. JOHNSON: Hello, all. That tree looks wonderful. Just thought I'd drop by on my way home and leave this. *(Puts package on table near easy chair.)*

IRENE: We sent something over to your house, too, Mr. Johnson.

MR. STEVENS: Don't tell me you've already put *The Chronicle* to bed, and you're going to spend Christmas Eve at home?

MR. JOHNSON: You bet I am, Henry. *(Casually)* By the way, have you read today's issue of *The Chronicle?*

MR. STEVENS: Not yet, Bill, I'm ashamed to say. (MRS. STEVENS *enters, her arm around* GINNY.)

MRS. STEVENS: Hello, Bill. What a nice surprise.

MR. JOHNSON: Hello, Connie. Merry Christmas. *(Turning to* MR. STEVENS) Then Virginia hasn't seen the answer to her letter! *(Excitedly)* I really should have called you—(GINNY *runs forward.)*

GINNY: Did you answer my letter, Mr. Johnson? Did you?

MR. JOHNSON: Of course I did, Virginia. *(He looks around, sees paper, picks it up)* It's right here on the front page.

MRS. STEVENS: So you were the one she was expecting a letter from, Bill.

MR. JOHNSON: Right. Virginia wrote a letter to the paper,

asking if there was a Santa Claus, and I thought it would be nice to print the answer so all the other children in town could see it. *(Showing* GINNY*)* Look— there's your name—Virginia Stevens—and the letter you wrote me. *(All crowd around.)*

GINNY: I can't believe it!

NORMA: What does it say, Ginny?

GINNY: I told Mr. Johnson that all the boys and girls at school say there isn't a Santa Claus. *(Looks at paper)* "I know you're a friend of Daddy's and I am writing to you because my Daddy says you always print the truth. Will you please tell me if there's a Santa Claus."

BOB: That's a great letter, Ginny.

MR. JOHNSON: Yes, it is, and I must confess I didn't write the answer myself. A man by the name of Francis Church wrote it a long time ago. In fact it was printed in the *New York Sun* in 1897, in answer to another little girl's asking if there was a Santa Claus—a letter very similar to yours, Ginny. *(Points to paper)* I mention that here.

MRS. STEVENS: I think I've read that editorial by Mr. Church.

MR. JOHNSON: You probably have—it's very famous, but I've never happened to reprint it. But since Ginny had the same name as the little girl who wrote the letter so long ago—

NORMA: Was her name Virginia, too?

MR. JOHNSON: Yes. *(Turning)* Well, I've got to be on my way. Have your father read the letter to you, Ginny— and I'm sure everything's going to be fine.

GINNY *(Happily):* Oh, thank you, Mr. Johnson!

MR. JOHNSON: You're welcome, Ginny. Have a Merry Christmas, all of you! *(Starts to exit)*

MRS. STEVENS: Can you stay a little while, Bill? I've just

put the tea on, and we have fresh cookies. We need a little bite to eat before we go caroling.

MR. JOHNSON: Thanks, no, I've got to be getting home. I'll see you tomorrow.

MR. STEVENS: Thank you, Bill. You don't know what this means to us. There was a major crisis developing.

MRS. STEVENS: Goodbye, and Merry Christmas. (MR. STEVENS *and* MR. JOHNSON *exit*.)

GINNY *(Still looking at paper):* Oh, I'm so anxious to have Daddy read the answer. Can he do it right now?

MRS. STEVENS: Sure he can. Let's all sit down and listen. Bob, will you go get the plate of sandwiches on the kitchen table? And Irene, the cookies are on the counter. (BOB *and* IRENE *exit*. MR. STEVENS *re-enters*.)

GINNY: Daddy, please read the letter—*(She hands him paper.* BOB *and* IRENE *enter with plates of food.)*

MR. STEVENS: You bet I will. Come on, Ginny, you sit with me. *(Others take food, sprawl on sofa and chairs,* MRS. STEVENS *at left.* GINNY *sits in* MR. STEVENS'S *lap).*

GINNY: Oh, Daddy, I can't wait!

MR. STEVENS: Now, after your letter, which we all heard, there's the letter that the other little girl wrote so long ago. Here it is. *(Reading)* "Dear Editor: I am eight years old. Some of my little friends say there is no Santa Claus. Papa says 'If you see it in the *Sun* it's so.' Please tell me the truth, is there a Santa Claus? Virginia O'Hanlon."

GINNY: Why, that's something like my letter, Daddy.

MR. STEVENS: And now, here's what Mr. Church answered way back in 1897. *(Reading)* "Virginia, your little friends are wrong."

GINNY: Daddy, there *is* a Santa Claus then—there is a Santa Claus! *(They all smile.)*

MR. STEVENS *(Nodding and continuing):* "They have been affected by the skepticism of a skeptical age."

GINNY: Skep-ti-cism? What does that mean?

MR. STEVENS: Well, it means that people don't believe in things enough—in good things, that is—and I think that applies to today just as it did in 1897.But listen to the rest, Ginny.

GINNY: All right.

MR. STEVENS *(Reading):* "They do not believe except what they see. They think that nothing can be which is not comprehensible by their little minds. All minds, Virginia, whether they be men's or children's, are little. In this great universe of ours, man is a mere insect, an ant, in his intellect, as compared with the boundless world about him, as measured by the intelligence capable of grasping the whole of truth and knowledge."

BOB: This is really good.

MR. STEVENS *(Continuing):* "Yes, Virginia, there is a Santa Claus. (GINNY *smiles again.*) He exists as certainly as love and generosity and devotion exist, and you know that they abound and give to your life its highest beauty and joy. Alas! How dreary would be the world if there were no Santa Claus!"

GINNY: Of course it would. That's what I told Tommy Jones.

MR. STEVENS *(Reading):* "It would be as dreary as if there were no Virginias. There would be no childlike faith then, no poetry, no romance to make tolerable this existence. We should have no enjoyment, except in sense and sight. The eternal light with which childhood fills the world would be extinguished."

GINNY *(Leaning against his shoulder):* I'm so glad there is a Santa Claus.

MR. STEVENS: "Not believe in Santa Claus! You might as

well not believe in fairies! You might get your papa to hire men to watch in all the chimneys on Christmas Eve to catch Santa Claus (GINNY *sits up*), but even if they did not see Santa Claus coming down, what would that prove? Nobody sees Santa Claus, but that is no sign that there is no Santa Claus."

GINNY: That's what I told the kids in school. We never see Santa, except sometimes in stores, and those men are just Santa's helpers. We'd never really see Santa Claus—he wouldn't want us to.

MR. STEVENS: Exactly. *(Reading)* "The most real things in the world are those that neither children nor men can see. Did you ever see fairies dancing on the lawn? Of course not, but that's no proof that they are not there. Nobody can conceive or imagine all the wonders there are unseen and unseeable in the world."

NORMA: I'll say. You realize that when you start to study science. You keep going back—this started that and that started this.

MR. STEVENS: That's right. *(Continuing)* "You tear apart the baby's rattle and see what makes the noise inside, but there is a veil covering the unseen world which not the strongest man, nor even the united strength of all the strongest men that ever lived, could tear apart."

GINNY: What does that mean, Daddy? The unseen world?

MR. STEVENS: Well, it means that—well, that the things we think in our minds are more real than the things we can touch with our hands. It means all the mysteries there are in the universe which no one can understand.

IRENE: That letter makes Christmas just about perfect, Dad.

MR. STEVENS *(Reading):* "Only faith, fancy, poetry, love, romance, can push aside that curtain and view and picture the supernatural beauty and glory beyond. Is it all real? Ah, Virginia, in all this world there is nothing else real and abiding. No Santa Claus? He lives and lives forever."

GINNY: Oh, Daddy.

MR. STEVENS *(Reading):* "A thousand years from now, Virginia, nay, ten times ten thousand years from now, he will continue to make glad the heart of childhood."

GINNY: Ten times ten thousand years—it hasn't been that long since 1897, has it? *(All laugh.)*

MRS. STEVENS: I should say not, darling. Not even a hundred.

MR. STEVENS: Besides, Virginia, the way it's used here, ten times ten thousand means always.

GINNY *(Happily):* Always! There'll always be a Santa Claus.

IRENE: That means forever, Ginny. *(Voices of carolers are heard offstage.)*

BOB *(Jumping up):* The carolers!

IRENE *(Running to window):* Here they come—oh, and look! It's starting to snow! Great big soft flakes!

MR. STEVENS: Didn't I tell you *The Chronicle* always prints the truth?

IRENE: I love singing carols in the snow—come on, everybody! (NORMA *picks up coat and hat.*)

BOB: We're late—they're probably wondering what happened to us. (IRENE *exits, with* NORMA.) See you all later. *(He exits.)*

MRS. STEVENS *(Calling):* Don't forget to bring the carolers in for the pies and hot chocolate when you finish.

BOB *(From offstage; calling):* We won't! Goodbye!

MR. *and* MRS. STEVENS, GINNY *(Ad lib):* Goodbye! Have fun! *(Etc.)*

GINNY *(Running to window):* There they go—they're

starting to sing with the others! *(Carolers are heard offstage.)*

MR. STEVENS: I can hear Bob's voice.

MRS. STEVENS: How beautiful! I'd just like to sit here and listen, but there's so much to do. *(Rising)* I'll get busy wrapping presents and straightening up this room.

GINNY: I'll help you, Mother. *(She picks up some Christmas paper and piles it on the tables behind the sofa.)*

MRS. STEVENS *(Crossing in front of sofa)*: No, Ginny, I wouldn't keep piling things up back there. *(Seeing tables)* What's all this? I suppose the children thought they'd put everything back here to get it out of the way. *(Moves behind sofa)* I'm going to take some of these things and—*(She starts picking paper, etc., off table.)*

MR. STEVENS: No—no, Connie, you mustn't touch—

MRS. STEVENS: But Henry, I've got to straighten up— *(Takes more off tables and puts them on sofa)*

MR. STEVENS: Connie, please—

MRS. STEVENS: What in the world? *(Removes more paper, etc.)* Why, there are two tables back here.

MR. STEVENS *(Giving up)*: All right, Connie, if you insist—have your surprise early.

MRS. STEVENS: My surprise? *(She has taken everything off new table.)* Henry—this is a beautiful mahogany table—the one I've been wanting!

MR. STEVENS *(Going over and lifting new table over to center of room)*: Your Christmas present, my dear. It was too big to hide so we tried to camouflage it.

MRS. STEVENS: Oh, Henry, it's beautiful. I never dreamed I'd own anything like this. *(Happily)* Oh, Henry, there is a Santa Claus!

GINNY: But of course there is, Mother. Didn't we just read about him?

MRS. STEVENS *(Laughing)*: That's right, darling!

GINNY *(More seriously):* It's different, though, from what I thought. I guess I'll understand it better when I'm older.

MR. STEVENS: But you're satisfied—?

MRS. STEVENS: You're happy about Christmas—?

GINNY *(Smiling):* Oh, yes! I guess the more things you know and understand about what Christmas means, the more wonderful it is! *(Carolers are heard singing, as curtain falls.)*

THE END

A Tree to Trim

by Aileen Fisher

A stodgy professor reluctantly writes a Christmas play, and comes to understand the true meaning of the holiday. . . .

Characters

MR. ARCHIBALD, *an author*
MISS ROSE, *his secretary*
SAM, *his handyman*
LARRY ⎫
LINDA ⎬ *the children next door*
LOU ⎭

SETTING: *Mr. Archibald's study.*
AT RISE: MR. ARCHIBALD *is pacing up and down, dictating to his secretary,* MISS ROSE, *who is seated at the desk, holding a shorthand pad.*

MR. ARCHIBALD (*Stopping his pacing for a moment*): "It is important for all students of twelfth-century history to remember that in Lancashire . . ." do you have that. Miss Rose?
MISS ROSE: Yes, Mr. Archibald.
MR. ARCHIBALD: Very good. Now, where was I?
MISS ROSE: "It is important for all students of twelfth-century history to remember that in Lancashire . . ."
MR. ARCHIBALD: Oh, yes. In Lancashire. . . . or was it in Cheshire?
MISS ROSE: I'm sure I don't know, Mr. Archibald.
MR. ARCHIBALD (*Puzzled*): Was it in Lancashire or was it

in Cheshire? Dear me, how could I ever forget such an important point?

MISS ROSE: Perhaps you could look it up in one of your books.

MR. ARCHIBALD: Of course I can, Miss Rose. Just what I was about to suggest myself. I'll look it up. (*Calls off right.*) Sam! Sam! Oh, where *is* that lazy handyman of mine? Sam!

(SAM, *a slow and silent but good-natured fellow, appears in the doorway, at right.*)

MR. ARCHIBALD: Ah, there you are, Sam. I want you to take these files back to my library, and bring me a copy of the *Encyclopedia of Mediaeval England.* (SAM *picks up some cardboard file boxes, precariously balanced one on top of another, and gingerly begins to carry them to the doorway. Halfway, he stumbles and drops the files, spilling the contents all over the floor.*)

MISS ROSE (*Alarmed*): Oh, Sam, did you hurt yourself? (SAM *looks sheepish.*)

MR. ARCHIBALD (*Growling*): Never mind whether he hurt *himself,* Miss Rose! What's important is whether he hurt *my notes!* Look at them: my precious files all over the floor! I see I can't trust *you,* Sam, to bring me the book I need. I'll have to get it myself! While I'm gone, I want you to pick up all the cards you dropped—and see that you put them back in the right files. (MR. ARCHIBALD *goes out.*)

SAM: What a grouch!

MISS ROSE (*Going over to* SAM, *who is still on the floor*): Never mind Mr. Archibald, Sam. He didn't mean to be cross with you. Here, let me help you. (*Together they begin to pick up the notes.*)

SAM: You're a real friend, Miss Rose, but I don't know how you put up with him.

MISS ROSE: I know Mr. Archibald *sounds* grumpy, but

that's because he has his mind on the book he's writing. He is a very serious historian, you know, and that's why he gets annoyed sometimes. You mustn't mind him, though.

SAM (*Smiling at* MISS ROSE): I guess if you can stand him, I can.

MISS ROSE: There! All the notes are back where they belong. (*There is a knock at the door.*) I wonder who that can be. Sam, you take the files into the library—and be careful! I'll see who's at the door.

SAM: Thanks a lot for your help, Miss Rose. (SAM *picks up files and goes off right.* MISS ROSE *opens door at left, and admits* LARRY, LINDA *and* LOU, *three children dressed in winter clothes. They look around tentatively.*)

MISS ROSE: Why, good afternoon, children! What a pleasant surprise!

LARRY: Good afternoon, Miss Rose.

MISS ROSE: What can I do for you?

LINDA: We're sorry to trouble you like this, but it's awfully important! (*Looks around*) Is Mr. Archibald in?

MISS ROSE: Well—yes, he is. But I'm afraid that Mr. Archibald is very busy right now, and can't be disturbed.

LARRY (*Crestfallen*): Aw—

MISS ROSE: Perhaps it's something that I can help you with?

LINDA: Thank you, Miss Rose, but— I guess we really need Mr. Archibald.

LOU: Yes. You see, we need the help of a writer. A real author!

MISS ROSE: What is it? You all seem so mysterious!

LARRY (*Eagerly*): Well—we thought that since Christmas is coming soon, this would be a good time for us to try to do something for somebody who wouldn't have much of a Christmas.

LINDA: There are lots of children in the orphanage who won't have much fun.

LOU: So Larry, Linda and I decided to do something about it.

MISS ROSE: What a wonderful idea! But I don't see why you need Mr. Archibald's help.

LINDA: We thought that perhaps—if he wanted to, of course—Mr. Archibald could write a Christmas play for us to put on at the orphanage on Christmas Eve.

LARRY: We'd write the play ourselves, but Christmas is only a few days away, and it would take *us* months and months to write one.

LINDA: Since Mr. Archibald is an experienced, *professional* writer—why, it wouldn't take *him* much time at all!

LARRY (*Glumly*): But I guess if he's busy . . .

MISS ROSE: I'll tell you what I'll do: I'll tell Mr. Archibald what you want, and though I can't promise a thing, I'm quite sure that when he hears your good idea, he'll want to do everything he can to help.

LINDA: Oh, would you, Miss Rose? That would be wonderful!

LARRY: Just think: a Christmas play by the famous writer, Mr. Archibald!

MISS ROSE (*As the children move to the door.*): Of course, it isn't exactly in his line; but I'll tell him.

LOU (*Going out*): Thank you so much, Miss Rose.

MISS ROSE (*Talking to the children who are now outside the room*): It was nice of you to think of him. (*Pause*) I'll certainly tell him. (MR. ARCHIBALD *enters, carrying a book, from right.*)

MISS ROSE (*Without seeing him*): Yes, I'll let you know. Goodbye.

MR. ARCHIBALD: Please close the door, Miss Rose. You're letting in enough of a draft to freeze my brain!

MISS ROSE (*Closing the door, hurriedly*): I'm sorry, Mr. Archibald. Did you find the information you wanted?

MR. ARCHIBALD (*Grumpily*): Yes. It was Lancashire all the time. I *knew* it was Lancashire! But all your chatter out here didn't help me any! You know I insist on perfect silence while I work!

MISS ROSE: I'm sorry, sir.

MR. ARCHIBALD: Whom were you talking to anyway, Miss Rose, at this time of day?

MISS ROSE: It was the children next door, Mr. Archibald. You know, Larry, Linda and Lou.

MR. ARCHIBALD: Oh. (*He looks at pages, scratches his head, then looks up.*) The children next door? What did they want? I've told their mother time and time again that they're not to bother me.

MISS ROSE (*Hesitating*): Well, it's—it's a rather unusual thing, sir. They—they want you to write a play for them.

MR. ARCHIBALD (*Exploding*): A play! Why on earth do they think I would write a play for them? I happen to be a historian, *not* a playwright. Did you tell them that?

MISS ROSE: Yes, I did mention it.

MR. ARCHIBALD: Here I am, in the midst of a new book about the twelfth century, and they think I should write a play! I hope you told them I could not waste my time writing plays.

MISS ROSE: I told them you were very busy.

MR. ARCHIBALD: I am indeed. (*He returns to his notes for a moment, then looks up.*) And what, may I ask, was this play to be about?

MISS ROSE: It's a play for Christmas.

MR. ARCHIBALD: Christmas! Why should an historian write a play about Christmas? If you ask me, there's altogether too much fuss made about Christmas these days, anyhow.

Miss Rose (*Timidly*): Well, you see, sir, the children want to put on a little play for the orphans over at the Children's Home on Christmas Eve. I—I think it's a very nice idea, sir. A thoughtful idea. Well, a *Christmasy* idea.

Mr. Archibald (*Sharply*): Oh, you do?

Miss Rose (*Bravely*): Yes, sir, I do!

Mr. Archibald (*Suspiciously*): And what did you tell the children, Miss Rose?

Miss Rose (*Timidly*): I said I thought you might possibly —perhaps—*maybe* write a play for them.

Mr. Archibald (*Jumping up, and letting the manuscript pages fall*): Oh, you did, did you? You ought to know better than that! (*Looks at pages*) *Now* see what's happened to my manuscript! And all on account of Christmas! (*He and Miss Rose scramble about picking up pages.*)

Miss Rose: Oh, dear! If we get these pages mixed up, we'll *never* be able to sort them out again!

Mr. Archibald: Why not? Aren't the pages numbered?

Miss Rose: Yes, sir, but you keep changing the order! Let me think: did page 16 come after page 4, this time—or after page 24?

Mr. Archibald: Authors are entitled to change their minds, Miss Rose.

Miss Rose: Yes, I suppose everyone should be able to change his mind.

Mr. Archibald (*Handing papers to Miss Rose*): That's good enough for now. I'll look them over again in the morning.

Miss Rose (*Taking the sheets to her desk*): Yes, sir. (*She sighs*) You've certainly done a lot of writing lately. (*Shakes her head, then looks at Mr. Archibald admiringly*) You know, I think you could write a wonderful play for Christmas, after all that practice.

MR. ARCHIBALD (*Pleased in spite of himself*): You do?

MISS ROSE: My, yes! A man with your imagination . . .

MR. ARCHIBALD: Well, maybe I could. Maybe I could. But why should I? It's all stuff and nonsense. Why should I waste my time on a little Christmas play, an important, famous, *professional* writer like me?

MISS ROSE: Why, Mr. Archibald! Those are the very words the children used!

MR. ARCHIBALD (*Lighting up*): They did?

MISS ROSE: That was why they wanted *you* to write the play for them—because they knew you would do such a fine job. I think it was Larry who said they came to you because you were an experienced, professional writer. No, I'm wrong. That was Linda! It was Larry who called you famous.

MR. ARCHIBALD (*Pleased*): They said those things about me, did they? How perceptive. Of course, I always *said* they were intelligent children! Larry called me a famous writer, eh?

MISS ROSE: That's right, Mr. Archibald. And I agree with them. I think you're the perfect person to write the Christmas play.

MR. ARCHIBALD: Well, maybe I could at that. I've always wanted to write a play, you know. Maybe—(*Stops suddenly*) No, it's ridiculous. I don't have the time.

MISS ROSE: But it wouldn't take long. Why, I'll bet you could write a whole play in an hour. After all, you did all of this difficult writing—(*Holds up paper*)—in a week.

MR. ARCHIBALD: I suppose you're right. It wouldn't take me too long. (*Thinks, then shakes his head.*) But I don't have a Christmas thought in my head.

MISS ROSE (*Picking up her stenographer's pad*): Let's see. The play could be about the Star of Bethlehem—or Santa Claus—or—

MR. ARCHIBALD (*Warming up*): Or what about a historical Christmas play? That's it! I'll do a historical Christmas play! (*Stops, shakes his head*) No. I need a change from history.

MISS ROSE: Well—what about a Christmas tree?

MR. ARCHIBALD: A Christmas tree, eh? Hmm. A Christmas tree! Miss Rose, that's it! A Christmas tree! A nice little fir tree, smelling like a balsam pillow. Or a nice little blue spruce with silvered needles. Ah! (*He calls out loudly*) Sam! I say, Sam! (SAM *enters from right.*) Sam, because of your carelessness as a handyman, I've decided to take that job away from you. (SAM *clasps his hands in a pleading manner.*)

MISS ROSE: Oh, Mr. Archibald . . .

MR. ARCHIBALD: Don't worry. Come here, Sam. You're going to be a stagehand instead. (SAM *does a spritely little skip over to* MR. ARCHIBALD.) Now, look. I'm going to write a play—a play for Christmas. This is the stage. (*He makes a sweeping gesture around room.*) Out there is the audience. (*Points at audience.*) All you have to do is use your imagination. (SAM *thinks a moment, then bows grandly to audience.*) No, no, Sam. You aren't going to be an actor. You're going to be a stagehand. A stagehand! (SAM *looks blank.*)

MISS ROSE (*Patiently*): What Mr. Archibald means, Sam, is that you will bring in the things we need for the play.

MR. ARCHIBALD: Right! For instance, if I say "Stagehand! I shall need an elephant!" all you will have to do is bring in an elephant. (SAM *looks panicky, his mouth open.*) But I'm sure I shan't need an elephant! (SAM *gives deep sigh of relief.*) Now let's see. Where were we, Miss Rose?

MISS ROSE: We got as far as the Christmas tree.

MR. ARCHIBALD: Oh yes, the Christmas tree. (*He bows to* SAM.) Stagehand, I shall need a Christmas tree. A nice, green Christmas tree—not too big, not too small, but just right. (SAM *nods slowly.* MR. ARCHIBALD *turns him around, heads him to the door, gives him a gentle push.* SAM *marches out.*) Now, Miss Rose, when we get the Christmas tree, what shall we do with it?

MISS ROSE: Put it right in the middle of the stage.

MR. ARCHIBALD (*Impatiently*): Of *course* we'll put it right in the middle of the stage! But that isn't enough, you know. We can't just say to the audience, "Here is a Christmas tree. Isn't it a pretty one? THE END!" Now can we?

MISS ROSE: Oh, no! The Christmas tree will have to *mean* something.

MR. ARCHIBALD: That's it, Miss Rose. What we need is a plan. A plot!

MISS ROSE (*Thinking hard*): A plan—a plot—I know! Let's have the tree be a *magic* Christmas tree, Mr. Archibald.

MR. ARCHIBALD (*Annoyed*): Now, see here, Miss Rose. I cannot write a play about magic. If the children want magic, they'll have to ask someone else. According to my history books, the existence of magic has been disproved in the 2nd, 4th, 6th, 8th, 14th, 16th, 18th and 20th centuries inclusive!

MISS ROSE (*Wistfully*): But there *is* a kind of magic about Christmas. (*Brightly*) And the way you find out things about the 12th century—that seems like magic to me.

MR. ARCHIBALD (*Happily*): It does? Very well then: Let the children have a magic Christmas tree.

MISS ROSE: What about a magic Christmas tree that will be very hard to trim?

MR. ARCHIBALD: Of *course* it will be very hard to trim.

MISS ROSE: And the whole idea of the play will be to get the tree trimmed somehow!

MR. ARCHIBALD (*Excitedly*): A tree to trim! A tree to

trim! Put that down, Miss Rose. The perfect title! "A
Tree to Trim," by Archibald Archibald. (MISS ROSE
writes.) Ah. . . . (*He rubs his hands as* SAM *enters
with a Christmas tree on a standard.*) Set the tree right
in the middle of the floor, stagehand. (SAM *goes to a
great deal of trouble getting the tree in the middle. He
paces the floor, measures with a yardstick, finally gets
it right. Admiring the tree, he goes out right.*)

MISS ROSE: That's just perfect!

MR. ARCHIBALD: In just what respect would you say this
was a magic tree, Miss Rose? (*Walking around it, examining it closely.*) It looks very much like an ordinary
Christmas tree to me.

MISS ROSE: The magic doesn't show, sir. You see, it has a
spirit hidden inside.

MR. ARCHIBALD: A spirit?

MISS ROSE: Why, yes. You know—the spirit of Christmas.

MR. ARCHIBALD: Of course! Just what I was going to say.
You took the words right out of my mouth. The spirit
of Christmas! Did you get that down, Miss Rose? (MISS
ROSE *begins to write quickly, then begins to talk as she
writes.*)

MISS ROSE (*Reading from her notebook*): ". . . and since
this tree contains the spirit of Christmas, it is a very
difficult tree to trim."

MR. ARCHIBALD: Just a minute, there! In writing a play,
the author must be logical; he must be reasonable! Just
because this is a magic tree with the spirit of Christmas,
why would *that* make it hard to trim?

MISS ROSE (*Looking at* MR. ARCHIBALD *in surprise*): Don't
you know? (*She laughs.*) You're only trying to fool me
by making believe you don't know!

MR. ARCHIBALD (*A little embarrassed, but trying to put
up a bold front*): Er—well, write it down, Miss Rose.
Write it down.

MISS ROSE (*Talking as she writes*): "The magic tree is hard to trim because it can be decorated only with wishes."

MR. ARCHIBALD: With wishes!

MISS ROSE (*Continuing*): "It can be decorated only with wishes that contain the spirit of Christmas."

MR. ARCHIBALD (*Slowly*): I don't think I make myself quite clear, Miss Rose.

MISS ROSE (*Still writing*): "Wishes that have the spirit of Christmas in them will turn into big golden stars on the tree."

MR. ARCHIBALD: Ah! Precisely! And wishes without the spirit of Christmas, Miss Rose?

MISS ROSE (*Looking up and flicking her hand*): Whiff! They won't be anything at all.

MR. ARCHIBALD: "Whiff!" A very suggestive word. Did you get all that down, Miss Rose?

MISS ROSE (*Writing*): Yes. I think you are doing very well, sir.

MR. ARCHIBALD: Don't mention it. Writing is my business, you know. Of course, play writing isn't quite my line, but since you promised the children. . . . (*Thinking*) Well, now, let's see. . . . We must get someone to trim the tree, mustn't we?

MISS ROSE: Yes.

MR. ARCHIBALD (*Thinking hard*): Hmm. Someone to trim the tree . . .

MISS ROSE: And you must give them a reward if they succeed.

MR. ARCHIBALD: To be sure. A reward. (*Rubs his hands.*) Why, I do believe it's more fun to write a play than to write about the history of the twelfth century!

MISS ROSE: Oh, isn't it! (*Suddenly*) You know, I think I have an idea.

MR. ARCHIBALD: Not really!

MISS ROSE: Why don't you get the children next door to trim the tree?

MR. ARCHIBALD (*Excited at the idea*): The obvious solution! The perfect solution. (*Calls out loudly.*) Stagehand! Stagehand! (SAM *comes in.*) We shall need the children next door—all three of them. Bring them in, stagehand. (SAM *nods and exits.*)

MISS ROSE: They'll be so pleased, sir.

MR. ARCHIBALD (*Turning his pockets inside out*): I suppose I shall have to hunt up a reward. They will probably get the tree trimmed in no time. Let's see (*Examines contents of pockets*) . . . some paper clips, keys, rubber bands, matches . . .

MISS ROSE (*Laughing*): You're trying to fool me again, sir. Looking in your pockets for a reward!

MR. ARCHIBALD (*Trying to laugh*): Of course, you mean . . .

MISS ROSE: That the reward isn't finished yet.

MR. ARCHIBALD (*Stops laughing, and repeats slowly*): Not finished yet . . .

MISS ROSE: Don't you like to tease, though! Of course, the best reward you could give the children is the play . . . and it isn't finished yet. (*Turns to notebook*) Look, we're not very far along.

MR. ARCHIBALD (*Sighing*): I do have a hard time keeping up with myself.

MISS ROSE: Of course, I don't know how you plan to end your play, sir; but I think that as soon as all the children think of a Christmas wish that turns into a big gold star, you should reward them by giving them the play.

MR. ARCHIBALD: Remarkable, Miss Rose . . . remarkable how you can read my thoughts!

MISS ROSE: Thank you, sir. (SAM *comes in with* LINDA,

LARRY, *and* LOU. *The children look around wonder-ingly.* MR. ARCHIBALD *paces up and down in deep thought.*)

LINDA (*In a loud whisper as she passes* MISS ROSE's *desk.*): Is he going to write us one?

MISS ROSE (*Nodding, indicating the notebook*): It's half done already.

LINDA: That's great!

LARRY (*Clearing his throat loudly*): Did you want us, Mr. Archibald?

MR. ARCHIBALD (*Stopping short*): Oh, hello there! Come in. Come in. (*As the children move up toward the tree,* SAM *goes out.*) Now, my dear children, I have hatched a little plot for you. Haven't I, Miss Rose?

MISS ROSE: Yes, indeed, sir. You certainly have.

MR. ARCHIBALD: Do you see this Christmas tree?

CHILDREN (*Looking at it carefully*): Yes.

MR. ARCHIBALD: I was wondering if I could get you to trim it for me.

CHILDREN (*Variously*): Sure! You bet! When do we start?

LARRY: We're good at trimming Christmas trees, Mr. Archibald. Where are the ornaments?

LINDA: Do you have some red balls, and blue ones, and yellow ones?

LOU: And a bright gold star for the top?

MR. ARCHIBALD: Ah, that's just it.

LARRY: What's just it, sir?

MISS ROSE: Mr. Archibald means he doesn't have any ornaments. You see, for many years he has been so full of the twelfth century, he hasn't had time to think of Christmas trees.

LARRY: But . . . what shall we trim it with, then?

LINDA: We could string cranberries.

LOU: And make popcorn balls.

MR. ARCHIBALD: No, no. That would never do. You see (*He speaks very impressively and mysteriously.*) this is a special kind of Christmas tree.

LINDA: Oh! Is it really? (*They peer at the tree.*)

LARRY: It doesn't look different, does it?

MISS ROSE: It is a magic tree!

CHILDREN (*Amazed*): Magic? Honest-to-goodness magic?

MR. ARCHIBALD: This magic tree can be trimmed only with . . . ah . . . ah . . . How would you put it, Miss Rose?

MISS ROSE: Only with certain kinds of Christmas wishes.

LARRY: With wishes! Christmas wishes! We never heard of doing that.

MR. ARCHIBALD (*Very much pleased with himself*): Just so, my dear children. You are taking part in something very unusual. You shall each take turns at wishing.

MISS ROSE: The right kind of wishes will turn into big gold stars.

CHILDREN (*Looking at each other in surprise*): Into stars!

MR. ARCHIBALD: And as soon as all of you make wishes that turn into stars, I shall give you a reward. I shall give you the play you wanted! (*He puffs out his chest.*)

LINDA (*Eagerly*): Oh, how wonderful! Our play!

MR. ARCHIBALD (*To* MISS ROSE): Are you getting this all down, Miss Rose?

MISS ROSE: I haven't missed a word, sir.

MR. ARCHIBALD: All right, then, let's begin. Linda, what is your biggest wish for Christmas?

LINDA (*Quickly, very eager*): Oh, I wish for lots and lots of presents.

MR. ARCHIBALD (*Calling*): Stagehand! (SAM *appears.*) Will you please bring us a wish for lots and lots of presents? (SAM *scratches his head, moves his tongue up and down inside his cheek, and goes over to* MISS ROSE, *who whispers something to him.*)

LINDA: Do you mean he can *bring* a wish?

LARRY: I didn't know a wish was anything you could carry.

LOU: Can he hang a wish on the magic tree?

MR. ARCHIBALD (*Looking rather baffled, raises his eyebrows at* MISS ROSE, *who confidently nods her head*): Well . . . ah . . . er . . . it will probably work out all right. Sam is a very good stagehand! (SAM *comes in with a soap-bubble pipe. He walks up to the tree, and blows some beautiful big soap bubbles on it, but of course they all burst and vanish. When the pipe will blow no more bubbles,* SAM *shrugs and goes out.*)

MISS ROSE (*Softly*): Whiff! Your wish was just a whiff, Linda.

LINDA: What did you say?

MISS ROSE: Don't mind me. (*She begins to write.*) I was just trying to write it all down.

MR. ARCHIBALD: H'mm. Linda, you didn't make the kind of wish that turns into a golden star on a magic Christmas tree. Now, why do you think that was? (*Scratches his head.*) Well, Larry, you try next. What's your biggest wish for Christmas?

LARRY (*Quickly, as if he had it all figured out.*): I don't wish for lots and lots of presents like Linda. All I want is a bicycle!

MR. ARCHIBALD: Stagehand! (SAM *appears.*) Will you please bring in a wish for a bicycle? (SAM *looks at* LARRY, *opens his mouth as if to say something, then saunters out.*)

LINDA: I wonder if your wish will work, Larry.

LARRY: Will it, Mr. Archibald?

MR. ARCHIBALD: Well, I . . . I'd rather not say. It would spoil the plot, you know. Nobody should ever know what's going to happen before it happens. Isn't that right, Miss Rose?

Miss Rose (*Writing*): By all means. (Sam *comes in with a big cardboard box. He sets it down near the Christmas tree and takes off the cover. The children lean over to look, then turn to each other in surprise.* Mr. Archibald *tiptoes over to look, too.* Miss Rose *stays at her desk and nods, as if she knew what was in the box without looking. Carefully* Sam *makes believe he is taking things out and hanging them on the tree. But there is nothing in the box. When* Sam *finishes, he turns the carton upside down, shakes it, and carries it out.*) Another whiff!

Larry (*Walking around the tree and looking*): My wish doesn't show for anything, does it?

Linda: Just like mine.

Larry: Are you sure, Mr. Archibald, that some wishes will really turn into stars?

Mr. Archibald: Certainly, certainly. They have to. It's the plot, you see. Miss Rose has it all down on paper; haven't you, Miss Rose?

Miss Rose: Oh, yes, indeed.

Mr. Archibald: It's Lou's turn now. Come, Lou, what is *your* biggest wish for Christmas?

Lou (*Slowly, as if she is thinking it out while she speaks*): Linda wished for lots and lots of presents for herself. Larry wished for a bicycle. And I wish . . . well, I wish everybody would get presents.

Mr. Archibald: Ah! Stagehand! (Sam *appears.*) Stagehand, will you kindly bring us a wish for everyone to get presents? (Sam, *baffled as usual, goes out.*)

Linda: I bet it won't work.

Larry: I think it has to be a wish for something besides presents in order to turn into a star. Doesn't it, Mr. Archibald?

Mr. Archibald: That would be telling! (*He walks over to see what* Miss Rose *has been writing.* Sam *comes in with a stool and a bright red Christmas stocking. He stands on the stool with his back to the audience and hangs the stocking near the top of the tree. As he climbs down, the red stocking—which has a string attached to it that* SAM *can pull—comes off; and there, at the top of the tree, is a bright gold star. It had been hidden behind the stocking.*)

CHILDREN (*Greatly excited*): Oh, a star! A golden star!

MR. ARCHIBALD (*To* MISS ROSE): By jove, it *is* a magic tree, isn't it?

MISS ROSE (*Coming around to see the star*): What a beautiful star!

LINDA (*Thoughtfully*): I wished for something for myself. Larry wished for something for himself. But Lou wished for something for other people. That's the magic, isn't it, Mr. Archibald?

MR. ARCHIBALD: Well, now . . . do you think we should answer that question, Miss Rose?

MISS ROSE: My, no. You mustn't give away your plot.

LINDA: Could I have another wish?

MR. ARCHIBALD: By all means, by all means. We must get this tree trimmed right away. What shall it be, Linda?

LINDA (*Laughing*): You know . . . now that I have another turn, I don't know what to wish!

MR. ARCHIBALD: Dear me.

MISS ROSE (*Helpfully*): Did you ever read the story of Tiny Tim, Linda?

LINDA: Oh, yes. That's in *A Christmas Carol.*

MR. ARCHIBALD (*Under his breath*): I didn't happen to write it, but it's a good story anyway.

MISS ROSE: And Mr. Scrooge? Did you like him?

LINDA: Goodness, no! Not until he stopped being mean and selfish. (*She suddenly jumps up and down excitedly.*) I know! I know what I'm going to wish. I'm going to wish that all the mean and selfish people in the world would turn out to be nice like Mr. Scrooge on Christmas Day.

MR. ARCHIBALD (*Approvingly*): I couldn't have done better myself. (*Calls out loudly*) Stagehand! We need another wish here! (SAM *enters.*) We need a wish for— how shall I put it?

MISS ROSE: A wish that all the mean "Mr. Scrooges" will turn out to be kind. (SAM's *jaw drops as he looks from one to another. He rubs his chin, pulls his ear, and goes out.*)

MISS ROSE (*Writing*): ". . . will turn out to be nice like Mr. Scrooge on Christmas Day."

LARRY: I wonder if it will work.

LOU: The magic tree will know.

MR. ARCHIBALD (*To* MISS ROSE): I'm doing pretty well, don't you think?

MISS ROSE: Yes. Yes. (SAM *comes in carrying a big, red Christmas bell. He goes to the tree and begins to hang it. He decides to put it on the right side of the tree. But, as he turns to leave, the bell—which, like the stocking, had a string on it—falls off, and there, shining and bright, is a gold star. It had been hidden behind the bell. SAM looks as surprised as the others. He picks up the bell, and goes out backwards.*)

LINDA: Another star!

MR. ARCHIBALD: I never thought I could do it.

LARRY: Do what?

MR. ARCHIBALD: Why, write a Christmas play . . . after all my work on the twelfth century.

MISS ROSE: Only one more star, and the children will get their reward!

MR. ARCHIBALD: That's right. Larry, how would you like another turn?

LARRY (*Scratching his head.*): Well, I can't think of anything fancy like Linda. All I can think of is something common. But I think it's a good wish.

LOU: What is it, Larry?

MR. ARCHIBALD: Come on, Larry, don't keep us in suspense.

LARRY: Well, it's just that I want to wish everyone a Merry Christmas! That's all.

MR. ARCHIBALD: Not bad. (*Calls out.*) Stagehand! (SAM *sticks his head in.*) What about bringing us a good old-fashioned wish for a Merry Christmas for everybody? (SAM *pulls his ear, scratches his nose, blinks, and disappears.*)

LINDA: Where in the world did you get this magic Christmas tree anyway, Mr. Archibald?

MR. ARCHIBALD (*Importantly*): I didn't get it anywhere in the world, Linda. I got it out of my head—didn't we, Miss Rose?

MISS ROSE: Of course. You made it all up. It's a play, you see, Linda.

MR. ARCHIBALD: You can always have magic in a play. (SAM *comes in with a holly wreath. He goes to the tree, left side, and attempts to tie on the wreath; but as he turns away, the wreath drops, just the way the stocking and the bell did. And there is a star—the third bright star.*)

CHILDREN (*Variously*): Another star! Three stars! Three golden stars!

MISS ROSE: How beautiful they are!

MR. ARCHIBALD (*Very pleased with himself*): Well, what do you think of that!

LINDA: It's the most wonderful thing I've ever seen.

LOU: The children at the orphanage will love a play about magic stars.

LARRY: Mr. Archibald, you said that if we succeeded in

decorating the tree, you'd give us the play for a reward. Have we earned our reward?

MR. ARCHIBALD: Let me see. Is the reward ready, Miss Rose?

MISS ROSE: All we have left to write is the ending. And the tree should have a few more decorations, don't you think?

MR. ARCHIBALD: Yes, yes, of course. . . . About the ending, Miss Rose. What do you think the ending should have in it? I mean . . .

MISS ROSE: Oh, Mr. Archibald, you're teasing again. Everyone knows what the ending of a Christmas play should have in it.

MR. ARCHIBALD *(Puzzled):* Everyone? *(Regaining his composure)* Why, yes, of course—everyone.

LARRY: Tell us, Miss Rose!

MR. ARCHIBALD *(Nodding):* An excellent idea, Larry.

MISS ROSE: Why, the ending of the play should remind everybody that the true meaning of Christmas is a warm feeling inside your heart . . . (SAM *comes in, unnoticed, and hangs an gold star on tree*.) a feeling of peace and good will.

MR. ARCHIBALD: Exactly.

MISS ROSE *(Tearing out the pages):* Here you are, children. There's nothing more to write.

LARRY: Do you mean it's finished? The play is finished?

MR. ARCHIBALD: Your reward. The play you wanted me to write. *(Notices tree)* Why . . . look at that, would you!

CHILDREN: More stars!

MR. ARCHIBALD: Where in the world . . .

MISS ROSE: The play isn't *quite* finished, the tree isn't *quite* trimmed. And we ought to sing a Christmas carol before you go.

MR. ARCHIBALD *(Suddenly):* One moment, please, Sam!

I say, Sam . . . *(Goes to door and calls)* Where is that stagehand, anyway? *(Exits)*

LARRY *(Looking at script):* "A Tree to Trim." That's a good title, Miss Rose. *(Reads)* "Characters: Mr. Archibald, an author. Miss Rose, his secretary. Sam, his handyman. Larry, Linda, Lou, the children next door." *(Looks up)* Why, the play is about *us!*

LINDA *(Eagerly):* Let's start to rehearse right away.

MR. ARCHIBALD *(Hurrying in):* Just a moment. Just a moment. Don't do anything rash. I've just thought of the perfect ending. What's Christmas without a carol? (MISS ROSE *hides a smile.*) Answer me that, children. Answer me that, Miss Rose. And, if I may quote a well-known motto of the twelfth century . . . there's nothing like killing two birds with one stone. So I suggest we finish the play with a carol while we hang the rest of our good wishes on the tree.

MISS ROSE: Why, Mr. Archibald! You're not only famous . . . you're a genius! *(Gaily they begin to sing a carol and hang the stars which* MR. ARCHIBALD *distributes.)*

MR. ARCHIBALD *(Thoughtfully, when tree is trimmed):* A tree to trim! How in the world did this all happen, Miss Rose?

MISS ROSE *(Laughing):* It didn't happen "in the world," Mr. Archibald.

MR. ARCHIBALD: It didn't? You mean it all happened in my head?

MISS ROSE *(Smiling):* Not in your head, either. It happened where the true spirit of Christmas lives . . . and where it will live forever. It happened . . . in your heart!

THE END

Christmas Coast to Coast

by Lewy Olfson

John Lannon comes home on Christmas Eve to find a pear tree and seven swans in his apartment. . .

Characters

JOHN LANNON, 25
PEGGY LANNON, *his wife*
MILKMAN
MRS. SCHULTZ, *pompous, matronly dancing instructor*
MISS GEORGE, *her middle-aged pupil*
TWO DELIVERY BOYS
MR. HENRIES, *Boy Scout leader*
JEFFREY LORD, *acrobat*
DULCIE BAKER, *television emcee*
THREE TV TECHNICIANS
EXTRAS, *as many as possible*

TIME: *The present. The day before Christmas, 10:30 in the morning.*
SETTING: *The Lannon living room, in their New York City apartment. There is a huge potted tree standing in the middle of the room.*

AT RISE: *The stage is empty. After a moment,* JOHN *enters through door, right, without seeming to notice tree. He is dressed in a warm overcoat and scarf, carries a briefcase.*

JOHN (*Calling out*): Hello, I'm home! Peggy? Anybody home? (*To himself*) " 'Twas the day before Christmas, and all through the house, not a creature was stirring, not even my wife." (*He starts toward the closet with his coat when opposite door opens and* PEGGY *enters. She is in her work clothes. She carries a pitcher of water. She seems surprised to see* JOHN, *and not particularly pleased.*)

PEGGY: What are you doing here?

JOHN (*Taken aback*): What do you mean? Don't you remember me? I'm your husband. John Lannon. I live here.

PEGGY: Don't be silly, John, of course I know who you are. But what are you doing home so early? You're supposed to be down at the newspaper, working.

JOHN: I know, honey, but I got the day off.

PEGGY: The day off! No, John, that's tomorrow. Tomorrow's Christmas, and tomorrow's the day you get off!

JOHN: But you don't understand, Peggy. I'm getting today *and* tomorrow off.

PEGGY: Really?

JOHN: Really. Tomorrow I get off because it's Christmas. Right?

PEGGY: Right. And today?

JOHN: And the boss gave me today off because I'm going to be on television.

PEGGY: But we're not supposed to be on television until this evening!

JOHN: Well, the boss thought I could use a few hours to rest. And then we'll be having a rehearsal, won't we?

You know, they say it's tough being on television. I'll bet this "Americans at Home" program isn't as easy as it looks.

PEGGY: You don't have to tell *me* that! I've never been so nervous in my life.

JOHN: I must admit I'm a little nervous myself.

PEGGY: You, nervous? That's ridiculous! After all those terrible stories you've covered for the newspaper? That awful murder case, and the series about juvenile delinquency! You have nerves of iron.

JOHN: Maybe that's why I got to be such a good reporter. Maybe that's why we've been selected to appear on the "Americans at Home" television show. But Peggy, what's wrong with you? You don't seem very happy to see me home.

PEGGY: I'm *not* happy to see you home.

JOHN: You're *not*! Well, *why* not?

PEGGY: Look, John, not only are *you* going to be on television, but *I'm* going to be on television, and this apartment of ours is going to be on television, too. Do you know how much work I have to do between now and the broadcast to get this living room fixed up like a typical Christmas living room?

JOHN: That's O.K., honey. Now that I'm home, I can help.

PEGGY: No, John. You'll only be in the way.

JOHN: I've never been in the way before when we've decorated for Christmas. *I* string the lights, *I* string the mistletoe, *I* string the popcorn . . .

PEGGY: Yes, but that's for ordinary Christmases. This one is different.

JOHN: What do you mean by "different"? Every Christmas is the same.

PEGGY: That's just the trouble. Christmas is always the

same, everywhere, all over the country. What fun will it be for people to tune in their TV sets and see the same old things they have themselves? Like lights, and mistletoe, and popcorn . . .

JOHN: But people *like* those things.

PEGGY: Maybe they do. But our Christmas — our television Christmas — is going to be different. No lights, no . . .

JOHN: *No lights!*

PEGGY: Right! And no popcorn and no mistletoe! Our Christmas is going to be unusual, and original, and different, and glamorous, and exciting!

JOHN (*Skeptically*): Just what did you have in mind?

PEGGY: Well . . . John, I want it to be a surprise.

JOHN: But I'm your husband! You can tell me!

PEGGY (*Considering*): No, I don't think so. You'll say I'm foolish, and you won't let me do it. And I have all the arrangements made. So you'll just have to leave the apartment until it's time for the telecast, and leave the rest to me.

JOHN: Leave the apartment! But, Peggy, it's below zero out there. I'll freeze!

PEGGY: Then sit in the subway. Or go to the library.

JOHN: Look, dear, I'm a patient man, but I won't be driven out of my house on the coldest day of the year! May I stay if I promise not to interfere with anything you've planned?

PEGGY: Do you promise not to ask any questions?

JOHN: I solemnly promise not to ask any questions.

PEGGY: All right, then. You can stay.

JOHN (*Seeing the tree for the first time and pointing to it*): Good grief! What's that?

PEGGY (*Going to the tree protectively, watering it from the pitcher*): Now, John, you promised you wouldn't ask any questions.

JOHN (*Trying to control his temper*): All right, I won't ask a question. I'll make a declarative statement — an order, in fact. Tell me what that thing is!

PEGGY: Well, dear, it's a tree.

JOHN: I can see that for myself! But what's it doing here?

PEGGY: That's part of the surprise, John. Now don't go back on your word!

JOHN: Peggy, do you mean to say that *that* is for our Christmas?

PEGGY: That's it, dear. It's sort of a Christmas tree!

JOHN: I've seen pine Christmas trees and spruce Christmas trees and juniper Christmas trees, and even *plastic* Christmas trees. But a fruit tree for Christmas? Never!

PEGGY: Dear, I know it's hard to understand, but just be patient and everything will become clear in a little while. Just have faith in me, dear.

JOHN (*Smiling*): O.K. I'm sorry I blew up at you, honey. I'm sure whatever you're doing is very clever, and will be just right for the television show.

PEGGY: Thank you for trusting me, John. When you see what I've planned, you'll be so proud of me! I know you will.

JOHN: Hey, what's that tag tied to the tree?

PEGGY: I don't know. I haven't had a chance to look. Probably tells what kind of tree it is.

JOHN: Oh. Would it spoil the surprise if I looked at it?

PEGGY (*On her way out the door*): Not at all, dear. Go right ahead. (*Exits*)

JOHN (*Going to the tree*): It's pretty, whatever it is. (*Looks at the tag and lets out a yelp*) Peggy! Come in here at once!

PEGGY (*Entering in alarm*): What is it, dear? You sound as though you've been shot!

JOHN: I just read the tag.

PEGGY: Oh, dear. You mean it's a . . . a poisonous tree?

JOHN: No, but it might as well be. The tag says this tree costs three hundred dollars!

PEGGY (*Alarmed*): Three hundred dollars! Oh, there must be some mistake!

JOHN: There certainly must be, and I think the mistake was in ordering it. It's a good thing you haven't paid for it! (*Pauses, looking at her*) You haven't paid for it, have you?

PEGGY (*Hesitating*): No, not exactly. I . . . I charged it.

JOHN: Then call up the store right now and tell them to take it back!

PEGGY: I'd like to, dear, but I can't. It seems there's some kind of state law that won't allow it. Something about tropical diseases. You know, the kind trees get. The man was very nice; he explained it all to me.

JOHN: For three hundred dollars, I'll *bet* he was nice!

PEGGY: Now don't get yourself all upset, dear. We can take it out of the housekeeping budget.

JOHN: Three hundred dollars? At what rate?

PEGGY (*Meekly*): Fifty cents a week?

JOHN (*Calmly, wonderingly*): Peggy, sometimes I wonder how I ever married you.

PEGGY: It was very simple, dear. You just said "I do."

JOHN: I see. I guess we're stuck with the tree. I hope there aren't going to be any more little surprises like that.

PEGGY (*Smiling winningly*): No, dear. Now be a darling and hang your coat in the closet. I have a million things to do.

JOHN: O.K. But remember; no more surprises!

PEGGY: Yes, John. (*She starts to exit.* JOHN *goes to the closet, opens the door, is about to hang up his coat, does a "double-take," slams the door, and leans against it as though he has seen a ghost.*)

JOHN (*Shakily*): Peggy . . .

PEGGY: Yes, dear?

JOHN (*Slowly, deliberately*): There are two birds in the closet. (*She hesitates, seeming to think. Actually she is stalling for time.*) Peggy, I said there are two birds in the closet.

PEGGY: Oh. Yes. I meant to tell you about them.

JOHN: How much did these two birds cost?

PEGGY (*Smiling brightly*): Nothing, dear. I borrowed them from Mr. Johnson across the hall. He was very sweet about it. He's going to watch them on television this evening.

JOHN: You mean the birds are going to be on the program with us?

PEGGY: That's right.

JOHN (*Sarcastically*): Wonderful! I've always wanted to do an animal act on television!

PEGGY: Now, John, there's really nothing to be upset about. I have everything under control. Why don't you go inside and take a nice, hot shower? That'll relax you.

JOHN: You know, that's the first good idea you've had today. I think I'll do just that. A nice, hot shower! (*He goes out through the door, left.* PEGGY *faces front, smiling blissfully. Suddenly, a look of horror and alarm crosses her face.*)

PEGGY: John! Wait! Don't go into the bathroom, John! John! (JOHN *reappears, looking resigned.*)

JOHN (*Calmly*): What, may I ask, is a flock of geese doing in our bathroom?

PEGGY: They aren't geese, John. They're swans.

JOHN: Oh, of course. I couldn't understand why we had a bathroom full of geese, but now that I know they're swans, that's a different matter. (*Pauses*) Peggy! What on earth are swans doing in our bathroom?

PEGGY: Don't get excited, John, that's part of the surprise. And they didn't cost anything, either. I borrowed them from the Bronx Zoo. They wanted the publicity!

JOHN: Wait a minute. Wait just a minute. Light is beginning to break.

PEGGY: That's fine, dear.

JOHN: Would there, by any chance, be *seven* swans in our bathtub?

PEGGY: That's exactly right, seven. I didn't think you were in there long enough to count them.

JOHN: And would the birds in the closet be partridges?

PEGGY: That's right, dear, from Mr. Johnson. I told you about them.

JOHN: And this tree. This wouldn't be a *pear* tree, by any chance, would it?

PEGGY: I should have known you'd recognize a pear tree! Didn't you get a merit badge in nature study when you were a Boy Scout?

JOHN: "The Twelve Days of Christmas!" Of course!

PEGGY (*Hurt*): Oh, John. You've guessed it! Now the surprise isn't a surprise any more.

JOHN: That's all right, Peggy. We've only covered three days so far. It seems I have nine more surprises left, don't I? (*The doorbell rings.*) Well, what do you know? Surprise number four just popped up.

PEGGY: Now, you sit right down, dear, and relax. I'll see who's at the door. (*She opens the door.* MILKMAN *in white coveralls stands there.*)

PEGGY: Oh, hello.

MILKMAN: Are you the lady that wrote this letter to the milk company? (*Looking at the letter he holds in his hand*) Mrs. Lannon?

PEGGY: Yes, that's right. Won't you come in? This is my husband, Mr. Lannon.

MILKMAN (*Shaking hands with* JOHN): How do you do? I'm the milkman.

JOHN (*Dully*): Pleased to know you.

MILKMAN: Now about this letter . . .

PEGGY: Oh, it's very simple. I just want to borrow eight of your milkmaids for a few hours today. You see, we're doing a television broadcast of the old Christmas carol, "The Twelve Days of Christmas," and we need eight milkmaids. Of course, we'd give the milk company credit. It would be wonderful publicity!

MILKMAN: I'm sure it would, Mrs. Lannon. The only trouble is, we don't have any milkmaids.

PEGGY: You don't? But that's ridiculous! How do you get the milk from the cows?

MILKMAN: We use electric milking machines.

PEGGY: I never thought of that.

MILKMAN: You don't suppose you could change the line of the song to "Eight milking machines a-milking," do you?

PEGGY: No, no, I don't think so. No, we've got to have real milkmaids.

JOHN (*Sarcastically*): Why don't you just get eight milkmen, dear, and put wigs and dresses on them?

PEGGY: Why, John, that's a wonderful idea!

MILKMAN: Lady, I think your husband was only joking.

PEGGY: Even if he was, it's a brilliant idea. Do you think we could find eight milkmen who are free tonight, who'd like to appear on national television?

MILKMAN: I don't know, Mrs. Lannon. I guess I could try.

PEGGY: Would you? Oh, that would be just wonderful!

MILKMAN: Of course you'd have to pay them the union rate. That's six dollars and seventy cents an hour.

PEGGY: Apiece?

MILKMAN: Yes, ma'am. That's a union rule.

PEGGY: Oh, dear! John . . .

JOHN: Now, Peggy —

PEGGY: Oh, please, John, say yes. I know it's costing you a lot of money, but even if we wanted to fix up a regular Christmas now with trees and lights and things, we wouldn't have time before the broadcast. And we've got to have *something* Christmasy when we go on the air.

JOHN: O.K. I guess you win. If you can round up eight milkmen, get them over here as soon as possible, and I'll pay them all.

PEGGY: Oh, thank you, John, dear. (*To* MILKMAN) And would you tell each of them to bring one of his wife's dresses and old hats? That way, at least, we'll save on the costume expenses.

MILKMAN (*Skeptically*): Each one should dress up like a woman, huh? O.K., I'll tell them.

PEGGY: I don't suppose *you'd* be interested in being one of my milkmaids, would you?

MILKMAN (*Hastily beating a retreat through the door*): No, ma'am! I have a sick grandmother at home I have to take care of.

PEGGY (*Calling after him*): Oh, I'm sorry. But thank you so much. And Merry Christmas! (*Closing the door*) Wasn't he a nice man?

JOHN: Yes, he was. Considering that he didn't call the mental health unit and ask them to come lock you up, I thought he was very nice, indeed.

PEGGY: Now, John. (*The telephone rings.*) You sit right there, dear, and relax. I'll get it. (*Into phone*) Hello? Oh, yes. Yes, of course. Send them right up. (*Hangs up*) That was the doorman. He called to tell me that the nine ladies dancing are here. They're on their way up.

JOHN: All of them?

PEGGY: Now don't be silly, John. Only two of them. It's the head of the dancing school that I called, and her star pupil.

JOHN: Well, if they come from a dancing school, they're probably pretty good. That's *one* thing in our favor.

PEGGY: I certainly hope so! (*The doorbell rings.*) Here they are now. (*She opens the door and admits* MRS. SCHULTZ, *a pompous lady, and* MISS GEORGE, *nervous.*)

MRS. SCHULTZ: Mrs. Lannon?

PEGGY: That's right. Won't you come in? You must be Mrs. Schultz.

MRS. SCHULTZ: That's right, Gladys Schultz, director of the "Chic Schultz Salon." So very nice to meet you. And this is my star pupil, Miss Minnie George.

PEGGY: How do you do, Miss George?

MISS GEORGE: Charmed, I'm sure.

PEGGY: Mrs. Schultz, Miss George, this is my husband, Mr. Lannon.

JOHN (*Rising*): How do you do?

MISS GEORGE: Please don't get up. I like to see a man comfortable!

JOHN: Then I'm afraid you're looking at the wrong man.

MRS. SCHULTZ: Let's not chat, shall we, but let's get right down to business. Now, Mrs. Lannon, you said when you called that you want to put nine of my best pupils on television.

PEGGY: That's right. This evening, on the "Americans at Home" show. We'll give you credit, of course.

MRS. SCHULTZ: And there's no charge for this opportunity?

PEGGY: Why, no, not at all.

MRS. SCHULTZ: Well, then, it sounds ideal!

MISS GEORGE: Just think: one of us ladies might be discovered by some important talent scout, and go to Hollywood and have a big career!

PEGGY: Yes! Wouldn't that be wonderful? (MISS GEORGE *begins circling* JOHN's *chair, her eyes closed, her body swaying in an exotic dance.)*

MRS. SCHULTZ (*To* PEGGY): Now what sort of dance did you have in mind? (*The doorbell rings.*)

PEGGY: Will you excuse me for a moment? There's someone at the door.

MRS. SCHULTZ: Certainly. (*She crosses to* MISS GEORGE.) That's it, Minnie, keep your chin up. *One,* two. three. *One,* two, three. (PEGGY *opens the door to admit* 1ST DELIVERY BOY, *carrying a covered bird cage in one hand and a large crate in the other.*)

1ST DELIVERY BOY: Mrs. Peggy Lannon?

PEGGY: Yes.

1ST DELIVERY BOY: Sign for these, please.

JOHN: Just a moment. Where are you from?

1ST DELIVERY BOY: The prop department at the network. These are for the broadcast this afternoon.

JOHN: Peggy, do you mean to say you've let the *network* in on this foolishness?

PEGGY: Of course, dear. I wouldn't want to get into any trouble without getting authorization for it first!

JOHN: All right, I'll sign for this stuff. At least there won't be any charge. (*He signs the slip.*)

1ST DELIVERY BOY: You mean I hauled all this stuff over here through the wind and snow, and I'm not even going to get a tip?

JOHN (*Giving him some change*): I take it back about there being no charge.

1ST DELIVERY BOY: Thank you, sir.

JOHN: Say, what's in these packages, anyway?

1ST DELIVERY BOY: Four live calling birds in the cage, and

six stuffed geese in the crate. Don't uncover the cage until you're ready to go on the air. Those birds make quite a racket!

JOHN: Nothing, I'm sure, to what my wife can do.

1ST DELIVERY BOY: How's that again, sir?

JOHN: Nothing. Merry Christmas!

1ST DELIVERY BOY (*Going*): Same to you, sir!

PEGGY: Now, ladies, where were we?

MRS. SCHULTZ: I had just asked you what kind of dances you wanted my girls to do on your program.

PEGGY: I thought a minuet would be nice.

MRS. SCHULTZ (*Horrified*): A minuet!

PEGGY: Or maybe a schottische! No, I think a minuet would be better.

MRS. SCHULTZ: But nobody dances the minuet these days! My students don't know how!

PEGGY: Then what would you suggest?

MISS GEORGE: Well, *I'm* an expert at the hustle! (*Does a few steps.*)

JOHN (*Aghast*): The hustle? For "The Twelve Days of Christmas"?

MRS. SCHULTZ: Perhaps you'd prefer the Latin hustle. (MISS GEORGE *goes into an active dance.*)

PEGGY: Ladies, it's too late to worry about it. Just have nine of your best dancers here as soon as possible for the dress rehearsal, and we'll take it from there!

MRS. SCHULTZ: Fine, Mrs. Lannon! I'm sure everything will work out perfectly!

PEGGY: I hope so. See you later! (*She shows them out. MISS GEORGE has continued to do the hustle. She does a kick just as she goes outside the door. Telephone rings. JOHN goes to answer it.*) And Merry Christmas!

(MISS GEORGE *sticks her head back into the room, just as* PEGGY *is about to shut the door.*)

MISS GEORGE: If I don't see you again, Mr. Lannon, have a nice holiday!

JOHN (*From telephone, into which he is talking*): Thank you! The same to you!

MISS GEORGE: I'll see you later, Mrs. Lannon!

PEGGY: Goodbye, now. (*She shuts the door.*)

JOHN (*Into telephone*): I see. I see. Yes, I'll tell her. Goodbye (*Tired*) — and a Merry Christmas.

PEGGY: Oh dear, John, I'm afraid to ask you who that was. From the look on your face I just know I've done something else wrong.

JOHN (*Almost too calmly*): No, dear. It was just one of your guests calling to check on the time his group was supposed to be here.

PEGGY: Oh, good. I'm glad at least *one* thing is all right. Which group was it, dear?

JOHN: It was the eleven pipers. You know: "Eleven pipers piping."

PEGGY: Good! Since that's one of the biggest groups, it was one of my biggest worries. I'm glad to know they'll all be here.

JOHN (*Patiently*): Tell me, Peggy, what made you decide to call the plumbers' union?

PEGGY: The plumbers' union? Oh, I just looked in the yellow pages under "Pipes," and that was the number they listed.

JOHN: Of course! How obvious! It must have sounded stupid for me to ask such a simple question. Did you know that union plumbers get fourteen thirty an hour?

PEGGY (*After a pause*): Oh. (*Smiling*) Well, dear, after the housekeeping budget has paid for the pear tree, you can collect for the plumbers. (*The doorbell rings.*)

JOHN: Now who could that be? Ten lords a-leaping, or three French hens?

PEGGY: Well, we'll know in a moment. (*She opens the door to admit* MR. HENRIES, *a middle-aged Scout leader in full Boy Scout regalia — short pants and all.*)

MR. HENRIES: Mrs. Lannon? (*He salutes smartly.*) Westborough Boy Scout Fife and Drum Corps reporting for duty.

PEGGY (*Saluting*): You must be Mr. Henries. How nice of you to come! But you didn't have to wear your short pants — especially in this below-freezing weather!

MR. HENRIES (*Heartily*): My good deed for the day!

JOHN: Hello, Mr. Henries. So you're the twelve drummers drumming!

MR. HENRIES: I beg your pardon?

PEGGY: Don't mind my husband, Mr. Henries. He's a bit nervous. We're going to be on television, you know.

MR. HENRIES: Well, all the boys are downstairs in the lobby rehearsing their drums. Whenever you want us, you just let us know.

PEGGY: I will, Mr. Henries, and thank you so much for your cooperation.

MR. HENRIES: The pleasure's all ours.

PEGGY: I'm sure you're just saying that!

MR. HENRIES (*Saluting*): Nope! Scout's honor! (*The doorbell rings.*)

PEGGY: Excuse me a moment, I'll get it. Just relax, John, dear. Relax!

JOHN (*Clenching his fists and pacing the floor*): Relax!

PEGGY (*At the door*): Yes?

JEFFREY LORD: Mrs. Lannon? I'm Jeffrey Lord.

PEGGY: Oh yes, of course. Come in, Mr. Lord!

JEFFREY (*Giving her a large box*): This package was in the lobby for you. I took the liberty of bringing it up.

There was a troop of Boy Scouts there, and I didn't
think it would be too safe.

MR. HENRIES (*Indignantly*): Sir!

PEGGY (*Smoothly*): How kind of you! Do sit down while
I open it, won't you?

JOHN: How do you do, Mr. Lord. I'm Mr. Lannon.

JEFFREY: It's a pleasure to meet you, sir. You're the man
to whom I give my bill, aren't you?

JOHN (*Weakly*): Your bill?

JEFFREY: Yes. Didn't your wife explain?

JOHN: No, I'm afraid not.

JEFFREY: It's quite simple. I'm the leader of a vaudeville
act. All my family are acrobats — perhaps you've
heard of us. The Lively Lords and their Terrific Tram-
poline.

JOHN: Don't tell me how many there are in the act; let
me guess. Would it be — ten?

JEFFREY: Why, yes. How clever of you!

JOHN: Ten lords a-leaping!

JEFFREY: Ordinarily, our television performance fee is a
thousand dollars. But since this is not a sponsored
show, I'll give you a break and make it seven hundred.
Quite reasonable, eh?

JOHN: Oh, quite!

PEGGY (*Who has opened the box and now holds up an
egg*): Look, John! The three French hens have arrived!
Aren't they cute?

JOHN (*Smiling bravely*): Just darling, darling! (*Door
opens and* DULCIE BAKER *enters. She is very brisk and
efficient. She wears a mink coat over her shoulders; she
whips this off and tosses it on the floor.*)

DULCIE (*Aggressively*): How do you do, Mr. and Mrs.
Lannon? I'm Dulcie Baker, the emcee of "Americans
at Home." I'm afraid the snowstorm has delayed

things miserably, and all of our live remote pickup gear is stuck in Manhattan. I do wish the weatherman would check with the network before he decides to send us a blizzard. It causes *such* inconvenience. However, we *did* manage to get one of our video-tape trucks through, so we're going to do the actual broadcast right away and put it on tape. I figure we should be able to begin the show (*Looks at her watch*) — in about fifteen minutes.

PEGGY *and* JOHN (*Gasping simultaneously*): Fifteen minutes!

DULCIE: That's right. But don't worry or get nervous; everything will be ready on time. Our crew is very efficient. (*Calls off*) O.K., fellows, bring in the stuff. (TV TECHNICIANS *begin to bring in miles of cable, microphones, a camera and other such paraphernalia.*)

DULCIE (*To* JEFFREY *and* MR. HENRIES): Would you two men move that easy chair out of the way? You'd better put it in the kitchen.

JOHN: But that's my chair!

PEGGY (*To* DULCIE): Are we really going on the air in fifteen minutes?

DULCIE (*Checking her watch*): Thirteen minutes, dear, but there's nothing to worry about. You're in safe hands when you're in the hands of Dulcie Baker. (*To the crew*) That's right, fellows, just move the camera in here.

MR. HENRIES: Mind if I use the phone, Mr. Lannon?

JOHN (*Dazed*): No, go right ahead.

MR. HENRIES: I'm going to have the Boy Scouts sent right up. I wouldn't want them to miss one minute of this excitement.

JOHN (*Numb*): Fine, fine.

PEGGY: Gosh! My hair isn't combed! My face isn't washed! I haven't dressed! I'm not ready!

DULCIE (*Efficiently*): Sorry, dear, but time, tide and the networks wait for no man. (*The doorbell rings.*)

PEGGY: Come in!

2ND DELIVERY BOY (*Appearing in the door*): Package for Mrs. Lannon from Cartier's.

JOHN: Cartier's! Cartier's the jeweler?

2ND DELIVERY BOY: That's right, sir.

PEGGY: Oh, of course. The five golden rings!

JOHN (*Putting his foot down*): I'm sorry, Peggy, that's going too far. I cannot afford to buy five twenty-four-carat gold rings from Cartier's!

PEGGY: They're only eighteen carats!

JOHN: No! Sorry, young man, you'll have to take them back.

2ND DELIVERY BOY (*Scratching his head*): You're the boss!

PEGGY: But, John! What can we use for rings? According to the song we have to have five golden rings!

JOHN (*Looking around the room desperately*): I don't know. We'll find something!

DULCIE: Quiet, everybody! I'm going to start testing mike levels!

JOHN (*Excited*): The curtains! (JOHN *and* PEGGY *rush to the windows and start pulling down the draperies, which are hung on large curtain rings. The front door flies open, and in come as many extras as possible: milkmen dressed as women, plumbers with lead pipes, Boy Scouts with drums, acrobats doing cartwheels, matrons doing the hustle.*)

DULCIE (*Standing calmly down center, full front, reading from a script*): Good evening, ladies and gentlemen of the viewing audience. This is Dulcie Baker, with another program in my "Americans at Home" televi-

sion series. Tonight, we are visiting the home of news-
paperman John Lannon and his charming wife, Peggy,
who are busy preparing for a peaceful, leisurely, quiet,
old-fashioned Christmas. (*The stage is utter pandemo-
nium and chaos, with people doing all the things called
for in the song "The Twelve Days of Christmas," and*
JOHN *and* PEGGY *pulling the rings off the draperies, as
the curtain falls.*)

THE END

A Christmas Promise

by Helen Louise Miller

Since Greg is too shy to talk to girls, he's more surprised than anyone to find that he has four dates to the Christmas dance!

Characters

MRS. EMILY COLLINS
MRS. MAY SPENCER, *her neighbor*
PATTY COLLINS, *17*
JEFF RAMSEY, *Patty's boyfriend*
GREG COLLINS, *15*
MR. AL COLLINS

SETTING: *The Collins living room, decorated for Christmas with a lighted tree, etc. Exit right leads to rest of house; left exit leads to front door. There is a telephone onstage. Mrs. Spencer's coat is on a chair.*

AT RISE: MRS. COLLINS *is displaying a tuxedo to her friend,* MRS. SPENCER, *who is sewing on a white evening gown.*

MRS. COLLINS: Don't you think the tailor did a wonderful job of cutting down this old tuxedo?

MRS. SPENCER: Why, yes, Emily. It looks brand new.

MRS. COLLINS: I hope Greg likes it. He's growing so fast, we can't afford to buy him a new tux, but he really needs one for the Christmas dance tomorrow night.

MRS. SPENCER: This evening gown for Kathy has miles and miles of stitches in it. I want it to be a surprise for her. Thank goodness I can work on it here, so she won't see it.

MRS. COLLINS: Speaking of surprises, I don't know whether to hang this tux in my husband's closet or pack it in a box.

MRS. SPENCER: The closet sounds like the best bet to me. At Christmastime the kids look everywhere for presents, except in the obvious places. Even if Greg did see it, he'd probably pass right over it as one of his father's suits.

MRS. COLLINS: I think you're right. Oh, May, I can hardly wait to see him in it. Greg's never had any interest in girls, but this year I'm determined to get him to that dance. This (*Indicating the tuxedo*) ought to do it.

MRS. SPENCER: Kathy is just eating her heart out to go. That's why I decided to give her this gown for Christmas, so she'll have something to wear, just in case.

MRS. COLLINS: What do you mean, just in case? The dance is tomorrow night. Doesn't she have a date yet?

MRS. SPENCER: Not yet, but you know the old saying. "While there's life, there's hope."

MRS. COLLINS: Wouldn't it be sweet if Kathy and Greg could go together? They'd make a lovely couple, and it would be thrilling for us. My son — your daughter — their first big dance!

MRS. SPENCER: Why, Emily, it would be marvelous! But what about Greg? Maybe he has a date already.

MRS. COLLINS: Heavens, no! I know Greg. He's so shy.

Asking a girl out is the worst part of the whole thing for him. This way it will be easy. After all, he's known Kathy all his life.

MRS. SPENCER: Emily, it's a wonderful idea! Kathy will be dying to go with Greg.

MRS. COLLINS: Then it's all settled. Now I'd better get this suit upstairs before Greg comes popping in here.

MRS. SPENCER: You might as well take this dress along with you, Emily. I'll come over later to pick it up when I'm sure Kathy is out. By the way, where's your daughter?

MRS. COLLINS: Patty? She's probably out with Jeff. He usually brings her home from school.

MRS. SPENCER: Jeff is such a nice fellow.

MRS. COLLINS: Yes, he's over here morning, noon and night, but we really don't mind.

MRS. SPENCER: Of course not. Well, Emily, thanks for letting me sew over here. I know you have a thousand things to do the day before Christmas.

MRS. COLLINS (*With suit and dress over her arm*): You know I love to have you. Now remember, not too many hints to Kathy. Greg will probably come over right after supper to ask her.

MRS. SPENCER: I hope so. (*Puts on coat*)

MRS. COLLINS: And don't forget our Open House tomorrow night. It's the first big party we've given in years. I had to talk my husband into it, but now I think he's more excited than I am.

MRS. SPENCER: Your husband Al will be the life of the party. He always is. We wouldn't miss it for the world. Goodbye and don't forget to speak to Greg.

MRS. COLLINS: Don't worry, I won't. (MRS. SPENCER *exits left and* MRS. COLLINS *exits right with clothes. The phone rings.* MRS. COLLINS *re-enters without dress and suit to answer phone.*) Hello . . . Oh, Jeff . . . . Why,

no, Patty isn't here. I thought she was with you . . . .
I don't know when she'll be in . . . . Of course, I'll
tell her . . . . Why yes, if you want to. Sure, it's all
right. You can come over and wait for her . . . .
What's the matter? Is something wrong ? . . . Well,
you sound upset . . . . I'm glad to hear everything's
O.K. . . . Yes, I'll be sure to tell her you called, but
what difference does it make if you're coming over
anyhow? . . . All right, all right. Goodbye. (*Hangs up*)
Honestly, sometimes I think Jeff is missing a few
marbles!

PATTY (*Entering left, in coat, with an armload of packages*): Look, Mom, I've got Jeff's Christmas present. I
can hardly wait to show it to you.

MRS. COLLINS: Are all those for Jeff?

PATTY (*Dumping her packages on sofa*): No, only one of
them, but wait till you see it. It's really super! It cost
me twice as much as I wanted to spend, but I guess
he's worth it, the big lug.

MRS. COLLINS: The big lug just called you.

PATTY: Jeff called? When?

MRS. COLLINS: Not more than two minutes ago. He
didn't say what he wanted, but he sounded upset, and
he wanted to come over and wait for you.

PATTY: Must be something important. (*Opens box*) Look,
Mom, isn't it perfectly beautiful? (*Holds up a brightly-
colored shirt*) Won't this absolutely knock his eye out?

MRS. COLLINS: It certainly will! Anyone who looks at him
will need sunglasses. What are your other packages?

PATTY: Surprises! And no peeking! I'm taking these upstairs before Greg barges in and starts snooping around.
(*Picks up her packages and starts to leave*)

MRS. COLLINS: Oh, Patty, you should see his tuxedo. It
looks perfect.

PATTY: When did it get here?

MRS. COLLINS: Just a little while ago. I hung it up in your father's closet. Take a look when you go up.

PATTY: I will. I hope Greg likes it.

MRS. COLLINS: Why wouldn't he like it? It looks as if it came right out of the store. You'd never dream it was a hand-me-down.

PATTY: Oh, I didn't mean that. I was just wondering if he wouldn't rather have had a different Christmas present — that backpack he's always talking about, for instance.

MRS. COLLINS: Well, he's getting the tuxedo whether he likes it or not. If he has a tux he has no excuse for not going to the Christmas dance. I have everything arranged. (*Doorbell rings.*) That's probably Jeff. (*Taking packages from* PATTY) Here, let me take those things.

PATTY: Thanks, Mother. Just stuff them into my closet. (MRS. COLLINS *exits. Doorbell rings again.*) O.K., I'm coming. I'm coming. (*Exits briefly, then re-enters with* JEFF)

JEFF: Where in the world were you? I was standing out there ringing the bell for ten minutes.

PATTY: Why didn't you barge right in the way you usually do?

JEFF: The door was locked. Pat, something terrible has happened.

PATTY: What? You do look funny. Mother said you sounded a little upset when you called.

JEFF: Not upset — frantic! Guess who arrived to spend the holidays with us — without a word of warning?

PATTY: From the way you sound it must be the Abominable Snowman!

JEFF: No, but you're close. It's Aunt Mabel and Cousin Millicent. (*Drops on sofa in tragic despair*) Can you believe it?

PATTY: That is pretty bad, but it could be worse. Isn't your cousin Millicent that stringy little kid who was here a couple of years ago — the one we used to call Pilly-Milly?

JEFF (*Groaning*): That's the one — Pilly-Milly! And to think she has to come *now*!

PATTY: Oh, well, it won't be so terrible. She's older now, probably has more sense and maybe even better looks. And besides you won't be seeing much of her, so why worry?

JEFF: But you don't understand. That's just the trouble. She *is* older, she *has* grown up, and I *will* be seeing her — especially tomorrow night.

PATTY: Tomorrow night! Why, tomorrow night is the Christmas dance. What are you talking about?

JEFF (*In agony*): Patty, sit down. This is going to be a shock. I don't even know how to tell you, but I can't take you to the dance.

PATTY (*Furious*): What? Jeff Ramsey, are you out of your mind? What are you talking about?

JEFF: I'm talking about my cousin Millicent. The family says I've got to take her to the dance.

PATTY: But that's impossible! You're taking me. We've had our date for ages.

JEFF: That's what I keep telling them. But they won't listen. My mother came up with this weird idea that the three of us could all go together, but I told her that was out.

PATTY: It sure is. I wouldn't be caught dead going with an extra girl. What got into your mother?

JEFF: It's Aunt Mabel. She seems to have her under a spell. There's no reasoning with her. She's determined to get Millicent to that dance.

PATTY: I still can't see why you have to be the victim. Why don't you get someone else to take her?

JEFF: At this late date? The day before the dance? Everybody has a date.

PATTY: Well, you'll have to get out of it some way, Jeff Ramsey, or I'll never speak to you again.

JEFF: I was afraid you'd take it like that.

PATTY: How did you expect me to take it? Standing me up the night before the big Christmas dance! Jeff, you're a spineless creature . . . you're a worm! You're worse than a worm — you're . . . you're an amoeba!

JEFF: Go ahead, call me all the names you can think of, but what can I do?

PATTY: What can you do? You can stand up and be a man. You can say you won't break your date with me. What can they do about it?

JEFF: Plenty! They can hold out on me.

PATTY: What do you mean?

JEFF: Money! I don't even have a nickel. I've spent every cent I own, and mostly on you. Mom promised to stake me to the dance as part of my Christmas present — flowers, tickets, dinner, the works! We're licked, I tell you, unless we can think of somebody else to take Millicent.

PATTY: What about Mark Miller?

JEFF: He's out. He's taking Judy Byers.

PATTY: I know! Pinky Hatfield! He never has a date. Come on, let's call him. He's a good friend of Greg's.

JEFF: Forget it! The Hatfields are out of town.

PATTY: We've got to find somebody.

JEFF: I tell you, it's no use. I've checked out everyone. There just isn't anybody. Our Christmas goose is cooked.

PATTY (*Jumping up in excitement*): Jeff, I've got it! I've got it! I know just the person.

JEFF (*Catching her excitement*): Who?

PATTY: Greg!

JEFF: Greg?

PATTY: Yes, Greg, my brother!

JEFF: But Greg doesn't go to dances.

PATTY: He's going to this one, my friend, and he's going with your cousin Millicent.

JEFF: But he's met Millicent. Unless he's lost his mind he'll never agree to take her to the dance.

PATTY: One girl's just like another to Greg. He doesn't care about any of them. He'll be glad enough to get a date without having to ask anyone.

JEFF: If he doesn't like girls, why would he go at all?

PATTY: It's Mother's idea. She thinks he should go this year and she's been working hard on him. He gave in about a week ago, and tomorrow she's giving him a tuxedo, so he can't back out.

JEFF: But maybe he has a date.

PATTY: Not Greg. He told me just last night he didn't have a date.

JEFF: Then you really think you can fix it?

PATTY: Just leave it to me. Now go home and tell Pilly-Milly she's going to the dance with the Don Juan of Hill Street.

JEFF: What a relief! Patty, you're one in a million. (*Nervously*) Suppose something goes wrong!

PATTY: Trust me, coward, nothing will go wrong. I've done plenty of favors for Greg in my time, and I know he'll do this for me.

JEFF: This calls for a celebration. Remind me to tell you sometime what I really think of you, Pat.

PATTY: I'll do that. Now move, and get things under control at your house while I take care of things here.

JEFF: O.K., Patty. Be sure to call me the minute you have Greg signed and sealed.

PATTY: Don't worry, I will. Oh, this is going to be a wonderful Christmas, Jeff! Even the weather seems right. There were little snowflakes when I was downtown.

JEFF: And they're getting bigger. Maybe we'll be having a white Christmas after all. See you later, Patty, and thanks for everything.

PATTY: Bye, Jeff. (JEFF *exits.*)

MRS. COLLINS (*Entering*): Has Jeff gone, Patty?

PATTY: Just left. And wait till you hear the awful mess he's in. His Aunt Mabel and that awful Cousin Millicent dropped in on them unexpectedly.

MRS. COLLINS: No wonder the poor boy was upset.

PATTY: But that's not all! Wait till I tell you!

MRS. COLLINS: I do want to hear about Jeff, dear, but right now I have other things on my mind. Your father, for instance — he doesn't have his boots with him, and it's beginning to snow. Would you mind taking the car and picking him up? The buses will be so crowded tonight.

PATTY: Sure, I'll go. (*Pulling on her coat*) I hardly get out of this coat, and I have to put it on again. Where are the keys?

MRS. COLLINS (*Handing keys to her*): Here they are. And be sure to finish your story about Jeff when you come back. I want to hear it.

PATTY: Believe me, it's right out of a T.V. comedy. By the way, if Greg comes home, tell him I want to see him.

MRS. COLLINS: I can't imagine where that boy is. I haven't seen him all day. Drive slowly, Pat. The streets are starting to get slippery.

PATTY: I will. Bye. (*She exits. Phone rings.*)

MRS. COLLINS: I wonder if that's Greg. (*On phone*) Hello . . . . Yes, this is Mrs. Collins . . . Who? Oh, Mr. Prentice, I've heard Al speak of you . . . . Why, no, he hasn't come home yet, but I'm expecting him shortly. My daughter just went to meet him . . . . Yes, I'll have him call you the minute he comes in. What's that number? . . . . Hotel Whitemarsh, 436-3347. Very well. . . . Thank you. Goodbye. (*She hangs up phone and writes number on pad; to herself*) I think he's one of the partners in Al's company. (GREG *enters left with an armful of packages.*)

GREG: Hi, Mom!

MRS. COLLINS: I'm so glad you're home, Greg. I have something very important to ask you. Why don't you come out to the kitchen and we can talk while I stuff the turkey.

GREG: I'll be right there. I have to take some things upstairs first. (*She exits. He puts down packages, takes off jacket and begins to open packages. First he pulls out a compact, opens it, and tries the powderpuff. Next he produces a bracelet which he puts on his own arm and admires. Finally he gets a perfume atomizer and squirts a little in the air. Meanwhile,* MR. COLLINS *enters left, wearing coat, and stands watching in amazement.*)

MR. COLLINS: What's this, Greg? Dress rehearsal for a beauty contest?

GREG: Oh, hi, Dad. Say, how do you think this smells? (*Sprays perfume*)

MR. COLLINS (*Sniffing*): Kind of exotic, I'd say. Is it hair tonic?

GREG: No! It's perfume. It costs a lot — five ninety-eight plus tax.

MR. COLLINS: I see. For your mother?

GREG: No. I bought some powder for Mom.

MR. COLLINS: Well, I'm sure Patty will like the perfume. (*Coming closer and seeing the bracelet*) I must say you outdid yourself. Perfume, a bracelet and a compact! Pat will be overcome.

GREG: They aren't for Pat.

MR. COLLINS: Don't tell me that at long last you've succumbed to the charms of a woman!

GREG: I guess you could say that. I met her today. I never thought any girl could be so great.

MR. COLLINS: Coming from you, Greg, that is quite an announcement. (*Takes off coat and moves toward phone table*)

GREG: Honest, Dad, I never knew it could happen like that.

MR. COLLINS: What could happen like what?

GREG: Love. It really knocks your socks off!

MR. COLLINS: That's nice, Greg. (*Noticing phone call memorandum on pad*) What's this? "Call J.P. Prentice at Hotel Whitemarsh." Now what on earth could he be doing there at this hour? Oh, sorry to interrupt, Greg. I've got to make a phone call. Tell me later, will you?

GREG: O.K. I'll take these things upstairs. (*Preparing to leave*) Dad, don't say anything about my girlfriend. I want to surprise the family.

MR. COLLINS: My lips are sealed. (GREG *exits.* MR. COLLINS *calls offstage.*) Emily! How long ago did this call come for me?

MRS. COLLINS (*Entering right*): Why, Al, you're home! I just sent Patty to meet you in the car.

MR. COLLINS: I left early and got a ride home with Tom Anderson. By the way, when did J.P. Prentice call? He was supposed to go back to Atlanta this morning.

MRS. COLLINS: Just a few minutes ago, dear. He seemed terribly anxious to talk to you. Isn't he one of the big brass from the main office?

MR. COLLINS: Yes. I'll call him right now. (MRS. COLLINS *exits. He dials phone.*) I'd like to speak to J.P. Prentice . . . . Oh, hello, J.P. What's up? I thought you'd be home by now. . . Well, no wonder. The storm's getting worse every minute. I guess all planes are grounded . . . . Say, that's tough. Marooned up here for Christmas. Well, you know where you're having Christmas dinner, don't you? . . . Sure. Right here with us. . . . No, no trouble at all. Emily would tear my hair out if I didn't ask you. Who's with you? Your daughter? . . . Well, bring her along. Always room for one more, I always say . . . . Oh, I'll bet she is disappointed . . . . (*Chuckling*) Yeah, fifteen is a bad age to be away from home at Christmas. I think I can cheer her up. The young people here always have a dance on Christmas night. Bring Sally along and I'll get her a date with my son Greg . . . . Sure, Greg's just about her age . . . Oh, he'll go for it, I know. I'm sure he doesn't have a date yet. O.K., then everything's settled . . . .We'll eat about three o'clock, but come over any time . . . . Great. And remember to tell Sally about that date. She'll be going to a dance after all. (*Laughing*) Well, that's O.K., J.P. I know you'd do the same for me . . . . Sure. Goodbye and Merry Christmas. (*Hangs up. Honk of automobile horn is heard from offstage.*)

MRS. COLLINS (*Entering right*): That's Patty tooting the horn. I'll bet she's stuck in the driveway. Al, can you go out and help her?

MR. COLLINS: Sure. I'll put the car in the garage and leave it in. What do you think, Emily? That was J.P. Prentice. His plane was grounded and he and his daughter are marooned here for Christmas. I asked them to have dinner with us.

MRS. COLLINS: Good. We'll have plenty. It must be dreadful to spend Christmas away from home. (*As* MR. COLLINS *exits,* GREG *enters. He is still in a daze.*) Hello, dear. This is the first time I've laid eyes on you since breakfast. Did you have a good day?

GREG: Super!

MRS. COLLINS: Good. Is your shopping all finished?

GREG: I think so.

MRS. COLLINS: That's a switch. You usually let things go till the last minute. Now, Greg, May Spencer was over here this afternoon finishing Kathy's evening dress. It's beautiful, all white and ruffly.

GREG: Yeah?

MRS. COLLINS: Kathy will look perfectly lovely in it. She's really very pretty. Have you ever noticed?

GREG: I guess so. Mother, did you ever know anyone could have eyes that are really and truly violet? Not blue — but real purply violet?

MRS. COLLINS: That's just what I mean, dear. Kathy's eyes are unusual. And her mother and I have a wonderful idea. We think it would be nice if you took Kathy to the dance tomorrow night.

GREG (*Shocked beyond words*): What?

MRS. COLLINS: Really, dear, it would make me very happy. I know you've never cared much for girls, but Kathy is so sweet, and her mother and I have been friends for years.

GREG: Are you asking me to take Kathy Spencer to the dance?

MRS. COLLINS: You could just go over and ask her after supper.

GREG: Ask Kathy? I'd rather eat a raw egg.

MRS. COLLINS: Why, Greg Collins, what a way to talk.

GREG: But Mother, she's awful. She's an absolute creep.

MRS. COLLINS: Now look here, Greg, you've grown up with Kathy and I'm not going to let you call her names. She's a lovely child, and besides, I promised her mother.

GREG: You what?

MRS. COLLINS: I promised May you'd take Kathy. She

is getting a lovely new dress and she's dying to go.

GREG: Then she can just die, because I'm not taking her.

MRS. COLLINS: Listen to me, Greg. I demand very little of you. In fact, I think I am entirely too easy on you. But this is one thing I am going to insist on. You're going to that dance and you're taking Kathy.

GREG: I won't, I tell you. I won't. I'll do anything else for you, Mother, but not this. You had no right to promise such a thing.

MRS. COLLINS: No right, indeed!

GREG: Absolutely no right. I'm old enough to lead my own life.

MR. COLLINS (*Entering right*): Calm down, Greg. What's going on? Who's old enough to lead his own life?

GREG: I am, and Mother has no business making promises that involve me.

MR. COLLINS: That's no way to talk to your mother, Greg.

GREG: But Dad, you don't understand. She's done something awful.

MRS. COLLINS: The awful thing I did, Al, was to ask Greg to take Kathy Spencer to the dance.

GREG: But she promised without asking me, Dad, and now she's trying to force me.

MR. COLLINS (*Clearing his throat*): Well, this is a predicament.

MRS. COLLINS: You know what a sweet girl Kathy is, Al. Why must he be so stubborn?

MR. COLLINS: Well, Emily, as a matter of fact, you did make a promise rather prematurely.

MRS. COLLINS: Al Collins, don't you dare side with him on this issue. May Spencer is a very dear friend of mine, and I'm not going to have her and her child disappointed.

MR. COLLINS: I'm afraid she'll have to be disappointed

this time, my dear. Greg simply can't take Kathy to the dance.

GREG: Good for you, Dad. Thanks.

MRS. COLLINS: But, Al, I promised.

MR. COLLINS: It so happens, Emily, that I, too, made a promise. J.P. Prentice has his fifteen-year-old daughter with him. She's brokenhearted because she's missing the Christmas dance at home, and I've promised him Greg would take her to the dance.

GREG *and* MRS. COLLINS (*Together*): What?

MR. COLLINS: I know how you feel, Greg, about not being consulted on this deal, but I had no time to ask you.

GREG: But, Dad, I can't take her.

MR. COLLINS: I'm sorry, but you must. J.P. Prentice is an important man in our company, and I'm not going to have him or his daughter disappointed.

GREG: But, Dad, this is terrible. I never heard of such a thing . . . a guy being rented out by his parents. I won't stand for it. I'll leave home first.

PATTY (*Entering right*): What's all the commotion? I could hear you shouting all the way out on the back porch. This is a fine way to spend Christmas Eve.

GREG: Christmas Eve or no Christmas Eve, I'm not going to be bullied into taking some strange girl to a dance.

MR. COLLINS: I'm not bullying you, son. I'm just telling you.

MRS. COLLINS: I must say, Al, I think you had a lot of nerve to promise Mr. Prentice without asking Greg.

MR. COLLINS: You're a fine one to talk. Didn't you do the same thing?

MRS. COLLINS: But that was different. Greg knows Kathy. After all, this Prentice girl is a total stranger.

MR. COLLINS: She's no stranger. She's my boss's daughter and Greg will have to take her to the dance.

GREG: Patty, can't you help me out of this? Can't you convince them it isn't fair to tell me whom I'm taking to the dance?

MR. COLLINS: You might as well keep out of it, Pat. My mind's made up. Greg has a date and it's Sally Prentice.

PATTY: But, Dad, this is terrible! I can't believe you did it! My life is ruined. I was counting on Greg, absolutely counting on him.

MRS. COLLINS: What on earth is wrong with you, Patty?

GREG: Wait a minute! What were you counting on me for?

MR. COLLINS: Nothing, Greg. She's just being hysterical.

PATTY: I'm not hysterical. I'm just upset. Jeff's family is making him take his cousin Millicent to the dance unless he can get somebody else, so I offered him Greg.

GREG: Did you hear that? She offered me, too! What am I, a burnt offering or something?

PATTY: But don't you see, if Greg doesn't take Cousin Milly, Jeff will have to take her and I'll be out in the cold.

MRS. COLLINS: This is too much for me.

GREG: Well, it's too much for me, too. You people ought to go into the rent-a-kid business. I'm getting out of here. When you finish fighting it out, let me know, but it just so happens I have a date of my own.

ALL (*Together*): What?

PATTY: Who?

GREG: I detect a note of surprise in your voices — more like shock, actually. Her name is Cookie — Cookie Hatfield.

MRS. COLLINS: Cookie Hatfield! I've never heard of her. Where does she live?

GREG: She's Pinky Hatfield's sister. I just met her this morning. She came home from boarding school last night.

PATTY: I never knew Pinky Hatfield had a sister.

GREG: Well, he does and she's going with me to the dance.

MR. COLLINS: Now look here, young man.

PATTY: Is Pinky home? Is he home now?

GREG: How should I know? He was home when I left his house this afternoon.

PATTY: Does he have a date for tomorrow night? Does he, Greg?

GREG: I don't know. I don't think so.

PATTY: I hope you're right. I'm going right over there now and sign him up for Milly. Wish me luck, folks. (*Exits*)

MR. COLLINS: Greg, I'm terribly sorry about this, but business is business.

GREG: And a date is a date, Dad.

MRS. COLLINS: What am I going to say to May Spencer? (*Phone rings. Picking it up*) Hello . . . . Oh, May. Yes, we were just talking about you . . . . Well, I haven't exactly asked him yet, I was just sort of leading up to it . . . . What? She doesn't want to go with him? . . . Well, for heaven's sake, why not? . . . What? Stop laughing, I can't understand you . . . . She thinks he's what? . . . Well, I must say I don't think that's very funny . . . . Oh, no, I'm not insulted, it's just that . . . Who's taking her? . . . Oh, a boy who's visiting the Emersons. Well, that's fine . . . . Oh, no, May, don't be silly, I'm not offended at all. As a matter of fact, I think Greg does have a date, two of them, if I'm not mistaken . . . . Yes, you heard me. I did say two . . . . I'll tell you about it later. Goodbye, May. (*Hangs up*)

GREG: What did Kathy Spencer call me?

MRS. COLLINS: Never mind what she called you. She has a date and that's that. If I ever get mixed up in something like this again, I'll have my head examined. (*Doorbell*) Now who could that be? (*Exits left*)

GREG: Can't you listen to reason, Dad? I really like this girl. She's the one I bought all the presents for.

MR. COLLINS (*Almost worn out*): I know, son, I know. But this Prentice guy is a big wheel.

GREG: How would you like to be shoved off to a Christmas dance with a girl you never saw?

MR. COLLINS: When you put it like that, it does seem a bit rough, but I did promise. (MRS. COLLINS *enters with a suit box.*) A special messenger just brought you this, dear. Did you order a suit?

MR. COLLINS: No. What is it? Here, let me see. (*Opens box and pulls out Santa Claus suit*) Oh, great. This is the final touch! This is all I needed.

MRS. COLLINS: A Santa Claus suit? What on earth for?

MR. COLLINS: For me. I completely forgot I promised to play Santa Claus for the Hermes Club tonight.

MRS. COLLINS: Oh, Al! Why did you ever promise such a thing? It's a terrible night. You'll be standing around in the snow for hours, and I'll bet your rheumatism will start again.

MR. COLLINS: I know, Emily, but a promise is a promise. That's why I can't give up on this Prentice deal. I'd give anything to get out of my debut as Santa, though.

GREG: Would you really give anything, Dad?

MR. COLLINS: Practically anything. What do you have in mind?

GREG: I was just thinking. I'll bet I could fill out that suit, and people say I have a nice way with kids.

MR. COLLINS: Do you mean you'd fill in for me?

GREG: Sure thing. Give me the suit. (*Pulls it on over his clothes*) You promised a Collins would play Santa Claus, and I'm a Collins.

MR. COLLINS: You're a good sport, son. Believe me, I appreciate this.

GREG: Listen, Dad. I'm not doing this for nothing. You said you'd give anything to get out of the job. Now pay up. Talk yourself out of the Prentice date and we'll call it even.

COLLINS (*Chuckling*): I guess you've got me over a barrel. Freeze to death as Santa Claus or do some fast talking to J.P. You win, Greg. I'll call him.

GREG: That's great, Dad. Go ahead, call him up right now.

MR. COLLINS: All right. I guess I can think of something. (*Phone rings*) Hello! . . . . Why, hello, J.P. I was just going to call you and you beat me to the draw. What? There's a plane going out after all? That's great . . . . Yes, the storm seems to have died down. Well, good luck, safe journey, and a Merry Christmas. (*Hangs up; mops brow with handkerchief*) Whew! That was a close one. They're going home.

GREG: Then I won't have to play Santa Claus after all.

MR. COLLINS: Oh, yes, you will. A promise is a promise.

MRS. COLLINS: And after this, let's each do our own promising.

MR. COLLINS: I second the motion. (PATTY *rushes in.*)

PATTY: I've got him. I've got him. Pinky's going to take Pilly-Milly to the dance.

MR. COLLINS: Then it looks as if we're all set for a merry Christmas after all. What do you say, Mr. Santa?

GREG: I say I'll do my best to make it a Christmas we'll never forget — and that's a promise, Dad. Shake?

MR. COLLINS: Shake. (*They shake hands as curtains close.*)

THE END

A Star in the Window

by Mildred Hark and Noel McQueen

A shopkeeper's kind heart and good will to all give a special meaning to Christmas and make a tinsel star shine with new brilliance. . . .

Characters

OTTO
ALMA, *his wife*
MAN
MRS. FLANAGAN
MR. BAKER
WOMAN
MR. JONES

TIME: *Christmas Eve.*
SETTING: *Small neighborhood novelty shop, decorated for Christmas. Door down right leads to street and door left leads to living quarters in the back of store. At left is counter with cash register, telephone, radio, and various items for sale on it. On right wall is show*

118

window, hidden from view by curtains. Upstage wall has shelves filled with books and other merchandise. At right end, on high shelves, are mirrors, one of which is tilted so it slants toward show window. On front of shelves is table loaded with lights, tinsel, stars, and other Christmas items. Near it is an old rocking chair. Christmas trees are stacked around the shop.

AT RISE: OTTO, *an elderly man, sits in rocking chair, reading. He wears glasses, which he peers over from time to time. Phone rings; without getting up, he puts book on counter, reaches for telephone and answers. He speaks with slight accent, not distinguishable as any certain nationality.*

OTTO *(Into telephone):* Hello. . . .Otto's Novelty and Gift Shop. . . .You want a Christmas star like the one in my window? Wait a minute. *(He puts phone down, rises, goes to table and rummages through Christmas tree ornaments. He picks up two tinsel stars, then puts them down again and returns to telephone.)* Sure, we have lots of them. . . .Two dollars. . . .Yes, that's all. . . . They are beautiful for two dollars. . . . Yes, just like the one in the window. . . .You come in, then. Goodbye. *(He hangs up, sits in rocking chair, and begins to read again.* ALMA, *his wife, an elderly woman, enters left. She goes to cash register, pushes one of the keys and the drawer opens.)*

ALMA: You're still reading, I see, Otto.

OTTO *(Looking up):* Aha, Alma, this time I catch you. Spending more money for Christmas.

ALMA *(With slight accent):* I almost forgot the lucky piece to put into the Christmas pudding. *(She takes coin out and shuts register.)* And you should see Mr. Turkey. He is all stuffed and ready for the oven.

OTTO: Fine, Alma, fine. Tomorrow we will have a wonderful Christmas dinner, and I will stuff myself, as usual.

ALMA: Ah, I know you, Otto. You'll give the best of it to the Spinelli children.

OTTO: Did you wrap their presents?

ALMA: Yes, everything is all ready. There's a present for Mrs. Spinelli, too. Otto, I'm glad you thought of inviting Mrs. Spinelli and her children. It gives us a chance for a happy Christmas.

OTTO: It makes all of us happy. Poor woman. Since her husband died, she hasn't been able to provide much. And you and I, Alma, have all the pleasure.

ALMA: I hope we have enough presents for them, Otto.

OTTO: If we haven't, I'll bring them into the store and say: Spinellis, help yourselves.

ALMA (*Laughing*): Ah, my Otto. A business man you are not. You would give everything in the store away, if I did not stop you.

OTTO (*Smiling broadly*): Ho, a lot of stopping you do, Alma. I remember the little girl who had only a dollar to buy a doll and you gave her a three-dollar one. (*Pauses*) But I guess you're right, Alma. I am not much of a business man. If I were, I'd have a great big store like Mr. Jones's downtown.

ALMA (*Thoughtfully*): Yes, Otto, you might have had a big store.

OTTO: Do you wish I had, Alma? Do you wish I was a go-getter?

ALMA: No, Otto. Mr. Jones has big business. He calls his store "the shop with the Christmas spirit." But to me, it's the wrong kind of spirit. Sell—sell—sell. Money—money—money. I like our way better.

OTTO (*Sighing*): But Alma, sometimes I worry that I don't give you much.

ALMA (*Laughing*): Don't be foolish, Otto. We have plenty

to eat, a place to live in the back of the store, and we have each other. What more could we want?

OTTO: Nothing, for me.

ALMA: Good. Now, Otto, it's Christmas Eve. Can you close up soon?

OTTO: Not yet, Alma. People in this neighborhood work late on Christmas Eve. They might need last-minute things. And a lady telephoned just now. She's coming for a Christmas star.

ALMA: Then you must wait. I'll get back to my pudding. *(Exits.* OTTO *turns to book again. Door from street opens, and* MAN *enters.* OTTO *keeps on reading.* MAN *stands for a moment, coughs to get* OTTO's *attention.)*

MAN: Are you the proprietor?

OTTO *(Looking up):* Oh, please excuse me, but I get so interested in my book. Old Christmas legends. *(Rises)* Can I help you?

MAN *(Smiling):* Yes. I would like a star for my Christmas tree. There was one in your window last night.

OTTO: Yes, of course. *(Puts down book, goes to table and picks up tinsel star)* Here we are. It's a nice star for two dollars.

MAN: Yes, very nice, but that isn't the one I wanted.

OTTO: No?

MAN: No. Late last night, I passed by after you closed, and saw the most beautiful star in your window.

OTTO *(Puzzled):* But this is the same star . . . just like the one in the window.

MAN: No, no. This is just an ordinary tinsel star. The one I saw must be much more expensive. It was beautiful. I've never seen anything like it. *(Tries to explain)* It was made of crystal, perhaps, and lighted from the inside.

OTTO *(Smiling and shaking his head):* Crystal? No, my friend. Not in Otto's little shop. You maybe saw it somewhere else.

MAN: It is possible, but I was quite sure—of course, I could have been mistaken.

OTTO: We all make mistakes. *(Door at right opens, and* MRS. FLANAGAN *enters. She is shabbily dressed.)*

MRS. FLANAGAN: Good evening, Otto.

OTTO *(Smiling):* Ah, Mrs. Flanagan, hello. I'll be with you in a minute. *(She starts looking at some of the Christmas trees.* OTTO *turns toward* MAN.) Why don't you try Mr. Jones's big store downtown? Maybe that's where you saw the star. If anyone has a crystal star, Mr. Jones will.

MAN: I will try there. Thank you. *(He starts for door, then stops and picks up package of Christmas tree lights from table.)* While I'm here, I might as well buy a set of these Christmas tree lights.

OTTO: Good. I'll make sure they work. *(Takes lights from* MAN, *goes behind counter and plugs in lights. They all light.)* That will be three dollars.

MAN *(Handing him money):* Fine. (OTTO *puts money in cash register, puts lights in bag, hands it to* MAN.)

OTTO: Thank you, sir. And a merry Christmas to you.

MAN: Thank you—and the same to you. *(Exits)*

OTTO: So, Mrs. Flanagan, you want a Christmas tree for the little ones, I'm sure.

MRS. FLANAGAN: Yes, Otto. *(Points to small tree)* I thought maybe this one.

OTTO: Such a little tree for such a big family?

MRS. FLANAGAN *(Sighing):* I'd like a big one, Otto, but they're so expensive.

OTTO: Expensive—that's not a nice word for Christmas.

MRS. FLANAGAN *(Laughing):* I know, but when it comes down to counting the pennies—

OTTO: Yes, of course, that's right, Mrs. Flanagan, but you

know, it's a funny thing this year. The little trees cost more than the big ones.

MRS. FLANAGAN *(Puzzled):* How can that be, Otto?

OTTO: Well, it's just that—so many people wanted the little ones this year, I guess it's what you call the law of supply and demand. Now, those little ones *(Points)* are ten dollars, but the big ones, outside—*(He takes her by the arm and leads her to outside door down right, opens it and points.)* See that big one leaning against the lamp post? It's really too big for most people in apartments. That kind of tree doesn't sell fast. Besides, it's already Christmas Eve. So—the price is only three dollars.

MRS. FLANAGAN: Why, it's a beautiful tree, Otto. You mean I can have that tree for three dollars?

OTTO: That's the price. (MRS. FLANAGAN *reaches into purse and takes out three dollar bills, which she hands to* OTTO.)

MRS. FLANAGAN: The children will love it. *(Smiles)* Otto, you're a fraud.

OTTO *(Beaming):* Now, is that nice to say? *(He goes to cash register and puts money into it.)*

MRS. FLANAGAN: God bless you, Otto, and a Merry Christmas to you and Alma. *(She starts out.)*

OTTO: Wait. There is some string outside. I'll tie the tree for you so you can carry it. *(He exits right with* MRS. FLANAGAN. *After a moment, phone rings.* ALMA *runs in.)*

ALMA: Coming, coming! *(Into phone)* Hello. Otto's Novelty and Gift Shop. . . .Christmas stars? Yes, we have them. They're two dollars. . . .Big, bright, all lighted up? No, I'm afraid not, sir. . . .But you couldn't have seen it, because we don't have them. . . .I'm sorry, sir. Goodbye. *(She hangs up, and* OTTO *re-enters with* MR.

BAKER, *a young man.)*

OTTO *(As they enter):* That's wonderful! Congratulations! Alma, here's Mr. Baker, and what do you think?

ALMA *(Excitedly):* The baby has come!

MR. BAKER *(Happily):* That's right. I wanted to tell you and Otto right away.

OTTO: It's a boy, Alma.

ALMA: Congratulations, Mr. Baker. And how is your lovely wife?

MR. BAKER: Fine—fine and so happy. We both are. *(After a pause)* You know, it's funny. A new baby—why, it's like a miracle.

OTTO: Miracles. Yes, they are all around us, if we just look.

MR. BAKER: That's true. *(Thoughtfully)* Miracles all around us. You know, Otto, that's something of the idea I'm trying to get into my book.

OTTO: Is the writing going well?

MR. BAKER: Yes, it really is. When I got home from the hospital, I started right in on the last chapter.

OTTO: The last chapter, that is good. See, Alma, soon it will be published.

ALMA: And a best seller, I hope.

MR. BAKER *(Laughing):* Oh, I don't know about that. Maybe no one will even want to publish it.

OTTO: But I know it is good. The parts you have brought me to read—they are like a fresh breeze in my head.

MR. BAKER: I know you like it, Otto, but how many people see things the way you do?

OTTO: Oh, I think many would, if they just had the chance. *(Shakes head)* Some of the new books—they show only the bad things that happen to people.

MR. BAKER: But the critics say life is like that.

OTTO: Yes. Life *is* like that sometimes, but it doesn't have to be. Life could be—why, it *could* be a miracle.

MR. BAKER *(Suddenly; with excitement):* Yes, that's it exactly! The idea is clear in my mind, but it's so hard to get it into my book.

OTTO: I know you will figure out a way.

ALMA: And when your book is published, Mr. Baker, we will put it in our window. Then we will have some new books, Otto, besides all of these secondhand ones. *(She gestures toward shelves of books.)*

MR. BAKER *(Laughing):* Alma, the reason you have so many secondhand books is because you've bought them from people like me. I've said to my wife, during the last year we have *eaten* my books.

OTTO: So—I did not pay you much for your books, Mr. Baker.

MR. BAKER: More than they were worth sometimes. And. . .I'm a little embarrassed to ask you, but I could use one of them right now.

OTTO: Oh? Which one is that?

MR. BAKER: The book of legends.

OTTO: Oh, of course. Only just now I was reading it. *(He goes to counter and picks up book he was reading and hands it to* MR. BAKER.) Here—you take it home again.

MR. BAKER: No—no, I can look at it now. It won't take but a minute to refresh my memory. I just thought if I could find an old Christmas legend that I could use in some way, it might help to dramatize the idea for my book.

OTTO: Fine. Sit down here and look for the story you want. (MR. BAKER *sits.*)

MR. BAKER: It seems to me there was one about a star. . . .*(His voice trails off as he starts looking through book.)*

ALMA: Star? That reminds me, Otto—a man called just now about a star. He said he saw one in our window last night—big and bright. He wants to buy one like it.

OTTO *(Surprised):* Why, another man came in and asked me the same thing. I told him he must have seen it at Mr. Jones's store.

MR. BAKER *(Looking up; happily):* Here's the story I want. "The Christmas Star." *(Reads)* "There is an old, old Christmas legend about the Christmas star. The villagers say a beautiful star like the one that led the wise men on the first Christmas is sometimes seen again. This star is really a band of angels, and often they are heard singing, so that men may not forget the miracle of Christmas."

ALMA *(Wistfully):* Yes, I heard that story when I was very little, in the old country. My grandpapa told it many times.

MR. BAKER: You mean he saw the star?

ALMA: No, *he* didn't. But when he was a boy, it happened in a village not far away. The big bright star came at midnight and some said they heard angels singing.

MR. BAKER: It's the same story, all right. Listen. *(Reads)* "The angels cannot draw near to the earth and cause the star to shine unless there is someone who has the true spirit of Christmas. And so, the villagers say, if the time should ever come when there is not one person who remembers the true meaning of Christmas, then the star cannot shine, and then darkness will come upon the earth."

OTTO: What a beautiful story!

MR. BAKER *(Thoughtfully):* And I think I can use it. It fits in with my idea—there's a character in my book who can tell the legend. *(Shop door opens and well-dressed woman enters hurriedly. She looks about the shop.)*

WOMAN *(Impatiently):* Could someone wait on me, please?

OTTO *(Turning to her):* Oh, I am sorry. Good evening.

WOMAN: I telephoned about the star.

OTTO: Of course, I remember.

WOMAN: I hope you have some left. I notice it isn't in the window.

OTTO: Oh, but it is still there—and we have lots more just like it. *(He goes to table and picks up a tinsel star and holds it out to her.)*

WOMAN: No—no, that's not the one.

OTTO: But my dear lady, you said you wanted a star like the one in the window. *(Goes to window, pulls curtain back and points)* See—the same thing.

WOMAN *(Crossly):* Now, really, I don't know what you're talking about. We drove past here late last night, and there was a beautiful star in the window. I phoned you just a little while ago, and you assured me you had more of them. Now you show me this cheap tinsel thing.

OTTO: But madam, this is all I have—it's all I've ever had.

WOMAN *(Indignantly):* You told me you still had them. I suppose you thought if you got me in here, you could make a sale. Well, you're mistaken. Badly mistaken.

OTTO: I am sorry, madam, but it's you who are mistaken.

WOMAN: It's misrepresentation, that's what it is. You ought to be reported to the Better Business Bureau! *(She storms out.)*

OTTO *(Shrugging his shoulders, but disturbed):* Well, what do you think of that?

ALMA: How can she talk like that to you? Misrepresent? You who always lean over backward. . . .

OTTO: Now, now, Alma. I guess she really thought I'd lied to her.

MR. BAKER *(Putting book down on counter, rising and coming toward them):* What's this all about, Otto?

OTTO: I wish I knew. I am beginning to wonder. At first I

thought nothing of it, but now if people are going to think I'm trying to cheat them—

MR. BAKER: Oh, that's ridiculous, Otto.

ALMA: But Mr. Baker, so many people say they saw a big bright star in our window last night, and we never had such a thing. Otto thinks it must be something in Mr. Jones's window, and people are just confused.

MR. BAKER: But how could they confuse your little place with the Jones store?

OTTO: I don't know—but Christmas time people rush around so, they don't know where they see things. Maybe Mr. Jones has a big bright star, made of crystal glass.

MR. BAKER (*Suddenly*): No, Otto, no! (OTTO *and* ALMA *look at* MR. BAKER, *perplexed.*) Not crystal glass—not at all!

OTTO: What do you mean?

MR. BAKER: Why, the legend we've just been reading— the Christmas star!

ALMA (*Catching* MR. BAKER'*s excitement*): Otto, do you think it could be—is it possible? Grandpapa told me—

OTTO (*Laughing*): No—no, Alma. (*To* MR. BAKER) Mr. Baker, you save that legend for your book. In Otto's little store, we have no such miracles.

MR. BAKER: But why not? You're the good people with the true Christmas spirit. It all fits.

OTTO: Hear him talk, Alma—no wonder he's an author. Such imagination.

ALMA: Yes, Mr. Baker, I suppose Otto is right. Even if it could happen, it would not happen to us.

MR. BAKER (*Laughing*): Well, all right—but it was an idea. I guess I'd better be getting back to my writing.

OTTO: Are you sure you don't need the book, Mr. Baker?

MR. BAKER: No—no, I'll remember it. (*Starts for door*) Merry Christmas to you both.

OTTO: Merry Christmas to you.

ALMA: And you take from us a merry, merry Christmas to your wife and new son.

MR. BAKER: Yes, I'll certainly do that. Thank you, and good night. *(Exits)*

ALMA: Ah, that Mr. Baker, he is so nice. *(She sighs.)*

OTTO: Why do you sigh, Alma?

ALMA: Did I? *(Pauses)* It's that woman—so unpleasant. Unpleasant things should not happen on Christmas Eve.

OTTO: Now, Alma, don't let all that foolish business upset our Christmas.

ALMA: It *is* foolish. I know that.

OTTO: It was all a mistake, Alma. Let us forget about the star we don't have.

ALMA: You are right. And I still have work to do. *(She starts left.)* Will you close up soon, Otto? It's very late.

OTTO: Yes, dear, I will. *(Door opens and MR. JONES, a well-dressed, middle-aged man, enters. ALMA stops as he enters, and stands near counter.)*

MR. JONES: Good evening. Merry Christmas!

OTTO *and* ALMA: Merry Christmas to you, sir.

MR. JONES: Yes, Merry Christmas—and thank goodness it's almost over!

OTTO: Why, what do you mean?

MR. JONES *(Sighing heavily):* I'm Jones from the store downtown. All this talk about the Christmas spirit. "Merry Christmas" with every sale, "Merry Christmas" with every phone call. I'm sick of it!

OTTO *(Very surprised): You* are Mr. Jones?

MR. JONES:Yes. I've been trying to get down here all evening, but it's been so hectic. Christmas is such a battle.

ALMA *(Quietly):* We don't think it's a battle, Mr. Jones.

MR. JONES: No—*(Looks around)* no, you wouldn't with a

little place like this. But with me it's different. I have terrific overhead. Have to keep pushing the clerks—telling them to sell, sell, sell! And I still have to think about good will. In fact, that's why I'm here. I'd like to make you an offer.

OTTO: An offer? An offer for what? I don't understand.

MR. JONES: Oh, yes, you do. This—this star you've had in your window . . . Everyone's talking about it—never saw such a real-looking star, they say—so bright and shining.

OTTO: Yes, Mr. Jones, that's what they tell me, too.

MR. JONES: Well, where is it? Why don't you have it in the window now?

OTTO: But I—I haven't changed my window. All day people have asked about a bright star. We thought all along it must be something you had in *your* window.

MR. JONES: No—no, I've nothing of the sort. Why, they say this star of yours is brighter than any light they've ever seen.

OTTO: Mr. Jones, look. *(He goes to window and pulls curtain back.)* I have never had any other star in my window but this. See? Just a tinsel star.

MR. JONES: Yes—yes, I see. *(He pulls out wallet crammed with bills.)* That's all that's there now. But later on you'll put that other one in. You have some unusual lighting effect or something that I don't know about.

OTTO *(Protesting):* No—no, I don't.

MR. JONES: Look, Otto, I don't know what your game is, but I could use this star of yours. Next week we have after-Christmas bargain sales. I need something to get the people in. If I could have that star in my window during the rest of the holidays, starting tonight, it would be worth—*(He pulls out some money.)* five hundred dollars. (OTTO *is speechless.* MR. JONES *pulls out some more money.)* Six hundred—seven hundred—

OTTO: Mr. Jones, please. You keep your money. I have nothing here that's worth that much.

MR. JONES: You have the star.

ALMA: Mr. Jones, we have told you the truth. We have no star.

MR. JONES: A thousand dollars—how about it?

OTTO: Mr. Jones, if I wanted to sell it, you could buy my whole store for that.

MR. JONES: All right, if you're going to be stubborn about it, I guess there's no use in my wasting any more time here.

OTTO: I am sorry, Mr. Jones.

MR. JONES *(Angrily): You're* sorry! What about me? Wasting my time when I'm all tired out, working late every night. Now I'll go home and my wife will expect me to be bright and cheerful. Tomorrow, too—big family dinner. Christmas, bah! I'm glad it's almost over! *(He exits, slamming door.)*

OTTO *(In disbelief):* Can you imagine? Glad Christmas is almost over.

ALMA: I feel sorry for him. He has the store of the Christmas spirit, but he misses all the real Christmas.

OTTO: Yes—yes. *(Sighs)* Alma, all this business about the star—I wish I knew. *(Shakes head)* I just don't know what to think.

ALMA: Now, now, Otto. We must forget about all this. It's all just some mistake.

OTTO: But what kind of a mistake? It is all so strange. Well, come, we will get ready to enjoy our Christmas.

ALMA: That's right, Otto. I'll see if there's a little Christmas music on the radio, while you close up.

OTTO: That will be nice. (ALMA *goes to radio, turns it on. Chorus singing "The First Noel" is heard*.) I think I'll leave the lights on in the window tonight. After all, it is Christmas Eve. (OTTO *pushes curtain back to reveal window, then pushes switch near front door and all onstage lights go off. A ray of light from above window curtain strikes tilted mirror that hangs on right end of shelves. The mirror reflects light back to star hanging in window, making it shine very brightly.* OTTO *stares at the star.)* Alma, look at the star in the window. See how brightly it shines.

ALMA *(Matter-of-factly):* It's from the street lamp outside.

OTTO *(Excitedly):* No, no, Alma. Come, look. *(He takes her arm and they cross to window.)* See, the light from the mirror up there, it shines back on our tinsel star. With all the other lights out, it makes the star shine and sparkle. I think we have solved the mystery!

ALMA: The star does sparkle, Otto—but not so much as people say. *(They step back from window.)*

OTTO: That's true. It shines some, and people imagine the rest. You see, at Christmas time, people's eyes are ready for miracles. *("The First Noel" continues softly in background.)*

ALMA: Wait till we tell Mr. Baker, with all his talk about the legend. *(She stops.)* Otto, listen, the singing—it's beautiful! Almost like angel voices.

OTTO: Let's take the radio with us, so we can listen to the carols tomorrow.

ALMA: Yes, that's a good idea. Let me unplug it. *(She leans down behind counter.)* Otto! *(She rises, holding up end of radio's cord.)* The radio was not plugged in!

OTTO *(Not realizing):* Oh, I remember. I pulled out the plug to test some Christmas tree lights and forgot to put it back.

ALMA: But, Otto—the music! Where is it coming from? There are no carolers outside.

OTTO *(Suddenly realizing):* Why, the music—it's . . . a miracle! *(Chorus gets louder.)*

ALMA *(Pointing; awestruck):* And Otto, look! The window—the light! *(Light in window gradually gets brighter, as music swells.)*

OTTO *(Singing along with chorus):* "And to the earth it gave great light, and so it continued both day and night." *(He puts arm around* ALMA *and they stand facing window as curtain closes.)*

THE END

Middle and Lower Grades

Happy Christmas To All

by Jeannette Covert Nolan

How "A Visit from St. Nicholas" was written. . .

Characters

DR. CLEMENT CLARKE MOORE
MRS. MOORE, *his wife*
EMILY, *Mrs. Moore's cousin*
BUD
2ND BOY } *Moore children*
GIRL

SCENE 1

TIME: *Six o'clock, Christmas Eve, December 24, 1822.*
SETTING: *The library of Dr. Moore's comfortable home in Chelsea, New York. Old fashioned desk, covered with books, is up right; fireplace with mantel is up left. Table is center and several chairs are scattered around room. Armchair, with footstool, is near fireplace.*

Rugs, small tables, etc., may complete the furnishings. Exit left leads to rest of house; up center is a door leading out and window, with sill, overlooking street.

AT RISE: DR. MOORE *is seated at desk, writing with quill pen. Sleigh bells and carol singing can be heard from outside.* MRS. MOORE *enters left, carrying tall red candle.*

MRS. MOORE: Clement?

DR. MOORE *(Without glancing up):* Yes, my dear?

MRS. MOORE: I'm sorry to disturb you. But something really dreadful has occurred. I don't see how I could have done such a thing! It was the confusion, I suppose. So much to think about. Tidying up the parlors, readying the spare bedroom for Cousin Emily, preparing the children's gifts and sweets. . . .*(Pauses)* Clement, you're not listening!

DR. MOORE *(Looking up; guiltily):* Eh? Yes, my dear?

MRS. MOORE: You haven't heard a word I've said!

DR. MOORE: Ah, but I have. You said you were confused, you had neglected the parlors, tidied up the sweets, and prepared the children's gifts for Emily.

MRS. MOORE *(Exasperated but smiling):* Nothing of the kind. You were *not* listening. I'm talking about the turkey.

DR. MOORE: What turkey?

MRS. MOORE: The Christmas turkey. For tomorrow.

DR. MOORE *(Nodding):* Ah, yes, of course. I prefer chestnut stuffing, a bit of sage, a hint of garlic—but just a hint—and a touch of spice. . . .

MRS. MOORE *(Crossing to him):* Clement, do come out of those dusty old books for once. *(Pauses)* There will be no stuffing at all. You see, there is no turkey.

DR. MOORE *(Half-rising; shocked):* No turkey! For Christmas! That's impossible! Why ever not?

MRS. MOORE: Simply because I've forgotten it—as I've been trying to tell you.

DR. MOORE *(Sinking back into chair):* But this is terrible! Something must be done about it!

MRS. MOORE *(Upset):* I agree, but what?

DR. MOORE: Without a turkey, it would scarcely be Christmas!

MRS. MOORE: I agree!

DR. MOORE: The children would be disappointed—

MRS. MOORE: And you too, Clement. I know how very fond you are of turkey.

DR. MOORE: I am indeed. *(Thoughtfully)* Let me see. . . .How can we solve the problem?

MRS. MOORE: Actually, there is no problem.

DR. MOORE: Eh? What do you mean?

MRS. MOORE: I mean, you must go to the market and purchase a turkey.

DR. MOORE *(Frowning):* At this hour?

MRS. MOORE: The shops are not closed yet.

DR. MOORE *(Shuffling papers on desk):* If I were not so— so occupied—

MRS. MOORE *(Firmly):* You will just have to put your writing aside, won't you?

DR. MOORE: Yes, I daresay. But—

MRS. MOORE *(Insisting):* Get your coat and hat, Clement. And do hurry.

DR. MOORE *(Reluctantly):* It's quite cold, snowing—

MRS. MOORE: But you never mind a little snow.

DR. MOORE *(Suddenly cheerful):* I would go, and gladly. But you see, I've lost my shoes. *(Stretches his feet out for her to see slippers)* You would scarely expect me to venture out in these?

MRS. MOORE *(Laughing):* Oh, Clement, you are only making excuses. You know you haven't lost your shoes.

Where are they?

DR. MOORE *(Solemnly):* I have no idea.

MRS. MOORE *(Circling chair, bends down and picks up shoes; holds them up):* I have! Here they are. Just where you put them every evening when you come home from your classes.

DR. MOORE *(Shaking his head):* Astonishing! *(Sighs)* Well, I suppose—*(Takes shoes, puts them on)* I have never before bought a turkey, you know. *(Stands)*

MRS. MOORE: High time you had the experience. *(She exits quickly left, returning with* DR. MOORE's *overcoat and black stovepipe hat.)* And your gloves, Clement. *(She helps him dress, tying muffler over hat and knotting it under his chin)* Now you will be snug. *(She pats him on back and gives him a little push toward door rear.)*

DR. MOORE *(Pausing, looking back):* I hope none of my students spies me. They might think it comical. Dr. Moore, Professor of Hebrew and Classical Languages at the General Theological Seminary—and strolling about Christmas Eve, carrying a plucked turkey over his shoulder!

MRS. MOORE: I wouldn't worry about it.

DR. MOORE: I doubt if my father would have consented to such an indignity. He was a gentleman and a scholar.

MRS. MOORE *(Edging him toward door):* Yes, yes, I know.

DR. MOORE: He officiated at the inauguration of President George Washington and at the death of Alexander Hamilton.

MRS. MOORE *(Impatiently):* Clement, you're hesitating merely because you're lazy. *(Firmly)* Let us just forget about the turkey. Take off your things; go back to your books. There is some salt cod in the house. I shall cook that for our Christmas dinner.

DR. MOORE *(Horrified):* Salt cod for Christmas!

MRS. MOORE: Yes, it's very good. And wholesome, too.

DR. MOORE *(Shuddering):* My dear! *(He bustles out slamming door behind him.* MRS. MOORE *smiles, hums softly to herself as she straightens up a chair or two, then exits left. After a pause,* BUD *enters from rear, carrying covered basket. He moves to center stage, whistles once mysteriously. Immediately,* 2ND BOY *and* GIRL *appear left.)*

GIRL *(In loud whisper):* Bud, did you get it? *(She closes door furtively.)*

BUD: No need to be so quiet. I passed Father on the street, but he didn't recognize me in the darkness.

GIRL *(Crossing to basket, lifting lid and peering in):* What a sweet, cunning one!

2ND BOY: Here, let me look. *(Crosses to center and peers in basket)* Yes, it's just right. Who gave it to you, Bud?

BUD: Mrs. De Paul.

GIRL: As usual!

2ND BOY: What did you tell her?

BUD: That we wanted a fine Christmas present for Father.

GIRL: As usual! And what did she say?

BUD: She laughed and she said she didn't think Father *could* be so very surprised.

GIRL: Because we've given him the same present for Christmas for the last three years.

2ND BOY: Well, Father always *is* surprised, though.

GIRL: Perhaps he only acts surprised.

BUD *(Indignant):* What's the matter? Are you sorry we planned this? Shall I take the present back to Mrs. De Paul?

2ND BOY: No, no! What else could we get now?

BUD: But if it isn't a surprise—

GIRL *(Softly, smiling down into basket):* It is so sweet!

But—*(Slowly)* next year we'll plan something quite different and original.

BUD: Sh-h! Who's coming? Father? *(He snatches basket, clamps on lid, and exits quickly. Knock is heard at rear as* BUD *re-enters. He goes to door, opens it.)* Oh—

CHILDREN: Cousin Emily!

EMILY *(Entering her arms laden with packages)*: So it is! Merry Christmas, darlings!

2ND BOY: I'll call Mother. *(Calls off left)* Mother! Cousin Emily's here!

BUD *(Politely)*: May I take your packages?

EMILY *(Chuckling)*: Thank you, no. I shall stow them away myself. They're secrets. *(She puts packages on table.)*

MRS. MOORE *(Entering and embracing* EMILY*)*: Dear Emily! Now we shall have the best of the holidays.

EMILY: A charming welcome. *(She takes off coat and hat.)*

MRS. MOORE: Children, what's in the basket in the hall?

BUD: It's our surprise for Father. It's—*(He whispers in* EMILY'S *ear.)*

EMILY: What, again? I'd think your yard would be swarming by this time!

BUD: No we keep them only until they grow large. Then we take them out to that farm.

2ND BOY *(Anxiously)*: Cousin Emily, we're afraid Father won't be surprised.

EMILY: Don't worry. He'll be delighted. But where is your father?

MRS. MOORE: At the market.

EMILY *(Surprised)*: Dr. Moore, the distinguished professor, at the market?

MRS. MOORE: He hated to go, but I insisted. And he should be back any minute. *(She glances out window.)*

Yes, here he is! (DR. MOORE *enters, his hat powdered with snow, a turkey over his shoulders. He puts turkey on table.*)

DR. MOORE (*Shaking hands with* EMILY): Emily, behold in me a much abused man.

EMILY: Doing the family marketing?

DR. MOORE: I had to . . . (*Muttering*) or eat salt cod.

MRS. MOORE (*Inspecting turkey*): I must say you did well, Clement. This is a beautiful bird!

BUD: Father, we have a gift for you. If you and Mother and Cousin Emily will sit down—(*He exits and returns with basket as others sit and he places basket in front of* DR. MOORE.)

DR. MOORE: For me? How nice! (*He starts to open it.*)

GIRL: Wait! Father, do you suspect what's in the basket?

DR. MOORE: No, I can't imagine. Fruit? Candies? A holly wreath? (*He taps forehead as if in deep thought.*) But I seem to hear a tiny scratching sound. Can it be something alive?

2ND BOY (*Excitedly*): Yes! It's alive!

DR. MOORE: Can it be—(*He removes lid.*) Well, well! A black kitten! Of all the splendid Christmas gifts. . .just what I've been wishing for.

2ND BOY: Honestly, Father?

BUD: We chose a black one, to match your clothes, sir.

GIRL: We gave you one last year, you know. And for several years before.

DR. MOORE: That is the very reason I didn't anticipate receiving one this year. (*He sets kitten on lap and strokes it.*)

EMILY: That looks like a superior kitten. May I have a closer look? (*She takes kitten from* DR. MOORE, *who rises, fumbles in pocket of his coat, and crosses to his desk.*)

DR. MOORE: And now I have a trifling surprise for you children.

BUD: But we don't get our presents till tomorrow morning.

DR. MOORE: True, but this is a little something special. *(He pauses.)* Something I wrote for you.

2ND BOY *(Flatly)*: Oh! Like—the books you're always writing?

DR. MOORE *(Slowly)*: Not exactly, no. *(He sits, spreads out crumpled piece of paper.)* Verses. Rhymes.

MRS. MOORE *(Amazed)*: Rhymes? Why, Clement!

DR. MOORE: I know it's a most extraordinary thing for me to do. But as I was walking along the streets, as I stood in the market—somehow rhymes about Christmas suggested themselves to me, so I jotted them down. I haven't yet finished, but would you care to—to—

MRS. MOORE *(Eagerly)*: Oh, yes, do read them, Clement!

DR. MOORE *(Reading)*:

" 'Twas the night before Christmas, when all through the house

Not a creature was stirring, not even a mouse;"

(Beginning timidly, he gains assurance, reading first ten lines of "A Visit from St. Nicholas.")

GIRL *(Interrupting enthusiastically)*: But, Father, this isn't a bit like the things you write! It's—it's wonderful!

MRS. MOORE: It really is, Clement!

DR. MOORE *(Smiling)*: Oh, it's nothing really.

EMILY: Nothing? A poem! I shall want a copy, Clement.

DR. MOORE *(Alarmed)*: No, no! I should be distressed if anyone ever knew I was so—so foolish. *(Picks up pen and writes rapidly)* It just spins out in the strangest manner. Well, shall I continue reading?

ALL *(Ad lib; enthusiastically)*: Yes, do read! Please, Father! *(Etc.)*

DR. MOORE:

"Away to the window I flew like a flash,
Tore open the shutters and threw up the sash. . . ."
(As he reads, lights dim and curtain falls.)

* * * * *

SCENE 2

TIME: *Evening, December 24, 1823.*

SETTING: *Same as Scene 1.*

AT RISE: DR. MOORE *is seated in armchair before fire, his slippered feet resting on footstool. He is reading newspaper.* MRS. MOORE *sits in another chair, stirring contents of a large bowl in her lap.*

DR. MOORE: Where are the children, my dear?

MRS. MOORE: Upstairs. Very busy with their Christmas tasks.

DR. MOORE *(Dryly):* I daresay I shall have the customary offering of a black kitten from Mrs. De Paul's cattery?

MRS. MOORE: The youngsters give you kittens because they themselves dote on kittens.

DR. MOORE *(Smiling):* We'll, that's an excellent rule for the selection of gifts. And is Emily coming?

MRS. MOORE: I—I think she is.

DR. MOORE: Good! There is never much alteration in our scheme of life, from season to season, is there? I prefer it so. Peace, serenity, nothing to upset routine. And this year the turkey was brought on schedule, and I'll not be forced to parade with it in public.

MRS. MOORE: I'm mixing the stuffing according to your taste.

DR. MOORE: Ah! *(He smiles, resumes readings. Suddenly, he rattles the pages, stares incredulously.)* Do my eyes deceive me? No! It is! It really is! That

ridiculous poem of mine, those silly whimsical verses I
wrote last Christmas! About Saint Nick! That drivel—
it's printed here, in the *Troy Sentinel,* where everybody
can see it! *(He kicks over the footstool and rises,
clutching newspaper. Agitated, he paces around the
room.)* This is terrible! A disgrace! Who could have
done it? *(Angry)* Well, say something. *(He stops.)* Did
you send my verses to the *Sentinel?*

MRS. MOORE *(Quietly):* No. No, I didn't!

DR. MOORE: But who else—*(Pausing)* Emily! Emily, of
course!

MRS. MOORE: Clement, I'm so sorry—

DR. MOORE: Emily! Even knowing my poor opinion of
them, Emily deliberately sent them to the paper!

MRS. MOORE: No, Clement. Please be calm. It wasn't like
that . . . not quite. Emily did make a copy of your
poem; she read it to a few friends, and they repeated it
to a few of their friends. Soon, she had a request from
the editor of the *Sentinel* for permission to print it—

DR. MOORE *(Furiously):* A request which she complied
with—without my permission. (MRS. MOORE *nods.*)
Emily is a meddling woman!

MRS. MOORE: She did not intend to annoy you, Clement.

DR. MOORE: Annoy? She has ruined me! *(He paces
about muttering.)*

MRS. MOORE: Oh, no! In her letter last month, Emily told
me—

DR. MOORE: So you knew it would be in the paper?

MRS. MOORE: Well, yes, I knew. But I—I hoped you
wouldn't notice. *(Puts bowl with stuffing on desk)*

DR. MOORE: Indeed? Everybody will notice. Hundreds
of people, thousands. And they will all think that Professor Clement Moore has lost his mind.

MRS. MOORE *(Defensively):* I am rather sure that they will
not think that. They'll read the verses with interest and

admiration. You should not be ashamed of that poem, Clement. You should be proud. It's lovely, a picture in words. Perhaps it will be reprinted—often. Perhaps it will be read years from now—twenty years. *(She gestures towards desk.)* Possibly not one of those books you've written will live as long or be as popular as the little poem you dashed off just for our children.

DR. MOORE: I can't believe that! *(Pausing, looking at her)* Are you weeping?

MRS. MOORE *(Wiping her eyes):* Only a bit. Forgive me.

DR. MOORE: But why?

MRS. MOORE: Well, our Christmas is spoiled. I'm—I'm so sorry.

DR. MOORE *(Moving to her; remorsefully):* My dear! How badly I'm behaving! *(Taking her hand)* I'm the one to apologize, and I do. *(Slowly)* The printing of the poem against my wishes is a minor incident. I have exaggerated its importance. What matters is that under this roof we shall be happy together on Christmas Eve.

MRS. MOORE: Oh, Clement, you are kind.

DR. MOORE: Dry your tears, my dear. *(Looking into bowl on desk)* Is there spice in the stuffing? Not too much. I trust.

MRS. MOORE: Will you sample it and tell me?

DR. MOORE: Yes, I will. *(Dips spoon in and nibbles from it)* Um-m. Delicate and delicious! *(They smile at each other. Rear door opens and EMILY enters.)* Ah, good evening, Emily.

MRS. MOORE: Emily! *(They embrace.)*

EMILY *(Walking shyly toward DR. MOORE):* Are you angry with me, Clement?

DR. MOORE: No. No, I have been somewhat startled, I admit. But not angry. *(He glances at MRS. MOORE.)* Would you say I displayed anger?

MRS. MOORE *(Stoutly):* Certainly not! *(She helps EMILY*

off with her coat. Voices are heard offstage and children enter, left, carrying a covered basket, which they deposit at DR. MOORE's *feet.)*

CHILDREN: Surprise! Surprise for Father!

MRS. MOORE: But you haven't greeted Cousin Emily, children.

CHILDREN *(Ad lib):* How are you Cousin Emily? We have a surprise for Father—*(Etc.)*

DR. MOORE: Well, well what can this be? *(Gazing at basket)* Candies? Fruit? A holly wreath?

CHILDREN: No, no!

BUD: No, sir!

GIRL: We said it would be a different present this year, and it is!

2ND BOY *(Dancing around):* Different! Very different! You will never guess!

DR. MOORE *(Aside to* MRS. MOORE): If it isn't a black kitten, then I'm truly mystified. *(He leans over basket.)* But surely I hear a tiny scratching sound. Something alive?

2ND BOY: Yes, alive!

DR. MOORE *(Lifting cover):* 'Pon my soul! A *white* kitten.

CHILDREN: Surprise, surprise!

GIRL: Would you have ever guessed?

DR. MOORE: Never. And I've been wishing for a white kitten.

GIRL: Father, do you remember the poem you read to us last Christmas Eve?

DR. MOORE: Yes, I remember it.

GIRL: It was such a nice poem. Will you read it again?

BUD: But Father said it was a "trifle." Maybe he didn't keep a copy.

DR. MOORE: As it happens, I've been providently supplied with a copy of that poem. *(He glances at* EMILY, *who smiles.)*

GIRL: Then will you read it, Father?

MRS. MOORE: You get into your nightgowns, children. Father will read it to all of us before the fire. *(Children and* MRS. MOORE *exit.)*

DR. MOORE *(Going to window):* A beautiful night, Emily. The snow is like a thick soft veil over the world.

EMILY: Yes. My dear Clement, just how it's going to be with that poem of yours. Everyone who reads it or hears it will remember it. *A Visit from St. Nicholas* will make you famous.

DR. MOORE *(Objecting mildly):* But the rhymes have no literary merit.

EMILY: They have such warm appeal!

DR. MOORE: They just seemed to come to me—out of the air.

EMILY: I think I recognize your St. Nick, though. He sounds like the butcher here in Chelsea.

DR. MOORE: Perhaps. When I bought the turkey there last year I noticed. . .*(Looking thoughtful)* "His eyes—how they twinkled! his dimples—how merry!"

EMILY *(Reciting):* "His cheeks were like roses, his nose like a cherry." Yes, that's our butcher, all right. But what prompted you to invent the reindeer?

DR. MOORE: Reindeer? I suppose I did invent them.

EMILY: Of course you did. No one ever described them before. "Now Dasher! now, Dancer! now, Prancer and Vixen!"

DR. MOORE: "On, Comet! on, Cupid! on, Donner and Blitzen!" *(Sighs)* Well, as I've told you Emily, the circumstances of my composing the poem were odd, to say the least. I can't explain it.

EMILY: Perhaps inspiration can never be explained, Clement. (MRS. MOORE *and children enter.)*

GIRL: Here we are, Father! *(All settle around hearth.)*

BUD: We're all ready, Father.

DR. MOORE *(Taking up newspaper and reading):*
" 'Twas the night before Christmas, when all through
the house
Not a creature was stirring, not even a mouse—"
(He continues; lights dim and curtain slowly falls.)

THE END

Whatever Happened to Good Old Ebenezer Scrooge?

by Bill Majeski

Ebenezer Scrooge decides that charity doesn't pay enough, and he reverts to his original nature . . .

Characters

EBENEZER SCROOGE
TV ANNOUNCER
INVESTMENT COUNSELOR
MEDIC
SMILEY
YAWNY
GROUCHY   *Seven Dwarfs*
SNIPPY
CUDDLY
DUMMY
SNOW WHITE
PRINCE
WITCH HAZEL
MIRROR, *offstage voice*

Scene I

SETTING: *TV studio, with two chairs, a table and a microphone. This scene is played in front of curtain.*

BEFORE RISE: TV ANNOUNCER *is seated at table, facing microphone.*

ANNOUNCER: Once again, ladies and gentlemen, we bring you another installment in our series called, "Whatever Happened To. . . ," a nostalgic trip into the past in which we follow up on personalities of days gone by. Tonight, in our studio, we have one of the literary world's most famous characters. He's from England and was known as one of that country's most hated misers, that is, until he was visited by three apparitions — the ghosts of Christmas past, present and future. They appeared courtesy of his old business partner Marley. The ghosts so unnerved our guest that he was transformed suddenly from a penny-pinching, miserly, coin-clutching rotter to an open-handed, charitable, decent human being. Would you welcome, please, Ebenezer Scrooge. (SCROOGE *enters and shakes hands with* ANNOUNCER.) Hello, Mr. Scrooge, and welcome to our show. How are you?

SCROOGE: Getting by — barely.

ANNOUNCER: After your transition to good guy you just seemed to drop out of sight.

SCROOGE: Had to. I gave up my business, lost all my money and filed for bankruptcy. Bang. All gone. Nothing left.

ANNOUNCER: You were running a thriving concern. Where did all the money go?

SCROOGE: You know how it is — you get a little weak. You get soft. After my Christmas visit to the Cratchits, I —

ANNOUNCER (*Interrupting*): That was Bob Cratchit and his family, wasn't it?

SCROOGE: Right. He was a clerk for me. In the old days he really slaved for me, and I was putting away money hand over fist.

ANNOUNCER: Then there were those three visits.

SCROOGE: Yep. That last one — from the ghost of Christmas future — that was a kick in the head. Wiped me out emotionally. That's when I became Mr. Nice Guy. Practically gave everything away.

ANNOUNCER: You gave everything away?

SCROOGE: Uh-huh. I turned altruistic, business-wise. Somebody would come in and order something, and I'd knock twenty, maybe thirty percent off the price. I'd extend credit and make loans at no interest. Just got too flabby financially. I ended up extending myself right into the poorhouse.

ANNOUNCER: You? Mean old Scrooge, old miserly Ebenezer, in the poorhouse?

SCROOGE: No, *that* Scrooge was rich and successful. It was the new, free-spending, open-hearted Scrooge in the poorhouse.

ANNOUNCER: Very interesting. What are your plans now?

SCROOGE: Frankly, I feel I've paid my dues by being nice. I've been putting my pennies aside day after day and now I'm about ready for a comeback. I want to go into business for myself again. Be my own boss. In fact, I'm on my way to see an investment counselor right now. (*Firmly*) Don't worry about old Scrooge — I'll be back on top again.

ANNOUNCER: We applaud your determination, Mr. Scrooge. (*To audience*) Formerly rotten old Scrooge, who became good old Scrooge, is planning a trip along the comeback trail back into the hard, demanding world of business. Will he succeed? (*Standing and turning to* SCROOGE, *who also rises*) Well, Mr. Scrooge (*Shaking his hand*), we wish you luck . . . (*Turning to audience*) I think. (*They exit. Curtains open.*)

* * *

SETTING: A business office. Table and chairs have been removed. A desk and chair are at center, with another chair beside desk. Ledger, pens, etc., are on desk.

AT RISE: SCROOGE *and* INVESTMENT COUNSELOR *are seated at desk.*

COUNSELOR: Well, Mr. Scrooge, glad to see you've brought your business to us.

SCROOGE (*Gruff, all business now*): Why not? You knock off the smallest percentage of my money. I'd be crazy to go someplace where they nail you but good.

COUNSELOR: Of course. What kind of business are you interested in?

SCROOGE: A money-maker, what else? I've been on the loser route too long. I want profit, dough, bread, the long green.

COUNSELOR: I think I get the picture.

SCROOGE: You'd better believe it. I've been rich and I've been poor, and rich is better.

COUNSELOR (*Flipping through ledger*): Here's a growing agricultural concern. A guy wants to sell his place out in the hinterlands. He grows mile-high beanstalks.

SCROOGE: Beanstalks? There's no jack in beanstalks. Not interested.

COUNSELOR: O.K., let's try something else. What about women's footwear.

SCROOGE: Footwear? Well, that's a step in the right direction. Tell me about it.

COUNSELOR: The company makes glass slippers. It's run

by a sweet young thing named Cinderella. But she's getting married to a nobleman.

SCROOGE: Glass slippers? I see right through that. No glass for me. As my former partner Marley warned me long ago, glass is a pain — and it can break you.

COUNSELOR: Ah, here's a nice item. A women's hairdressing establishment. Records show you have a fifteen percent profit margin — and you take it right off the top.

SCROOGE: Fifteen percent? Not high enough.

COUNSELOR: This Rapunzel knows everything about hair.

SCROOGE: What's to know about hair? Tell Rapunzel to keep her hair to herself and to keep the fifteen percent. Look, fellow, maybe I'm not getting through to you. I want a winner. I want something that'll keep me active, forceful, driving — in a word, mean. Something with a solid bottom line. Now either find that for me or I go elsewhere.

COUNSELOR: Ah, here's just the thing. How about a small factory that makes Christmas bells?

SCROOGE: You mean those things that jingle when people come into a store?

COUNSELOR: That's right.

SCROOGE: You know, you've got some weird enterprises here. Glass slippers, mile-high beanstalks — it sounds as if you're out in never-never land. Now you give me a bell factory.

COUNSELOR: We are a little offbeat, but remember, in all these businesses they work for low wages. In the bell factory you'll have seven employees, all of them dwarfs —that means low overhead. Low overhead, get it? Dwarfs. That's a joke.

SCROOGE: I'll be the judge of that. Tell me more about these bells.

COUNSELOR: Well, as I said, they're Christmas bells. You

know, jingle bells — the kind you hang on your tree, your front door, or a one-horse open sleigh.

SCROOGE: Christmas bells, huh? How ironic. Christmas.

COUNSELOR: Cheap labor. Minimum expenses. Good profit. See? (*Shows book to* SCROOGE, *who studies it*)

SCROOGE: O.K. You said the magic word — money! I'll take it.

COUNSELOR: Fine. It's called the Best Bell Business, Inc.

SCROOGE: You're going to see old Scrooge fill the world with Christmas bells and fill his pockets with jingling coins. Goodbye. (SCROOGE *rises, shakes* COUNSELOR'*s hand and starts to exit.*)

COUNSELOR: And Merry Christmas!

SCROOGE: Bah! Humbug! (*Curtain*)

*   *   *   *   *

SCENE 2

TIME: *A few days later.*

SETTING: *The bell factory. There is a long table at left with a couple of benches around it. Scrooge's desk is at right.*

AT RISE: SCROOGE *is seated at desk. He rises, looks at watch impatiently and begins to pace.*

SCROOGE: Five minutes to seven and my workers haven't shown up yet. They should be here by now. I'll show them what it's like to work for a *real* boss. The old Ebenezer Scrooge is back. (*Seven Dwarfs enter, singing "Hi-Ho, Hi-Ho," wearing beards, funny costumes, etc.* SCROOGE *scrutinizes them as they do a short drill and an abrupt about-face and end up in a straight line across stage.* SCROOGE *shakes his head slowly.*) What did I buy, a platoon of short Marines? (MEDIC *steps forward.*)

MEDIC: Mr. Scrooge?

SCROOGE: I'm not Good-Time Charlie, the last of the big-time spenders.

MEDIC: My name is Medic, and I'm foreman of the Best Bell Business, Inc. I'd like to introduce you to the rest of your staff.

SCROOGE: Hm-m-m. I'm not sure I want to meet them. But let's get it moving. Medic, huh? Are you a real doctor?

MEDIC: No, it's just a nickname.

SCROOGE: Too bad. It would be nice to have a doctor working here. With this crew I have the feeling there are going to be a lot of little accidents.

MEDIC: Our safety record is impeccable. We haven't had so much as a hangnail in the past five years.

SCROOGE: O.K. Now get on with the introductions.

MEDIC: Here's Smiley. (SMILEY *steps forward, smiling broadly.*)

SCROOGE: What's he smiling about?

MEDIC: He's Smiley.

SCROOGE: I can see that. About what? What's there to smile about? Cost of living skyrocketing, taxes spiralling upward, Internal Revenue Service breathing down our necks. . . .

MEDIC: That's his name — Smiley. (SMILEY *bows, still grinning broadly.*)

SCROOGE: Smiley? Ought to call him Silly. (*At this,* SMILEY *bursts out into a loud roar of laughter and steps back into line.*)

MEDIC: He likes your jokes, Mr. Scrooge.

SCROOGE: He looks as if he'd laugh at a sponge cake. Go on.

MEDIC: This is Grouchy. (GROUCHY, *sour-faced and cranky, steps forward.*)

SCROOGE: What's he sore at?

MEDIC: He's mad at the world. He's cynical, cranky, cantankerous, rude and nasty.

SCROOGE: My type of guy.

MEDIC: But underneath it all, a soft-hearted man.

SCROOGE: Oh . . . well, I'll withhold judgment. (GROUCHY *steps back into line.*)

MEDIC: Next — Yawny. (YAWNY, *working on a big yawn, steps forward and stretches.*)

SCROOGE: This guy's got to go. What kind of production can he turn out?

MEDIC: He's a good worker, Mr. Scrooge. (SCROOGE *does a double take as* YAWNY *gives a huge yawn.*)

SCROOGE: Did you see that? When he yawned, his ears disappeared. Does he run around all night or something?

MEDIC: No, he sleeps twelve, fourteen hours a night.

SCROOGE: As long as he doesn't sleep during the day.

MEDIC (*Beckoning to* SNIPPY): Next we have . . . . (YAWNY *steps back as* SNIPPY *steps forward.*) He's Snippy.

SCROOGE: He won't get snippy with me. O.K., who's next in this rogues' gallery?

MEDIC: Cuddly, you're next. (*No action. No one steps forward.*) Cuddly, please step forward. (CUDDLY *tries to duck behind others. They grab him and push him forward. He reluctantly stumbles out a few paces.*)

SCROOGE: What's he ashamed of?

MEDIC: He's a little shy.

SCROOGE: A little shy? Why is his face so red?

MEDIC: He's blushing.

SCROOGE: Did I say something out of line?

MEDIC: No. He always blushes. That's why girls like him and call him Cuddly.

SCROOGE: Well, there'll be no cuddling on company time, fellow. Next.

MEDIC: Dummy!

SCROOGE (*Whirling on him*): What did you call me?

MEDIC: Dummy, sir. Not you. Dummy's our last worker. He's Dummy. (DUMMY *steps forward, thumb in mouth.*)

SCROOGE: Oh, I see. I probably could have guessed. Is he O.K. upstairs? I mean, is he playing with a full deck?

MEDIC: Dummy is perfectly normal.

Scrooge (*To* DUMMY): Hey, Dummy. How long have you been working for Best Bells? (*Silence*) I asked you a question. Answer me.

MEDIC (*Tugging* SCROOGE*'s sleeve*): He doesn't talk.

SCROOGE: He can't talk?

MEDIC: He won't talk.

SCROOGE: He refuses to talk?

MEDIC: Yes, sir.

SCROOGE: Has anyone ever heard him talk?

MEDIC: Once, sir. At breakfast, eleven years ago.

SCROOGE: What did he say?

MEDIC: He said he didn't like the cereal.

SCROOGE: Well, at least he won't spend time gossiping around the water cooler . . . or talking behind my back. O.K., now I'd like to say a few introductory words. (MEDIC *steps over with other dwarfs and they stand in a row preparing to listen.*) Now listen up. I want to say a few words before you get back into the workshop and slave your heads off for me. I believe in incentive working, but I don't believe in paying bonuses. I've checked the production figures, so I know what you can do. Not bad. But you'll improve. My name is Ebenezer Scrooge, and I came up the hard way. I was from a poor, humble family. My family was so poor my parents couldn't afford to buy me shoes. They just painted my feet black and laced up my toes. I went into business with a guy named Marley, and I was successful. A series of bad breaks, like being nice, sent me tumbling down to the bottom. But I'm back now. Old Ebenezer Scrooge is back and you boys have got him. From now on, you get a ten-minute coffee break in the morning — Wednesday morning. Cut down on your lunch hour. Take bigger bites — it'll go down faster. I demand excellent workmanship and industriousness, and I want you here working at seven o'clock every morning. Any questions? (MEDIC *raises his hand and steps forward.*) Yes?

MEDIC: Can we start now? You've kept us from working for ten minutes now. The men want to work.

SCROOGE: Oh . . . yes, by all means. Go. Dismissed. (*Dwarfs march off at fast pace.*) I think I may have bought out Weirdo City. (*Sound of bells jingling is heard offstage.* SCROOGE *cocks his head and smiles.*) But money talks . . . or jingles. (*He exits, rubbing his hands together. Curtain*)

*   *   *   *   *

SCENE 3

SETTING: *The witch's place. This scene is played before the curtain.*

BEFORE RISE: WITCH *enters left, cackling, crosses right and gazes offstage as if looking into mirror.*

WITCH:
Mirror, mirror, on the wall,
Who is the fairest one of all?

MIRROR (*From offstage*): Snow White. (WITCH *throws a mild tantrum, stamps her feet, etc.*)

WITCH (*Enraged*): Still the fairest? After my expensive ten-week mail-order beauty treatment? Well, I'll take care of little Snow White. A flavorful apple, garnished with my own special sleeping potion, should take care of that little chickie. Then *I* will be the fairest one of all. And isn't that what every woman wants? Sure, I have untold wealth and my health, but I want to be number one in beauty. When I'm number two I have to try harder and it's getting me down. (WITCH *cackles wickedly and exits. Curtains open.*)

* * *

SETTING: *Same as Scene 2.*

AT RISE: *Dwarfs march in, singing "Hi-Ho, Hi-Ho," unenthusiastically. They sit wearily on benches and on floor.*

MEDIC: Boy, that Scrooge is a harsh taskmaster.

CUDDLY (*Hesitantly*): He treats us like animals.

GROUCHY: All he needs is a whip and a chair.

SMILEY: But the factory is doing well. Christmas is coming, and we're all working and we're healthy and happy.

GROUCHY: I'll be happy some other time. Right now I'm too busy thinking bad thoughts about Scrooge. (SNOW WHITE *enters. The dwarfs rise to greet her.*)

SNOW WHITE: Hello, fellows.

DWARFS (*Ad lib*): Hello, Snow. Hi there, Miss White. Glad to see you! (*Etc.*)

SNOW WHITE: How's your new boss treating you?

MEDIC: Not bad, all things considered.

YAWNY (*Suppressing a yawn*): I must admit he's fair. He treats us all alike.

GROUCHY: Right. He treats us all like dogs.

SNOW WHITE: I never met the man.

GROUCHY: You'd be smart to keep it that way. (SCROOGE *enters, sees gathering and stops short.*)

SCROOGE: What is this? A loafers' convention?

MEDIC: We were just —

SCROOGE (*Interrupting*): You aren't "just" anything. You're standing out here gabbing with a woman.

SNOW WHITE: Mr. Scrooge? I'm Snow White.

SCROOGE: That doesn't interest me. You're distracting my men. I don't need any recreation department here. I want to hear the bells ring in the factory, not in their skulls.

GROUCHY (*To* SNOW WHITE): He's all heart.

SCROOGE: What was that?

GROUCHY: I said — she must part.

SCROOGE: Absolutely. You'll have to leave, young lady.

SMILEY (*Grinning*): We still have two minutes left on our break.

SCROOGE: Well, walk slowly back to the shop.

YAWNY (*Yawning*): Aw, let her stay for another minute.

SMILEY (*Laughing*): She's good for our morale. Look at me, I'm laughing.

SCROOGE: You'd laugh if you were caught in a blizzard without shoes and a polar bear was chasing you.

SNOW WHITE: That's all right, boys. I really must go. I'm meeting a witch.

CUDDLY (*Shyly*): Which witch?

SNOW WHITE: Hazel.

SMILEY: Hazel the rich witch?

SNOW WHITE: Yes, I think so.

MEDIC: She may be a rich witch, but she's a bad apple.

GROUCHY: Don't go, Snow. She's rotten to the core.

SNOW WHITE: Oh, she's all right, once you get to know her.

SMILEY: She's mean.

SCROOGE: I'll show you the meaning of mean if you don't get back to work.

MEDIC: Mr. Scrooge, our production is twenty percent above normal.

SCROOGE: Twenty is not thirty. It's not even twenty-five. Goodbye, Miss White.

SNOW WHITE: Goodbye, all. (*She exits.*)

DWARFS (*Ad lib*): Goodbye. Be careful. Watch that witch. (*Etc.*)

SCROOGE: All right, all right. Your two minutes are up. Back to work, on the double. (*Dwarfs march offstage. Sound of bells jingling is heard.* SCROOGE *smiles to himself and rubs his hands together. Lights dim to indicate the passage of time. They come up on* SCROOGE *poring over some papers at his desk.* MEDIC *enters.*)

MEDIC: You rang, Mr. Scrooge?

SCROOGE: Yes. I must admit, you men are showing me something. Production zooming, profits up a pile — er, a little bit — and I'm feeling great. I'll have to watch it. The other day I caught myself smiling.

MEDIC: I'm pleased, Mr. Scrooge.

SCROOGE: But we can't relax. Our busy time is coming up. That calls for hard work, overtime and double overtime. We can't let up one second.

MEDIC: Right. (*Dwarfs, frantic, usher in* SNOW WHITE, *who can barely walk, and guide her to bench, where she lies down.*) What happened?

GROUCHY: The witch got her with one of the apples.

SCROOGE: Do you mean she got conked on the head with an apple and passed out?

SMILEY: No. She ate a bad apple the witch gave her.

SCROOGE: O.K., call a doctor. Send her to the clinic.

MEDIC: You don't understand, Mr. Scrooge. Whoever eats one of the witch's apples falls into a death-like sleep.

YAWNY (*Yawning*): And stays asleep, lucky thing.

SMILEY: She stays asleep until she is awakened by a kiss from a prince.

SCROOGE: What? What are you handing me?

MEDIC: It's true, Mr. Scrooge.

SMILEY: A real, live handsome prince must kiss her into wakefulness.

SCROOGE (*Sarcastically*): I get it, I get it. Then they live happily ever after. Well, what are you waiting for? Go out and find a prince.

SNIPPY: Where are we going to find a prince? Answer me that.

SCROOGE: Don't get snippy with me, Snippy.

MEDIC: Perhaps you know where to find a prince, Mr. Scrooge.

SCROOGE: What do I know about princes? Look in the yellow pages. Only get her out of here. She can't stay here in that condition.

CUDDLY: Why . . . uh . . . why don't you . . . uh . . . kiss her, Mr. Scrooge?

SCROOGE: Me? Why, I hardly know her. Besides, I'm no handsome prince.

GROUCHY (*Aside*): That's for sure.

MEDIC: The men would like a little time off — without pay, of course — to go out and locate a prince.

SCROOGE: Impossible. It's the busiest part of the year.

SMILEY: We'll work twice as hard when we get back.

YAWNY: We'd be (*Yawning*) dynamite.

SCROOGE: I'd lose a pile of profit.

GROUCHY: But we'd have Snow White alive and well.

CUDDLY: We all like her. She's so nice to us.

SCROOGE: Can't do it.

SMILEY: Please, Mr. Scrooge . . .

YAWNY: Just till we find a prince . . .

MEDIC: Be a sport, Mr. Scrooge . . .

SCROOGE: Let me kick it around for a few minutes. (*Dwarfs watch anxiously as* SCROOGE *goes to stage right by himself.*) Let's see. Seven people looking for one prince . . . twenty minutes per person . . . lots of time away from the workbench . . . dollars down the drain . . . What would Marley have done? Would he have been tough on them? No, he's the guy who gave me bad dreams about Christmas future just because I was a little short with Cratchit and a few others . . . All right, Marley, you win. (*To dwarfs*) O.K., you can let Snow White stay here. We'll hold up production. You can go out there and find that prince with the magic lips. (*Dwarfs cheer.*)

SMILEY: Mr. Scrooge is the best boss, after all.

GROUCHY: Yeah . . . after all the rest. (*Dwarfs exit. SCROOGE looks over at SNOW WHITE, then sits down, thinking. He yawns, stretches and then leaves. Stage is now empty except for the sleeping SNOW WHITE. PRINCE enters, led into room by dwarfs. He looks around and spies SNOW WHITE. He walks over to her and kisses her gently. She stirs, awakens. She stands up. PRINCE takes her in his arms and they walk off together, as she looks lovingly up into his eyes. Dwarfs follow them off happily. WITCH enters onto empty stage. She looks at "mirror" on wall. She checks her teeth, pats her hair, and shakes head.*)

WITCH: I don't know. Maybe those beauty courses aren't doing any good. I don't know about this mail-order stuff. The beauty treatments aren't working for me, but now my mailman is prettier than I am. Oh, well . . . . Maybe I should get some beauty sleep. (*She yawns, then lies down on bench that SNOW WHITE has just vacated. SCROOGE enters. He looks at bench.*)

SCROOGE: Look at that. Still snoring away. And where are those clowns? This prince hunt is costing me a pretty penny. They'd better get back soon, because I've just stopped being Mr. Wonderful. (*WITCH stirs.*

SCROOGE *looks at her as she sits up*.) Ah, she's coming out of it. (WITCH *turns to* SCROOGE, *who does double take, blinks eyes and shakes his head*.) You've changed!

WITCH: Changed?

SCROOGE: I mean, that wasn't exactly a beauty nap you just had, Miss White.

WITCH: I'm not Miss White. I'm Hazel.

SCROOGE: The witch?

WITCH: The rich witch.

SCROOGE: Rich witch? (*Warmly*) Well, I'm really pleased to meet you. I'm Ebenezer Scrooge. I'm a prince of a fellow . . . in a manner of speaking.

WITCH: Did you kiss Snow White?

SCROOGE: Kiss her! I never even held her hand. No, that's not my line of work. I'm a manufacturer. This is my factory.

WITCH (*Glancing around*): You seem to be doing well.

SCROOGE: We're moving along. No complaints. We'll do better, too. What do you do?

WITCH: I deal with apples, potions, things like that.

SCROOGE: Hold it. Are you the one who gave Snow White that bad-news apple?

WITCH (*Nodding*): Yes . . . . I feel very bad about it now. I guess just talking about it made me feel better. You know, being a witch can be lonely — no matter how much money I have.

SCROOGE (*Eagerly*): Money . . . do you have money?

WITCH: Oodles and oodles. But still . . . I'm a witch. It seems I have to use a few tricks now and then to keep me on speaking terms with the world.

SCROOGE: I know what you mean. I've been known to re-sort to trickery myself once in a while.

WITCH: When you're not blessed with beauty, I guess you can get pretty nasty.

SCROOGE: True — how true.

WITCH: So I compensate with dirty tricks and money.

SCROOGE: Dirty tricks and money. What a combination!

WITCH: Do you understand me?

SCROOGE: I certainly do, young lady. You're all right in my book. (*They look at each other fondly. Dwarfs come in, leading* PRINCE *and* SNOW WHITE.)

DWARFS (*Ad lib*): We're back! We found the Prince. He kissed Snow White. She's awake, for good. (*Etc. They see* WITCH *and cringe, backing off.*)

MEDIC: What's the witch doing here?

SCROOGE: Hazel and I were just chatting a bit.

YAWNY: You know her?

SCROOGE: We are fast becoming close friends.

SMILEY: But . . . but, she's a . . .

SCROOGE: I know all about it.

WITCH: I told him everything.

GROUCHY: Which witch is she? The rich witch?

WITCH: Yes.

SCROOGE: You bet your beard she's rich.

GROUCHY: Prove it.

WITCH (*Sighing*): If I must . . . . (*She crosses right and gazes offstage, as if looking into mirror, as before.*)
Mirror, mirror, on the wall,
Who is the *richest* one of all?

MIRROR (*Offstage*): You are the richest, Witch Hazel.

SCROOGE (*Jubilantly*): That's my type of woman! Men, you can all have the weekend off. (*Dwarfs cheer. They separate and form two lines.* SCROOGE *and* WITCH *walk arm in arm between lines. Dwarfs begin jingling bells.*)
Is there a preacher in this burg?

PRINCE: Three blocks down you'll find Parson Brown.

SCROOGE (*Patting* WITCH*'s arm*): Let's go, my lovely. We'll see him and then we'll go someplace and count our money — er, blessings! Count our blessings! (*They exit with dwarfs cheering and jingling bells.* SNOW WHITE *and* PRINCE *start off behind* SCROOGE *and* WITCH. *It becomes a grand, noisy exit, as dwarfs, bells ringing, follow them merrily along offstage. Curtain*)

THE END

Santa Claus Is Twins

by *Anne Coulter Martens*

---

*Only one Santa was expected, but two show up
— and one of them may be in trouble. . .*

Characters

DONNA, *14*
BETSY
MACK } *her friends*
FREDDY
MRS. SHELDON
WOODROW, *her son, 6*
OFFICER PERKINS
MRS. AVERY
SHARON, *her daughter*
PARENTS
CHILDREN } *extras*

TIME: *Saturday morning, a few days before Christmas.*
SETTING: *The recreation room in Donna's home.*
AT RISE: DONNA *and* BETSY *are putting Christmas decorations on a highbacked chair.* FREDDY *stands on a
small stepladder behind sofa, attaching to the wall a*

sign that reads: TOYS FOR TOTS. *Above it is another sign reading,* OUR CLUB PROJECT, *and beside this is a sign reading* HAVE YOUR CHILD'S PICTURE TAKEN WITH SANTA CLAUS. *An open costume box is on the coffee table with a Santa Claus suit and some jingle bells hanging over side.*

FREDDY: What time is it?

DONNA (*Looking at her watch*): Ten of ten.

FREDDY: I thought Mack was supposed to be here to help.

DONNA: Mack's late, as usual. He has no sense of time at all.

BETSY: And he knows we want to make as much money as we can for the Gifts-for-Children project.

DONNA: If the Fire Department can make time for this, I should think Mack might make some effort to get here.

FREDDY: How much do you think we'll make on this picture-taking?

DONNA: A lot, I hope. The more we make, the more the Fire Department will have to buy toys for needy kids. (*Goes to costume box.*) Mack was going to borrow a new Santa suit for you, but if he doesn't get here soon, you'll just have to wear this old ratty one. (*Holds up a red jacket with white trim*)

FREDDY (*Sitting on top of ladder*): Playing Santa Claus really isn't my thing.

DONNA: Now, Freddy. Where's your Christmas spirit? (*Telephone rings.*) I'll get it. (*Into phone*) Hello . . . Certainly Mrs. Sheldon, we'll be ready to take a Polaroid picture of your little boy at ten o'clock sharp. (*Picks up appointment book*) Yes, I know you're very busy, but there won't be any delay. . . . Of course, Mrs. Sheldon. Ten o'clock, on the dot. (*Hangs up*) Oh, dear!

BETSY: What's the problem?

DONNA: Mrs. Sheldon. You know what a grouch she can be. She practically chewed my ear off! What if she gives us a hard time?

BETSY: Our schedule would go haywire! Let's hope she doesn't. (*Checking camera on desk*) The camera's loaded and ready. I'm glad we could get the film at cost.

DONNA: I guess everybody likes to help out as much as possible at Christmas.

FREDDY (*Getting down from ladder*): The more I think about it, the more I realize I'm just not the Santa type. You should have asked Mack. (*Takes ladder behind screen*)

DONNA (*Sarcastically*): We did. He said he'd rather supervise.

BETSY: Then why isn't he here?

FREDDY (*Coming from behind screen*): Should we call his house to see if he's left yet?

DONNA: Good idea. (*Picks up phone, dials*)

FREDDY: You did a great job decorating this chair. And those lollipops look terrific. (*Reaches toward box on coffee table*)

BETSY (*Stopping him*): Oh, no, you don't! These are for the kids who have their pictures taken.

DONNA (*Into phone*): Hello . . . Mrs. Barnett? . . . This is Donna. Has Mack left yet? . . . Half an hour ago? He must have been sidetracked somewhere. We're waiting for him to bring the Santa suit . . . Thanks anyway. (*Hangs up*)

BETSY: I guess Freddy will have to wear this old suit after all!

DONNA (*Holding up the red jacket*): You'll need a couple of pillows to fatten you up.

FREDDY (*Unhappily*): Can't we wait a few more minutes for Mack?

DONNA (*Shaking her head*): Time's running out.

BETSY: Come on, Freddy, let's hear you give us a "Ho, ho, ho!"

FREDDY: I'm too nervous. (*Clears his throat and speaks in a flat unconvincing voice*) Ho, ho, ho. (*Sighs*) See? I told you I'm no good as Santa.

BETSY: Don't worry, Freddy. You'll be great. (*Pauses*) Anyway, you're elected.

DONNA (*Matter-of-factly*): Here, put this jacket on. (*Hands it to him*)

BETSY: All you have to do is ask each child if he's been good and what he wants for Christmas.

DONNA: And don't forget that you are supposed to be jolly!

FREDDY (*Resigned*): How do I get myself into these situations? (DONNA *takes red pants out of box and hands them to* FREDDY.)

DONNA: Here are the pants. (*Reaches into box again*) Your hat and boots are in here, too. (*Takes them from box and gives them to* FREDDY)

FREDDY (*Putting on costume*): I'll be quite a sight, all right! (DONNA *takes beard and bells from box.*)

DONNA (*Handing beard and bells to* FREDDY): There, that does it! You're all set now. (FREDDY *adjusts beard, puts on hat and boots, and rings bells.*)

BETSY: You're dynamite as old Saint Nick. (*Pats him lightly on the back*) We really appreciate the way you've volunteered to do this, Freddy.

FREDDY (*Ringing bells again; then in unenthusiastic voice*): Ho, ho, ho.

DONNA: Try putting a little more pep into your ho-ho-ho. You're supposed to be jolly, remember?

FREDDY (*Not doing much better*): Ho, ho, ho. (FREDDY *holds out his arms, the bells in one hand, and* DONNA *places box on extended arms.*)

BETSY: Take these cushions, too. (*She piles two sofa cushions on top of the box.*)

FREDDY: This isn't exactly the kind of "pack" Santa's supposed to carry.

DONNA: Very funny. (*Points left*) You wait out there, and we'll signal when you're to come in. (*He starts toward left.*)

FREDDY: What's the signal?

DONNA: We'll sing "Jingle Bells." O.K.?

FREDDY: I should have stayed in bed. (*Sighs and exits*)

BETSY: Poor Freddy.

DONNA: At least he's reliable. That's more than we can say about Mack.

BETSY: If only his voice didn't squeak!

DONNA: And the suit is sort of ratty. That Mack has no sense of time or responsibility! (*Telephone rings.*)

BETSY (*Into phone*): Hello. . . . Just a moment, Mrs. Avery, and I'll check. (*Looks in appointment book*) Yes, we can take your daughter's picture with Santa at ten-fifteen. Thank you for calling. (*Hangs up*)

DONNA: We're booked solid from ten to twelve. Not bad, Betsy.

BETSY: And with all the posters I've put up, there are sure to be some drop-ins. (*Pauses*) I do wish we had a better Santa suit, though.

DONNA: Once the children are sitting on Santa's lap, it will be all right. They'll never notice. (*Annoyed*) That Mack makes me so angry! (*There is a quick knock, and* MACK *enters, carrying a costume box and a small Christmas tree on a stand. He wears a heavy turtleneck sweater in a bright pattern.*)

MACK (*Jauntily*): Are you talking about me? (*Puts costume box on coffee table*)

DONNA: Mack! What do you mean by getting here so late? We've been waiting for you for half an hour. You look like a clown in that ridiculous sweater.

MACK: So I'll be Santa's clown. What are you two so upset about?

BETSY: Freddy had to put on the old Santa suit because you were so late. Our first customer will be here at ten sharp (*Looks at watch*) — in about two minutes!

DONNA: Where were you, anyway?

MACK: I stopped to buy you a bargain tree. (*Holds up tree*) Cute, huh? I bought it from a kid on the corner down the street and paid for it out of my own pocket.

DONNA: Sure, it's a nice tree, and thanks. (MACK *puts tree on desk.*) There are some miniature lights in the garage. They'd look pretty on it.

BETSY: I'll go get them. (*Exits left*)

DONNA (*Looking at costume box* MACK *brought*): I don't know what we'll do with this costume now. We don't need two Santas.

MACK: Sorry. I must have lost track of the time. (*Takes a white beard from box and holds it to his face. Speaks in a deep voice*) Ho, ho, ho!

DONNA: It's not funny.

MACK: Are you mad at me?

DONNA: Yes, I am! I'm furious.

MACK: Oh, come on, it's no big deal.

DONNA: Not to you, maybe, but it is to us. When you promise to be somewhere at a certain time, you should be there.

MACK (*Mocking*): Are you going to tell Santa I was a bad boy?

DONNA (*Still angry*): I just wish I could.

MACK: Maybe there's still time to put this suit on Freddy. (*There is a knock on door.*)

DONNA: It's too late. That must be Mrs. Sheldon. She's our first customer, and she may be touchy! Mack, put this extra suit out of sight, behind the screen. (*Puts box in his arms*) Hurry! (*He takes box and goes behind screen.* DONNA *calls*) Come in, please! (MRS. SHELDON *and* WOODROW *enter right.* BETSY *enters left with a string of small lights and begins putting them on tree.*)

MRS. SHELDON: Hello, girls.

WOODROW: Where's Santa Claus?

BETSY: He'll be here in a minute.

MRS. SHELDON: This has been such an upsetting morning for me. Sit down, Woodrow, and be very quiet. (*Points to a chair, where* WOODROW *sits.*) He's such a good little boy. (*Looking around*) I'm looking for a nasty young man in a loud turtleneck sweater. (MACK *peers over top of screen, then ducks down.*) Did he come in here?

DONNA (*Uneasily*): Why would he come here?

WOODROW: Wow! Look, lollipops! (*He dashes over to box of lollipops, grabs one, rips the wrapper off and puts it into his mouth.*)

MRS. SHELDON: Woodrow, that's a no-no! (*Reaches for lollipop, but* WOODROW *backs away.*) I never allow sugar because it's bad for him.

BETSY: I'm sorry. We didn't know. (*As she reaches to take lollipop from him,* WOODROW *runs to other side of room.*)

MRS. SHELDON: Wait till Santa hears about this!

WOODROW: I'll bet Santa likes candy.

MRS. SHELDON: Never mind that. Now, look at you.

Your face and hands are all sticky. (*To* DONNA) Does he have time to wash up before you take the picture?

DONNA: Sure. (*Pointing*) Right there — first door to the left.

MRS. SHELDON: March, Woodrow. (WOODROW *goes out left, still sucking the lollipop.*) He's usually so obedient. But after what happened this morning, I'm just too jittery myself to keep a close eye on him.

BETSY (*Putting lights on tree*): What happened, Mrs. Sheldon?

MRS. SHELDON (*Pacing about*): I could *cry*. You know that beautiful evergreen tree on my front lawn? Some vandal sawed the top off it!

DONNA: Who would do such a thing? (MACK *again peeks over the screen, unseen by* MRS. SHELDON.)

MRS. SHELDON: The boy in the turtleneck sweater, that's who! The police station is sending an officer over here, to investigate the vandalism.

BETSY: Did you call the police?

DONNA (*Breaking in excitedly*): And did you tell them to come *here?*

MRS. SHELDON: Yes! I want that boy punished, and there's no time to lose. Not half an hour ago I saw him walk right past my house.

DONNA: Do you know him?

MRS. SHELDON: Not by name. But I'd recognize that sweater anywhere. (MACK *looks over top of screen, puts his hand to his neck, then ducks down.*)

DONNA: But why would he do such a thing?

MRS. SHELDON: That boy is out for revenge, because I complained about him in the supermarket yesterday.

BETSY: What did he do?

MRS. SHELDON (*Self-righteously*): He rammed his shopping cart into me just as I was picking up a carton of eggs!

DONNA: It must have been an accident!

MRS. SHELDON: No! I'm sure he did it on purpose. (*Pompously*) The manager made him pay for the eggs.

BETSY: Couldn't it have been an accident?

MRS. SHELDON: I'm sure it wasn't.

DONNA: Maybe you stopped short, and he couldn't stop in time.

MRS. SHELDON: Since when does a person have to give a signal to stop at the egg counter? No, he did it deliberately. (*Getting worked up*) He probably followed me home and then came back this morning to ruin my tree. This time I'll have him arrested! (MACK *pops his head up, then down.*)

DONNA: Isn't that a little drastic?

MRS. SHELDON: After what he did to my tree? It had a perfect shape, and now this much is sawed right off the top. (*Indicates about twelve inches*) Just about the size of that little tree you have.

DONNA: Really? (*Looks uneasily at tree.*)

MRS. SHELDON: There were a few brown needles near the top and I was considering spraying. (*Goes to look at their tree closely*) Brown needles! This looks just like it!

DONNA (*Nervously*): That's not possible, Mrs. Sheldon.

MRS. SHELDON (*Imperiously*): Where did you get this little tree?

BETSY (*Indignantly*): You don't think one of *us* . . .?

MRS. SHELDON: No, no, it was that boy. But where did you get it?

BETSY (*Quickly*): It was a gift from a friend.

MRS. SHELDON: What is your friend's name?

BETSY: I forgot. Do you remember the name, Donna?

DONNA: It just escapes my mind.

MRS. SHELDON: I'd certainly like to know! While you're thinking (*Goes left*), I'll see what's keeping Woodrow.

I do hope he's not running water in your bathtub, because that's a no-no. (*She exits left.* MACK *dashes out from behind screen, tugging at the zipper at the neck of his sweater.*)

MACK: The zipper's stuck!

DONNA: Mack, was it you?

MACK: Never mind. Just help me. (BETSY *tries to release zipper.*) I've got to get out of this sweater or I'll spend Christmas in jail!

BETSY (*Trying to work zipper*): It won't budge.

DONNA: Tell us, Mack. Did you saw off the tree?

MACK: No. I told you the truth about where I got that tree. But the eggs in the supermarket — that *was* an accident, and I paid for them!

BETSY: She'll never believe you.

MACK (*Anxiously*): But you do, don't you?

DONNA: Well . . . I guess so. (BETSY *struggles with zipper*)

MACK: Come on, hurry up with that zipper!

BETSY: I think the zipper's broken. (*There is a knock on door right.*)

DONNA (*Tugging at zipper*): Betsy, go peek and see who it is. (BETSY *hurries out right.*)

MRS. SHELDON (*From off left*): Come on, Woodrow, dear.

MACK (*Frantically*): I can't go that way. She'll see me!

BETSY (*Looking in from doorway*): The policeman! Beat it, Mack! (*Goes out right, as knock on door is repeated*)

MRS. SHELDON (*Offstage*): Don't dawdle, Woodrow. (MACK *dashes behind the screen just as* MRS. SHELDON *enters left with* WOODROW, *and* OFFICER PERKINS *comes in right with* BETSY.)

BETSY: Officer Perkins is here to see you, Mrs. Sheldon.

MRS. SHELDON: It was good of you to come so promptly, officer.

PERKINS: Are you the woman who phoned about some vandalism?

MRS. SHELDON: Yes, in my yard down the street. I have an appointment here, but I'll be ready in a minute. (WOODROW *stands up on chair*) That's a no-no, Woodrow. (*He ignores her.*) Santa Claus will be here in a few minutes.

PERKINS (*Taking out small notebook and pencil*): Just what was the nature of this vandalism?

MRS. SHELDON: The top of my prettiest evergreen was sawed off. (*Points to little tree*) See? I'm sure this is it!

PERKINS (*Going to it*): Do you really think this is it?

MRS. SHELDON: I'm positive. (MACK *sneezes from behind screen. As* MRS. SHELDON *and* PERKINS *turn,* DONNA *sneezes quickly.*)

DONNA: Excuse me, please.

PERKINS: May I ask where you girls got this little tree?

MRS. SHELDON: *They* say it was a gift. *I* think they're covering for somebody.

PERKINS (*To girls*): Is that true?

DONNA: Officer, I give you my word we don't want to obstruct justice.

BETSY: If we knew who sawed off the tree, we'd tell you. (MACK *sneezes again and so does* DONNA.)

DONNA: I hope I'm not catching a cold.

PERKINS (*To* MRS. SHELDON): Can you give me a description of the vandal?

MRS. SHELDON: He was a very ordinary looking boy. (*There is a noise behind screen;* DONNA *quickly pushes a book off the desk.*) What was that noise?

DONNA: I dropped this book. (*Picks it up*)

MRS. SHELDON: As I was saying, he was ordinary looking. But I remember one thing — he was wearing a very loud turtleneck sweater. It was so loud, nobody could forget it!

BETSY: Lots of boys wear turtlenecks.

MRS. SHELDON: Not like this one. (WOODROW *jumps up and down on sofa.*) That's another no-no, Woodrow! (*He keeps on jumping, as she turns to others.*) I believe in reasoning with children. Woodrow is always such a good little boy. (*Another noise is heard from behind the screen.*)

WOODROW: I heard a noise.

PERKINS: Where? (WOODROW *points to screen.*)

MRS. SHELDON: That screen. Hm-m-m. Someone could be hiding back there.

DONNA (*Quickly*): It's just an ornamental screen, Mrs. Sheldon.

BETSY: There's nothing but a stepladder back there.

PERKINS: Is that all? Maybe I'd better take a look.

DONNA: I'll check. (*Goes behind screen, calling*) Yes, I'm happy to report that the stepladder's still here. (*She remains behind screen.*)

PERKINS: A stepladder didn't make that noise we heard. Let me take a look.

DONNA (*Coming out from behind screen*): Surprise! (*She brings* MACK *out from behind screen; he is dressed in Santa suit, carries jingle bells.*)

MACK (*Heartily, ringing bells*): Ho, ho, ho!

MRS. SHELDON: Why, it's Santa Claus! (WOODROW *hides behind her.*) Don't be afraid, darling. Santa likes good little boys. Don't you, Santa?

MACK: Ho, ho, ho! (DONNA *guides* MACK *to high-backed chair, and he sits down.*)

DONNA: Any time he's ready, I'll take the picture.

WOODROW (*Turning to his mother*): I want to sit on Santa's lap.

MRS. SHELDON: Why, of course, dear. Go sit on Santa's lap. Isn't that sweet?

BETSY: Santa will be delighted.

MACK (*Half-heartedly*): Ho, ho, ho.

MRS. SHELDON (*Setting* WOODROW *on* MACK'*s lap*): Before you get your picture taken, tell Santa what you want for Christmas. (*To others*) He's so good that I'm sure he'll get all he wants.

PERKINS: This is a great idea. It puts me right in the Christmas spirit. (*He begins to sing "Jingle Bells."* MRS. SHELDON *joins in. They are looking at* MACK, *their backs to the door left, as* FREDDY, *also dressed as Santa Claus, comes in left and crosses to sofa, ringing his bells.* MACK *sees him and quickly rings his own bells.* DONNA *signals* FREDDY *to go back.* BETSY *hurries over to him and pushes him down behind sofa.*)

MACK: Speak up, sonny. What would you like for Christmas? (WOODROW *whispers in his ear.*) A bike, eh?

MRS. SHELDON: Well, maybe. (BETSY *walks toward screen, covering* FREDDY *as he creeps to screen.*)

MACK: What else? (WOODROW *whispers again.*) A walkie-talkie set? Well, I'll think about it.

MRS. SHELDON: I never have to punish him, Santa.

MACK: Fine! Anything else? (WOODROW *whispers to him.*) A new tool set? I guess that means you already have an old one. (WOODROW *whispers to him.*) I see. You broke the little saw.

MRS. SHELDON: This morning, yes. His saw is absolutely destroyed. The poor darling was so distressed about it.

DONNA: I can imagine. (*Picks up camera*) Ready for the picture?

MRS. SHELDON: Smile, Woodrow.

DONNA: A nice big smile. (*All look toward camera as she takes picture. At the same time,* BETSY *shoves* FREDDY *behind the screen.*) Very good. All done!

BETSY (*Coming from screen*): It won't take long for the picture to develop.

MRS. SHELDON: Good. I don't like to keep the officer waiting.

DONNA (*To* MRS. SHELDON): Would you please pay Betsy? She's the treasurer of our club. (*To* OFFICER PERKINS) We're giving the money to the Fire Department to buy toys for needy kids.

PERKINS: Very enterprising of you. (MRS. SHELDON *gives* BETSY *some money, and* BETSY *puts it into desk drawer.*)

BETSY: Thank you. I know it'll be a great picture. (FREDDY *peeks over screen, then ducks down again. Screen wobbles.*)

MACK (*As* WOODROW *whispers again*): Oh, you want a model plane, too? (WOODROW *whispers*) And a cowboy suit and a wagon and an electric train? Slow down there, young fellow.

BETSY: Santa has to save some things for other little boys.

MACK (*As* WOODROW *whispers*): And finger paints? And balloons? And a big box of candy?

MRS. SHELDON: Candy's a no-no, Woodrow, dear.

DONNA: O.K. The picture's ready.

MRS. SHELDON: Let me see. (*Goes to look at it.* DONNA *holds it up for her to see.*)

DONNA: It's still a little damp, so be careful.

MRS. SHELDON: Adorable. Woodrow is such a photogenic child. (*As* DONNA *mounts the picture,* FREDDY *peeks over the screen again and* WOODROW *sees him.*)

WOODROW (*Pointing*): Look! Look!

MRS. SHELDON: Quiet, darling. We'll be on our way as soon as the picture's ready. (*Beckons to him*) Come to Mother, Woodrow. (*He stays on* MACK's *lap.*) How sweet. He wants to stay with Santa! (*A sound is heard from behind the screen, which wobbles again.*)

WOODROW (*Pointing to screen*): That thing's moving!

BETSY (*Quickly*): Woodrow, you mustn't keep your mother and the officer waiting. (*Takes his hand, but he pulls it away.* DONNA *gives the picture to* MRS. SHELDON.)

DONNA: Here you are, Mrs. Sheldon. Thanks for coming.

MRS. SHELDON: Glad to help a good cause. (*Screen wobbles.*) That screen *did* move!

BETSY: How could it? (*Suddenly,* FREDDY *loses his balance and knocks screen over.*)

PERKINS (*Startled*): Santa Claus is twins! (*Helps* FREDDY *to his feet*)

FREDDY (*Weakly*): Ho, ho, ho!

WOODROW (*Looking from* FREDDY *to* MACK): Another Santa!

MRS. SHELDON: I don't understand. (WOODROW *runs to* MACK, *yanks his white beard, pulling it off. Startled,* MACK *stands up. Without beard, they can see his sweater.*) Look at that sweater! He's the one who broke my eggs! He's the vandal!

MACK: I am not!

MRS. SHELDON: Do you deny that you brought that little tree in here?

MACK: No, but —

PERKINS: Mrs. Sheldon, are you sure you want to lodge a complaint?

MRS. SHELDON: I certainly am.

PERKINS: All right, young man, you'll have to come along with me.

DONNA: He's innocent, officer! Tell him who sold you that tree, Mack. I think you know now who cut it.

MACK: I can't, Donna. I hate to be a squealer.

DONNA: Maybe there's another way. (*Bends down beside* WOODROW) You broke your little saw this morning, didn't you, Woodrow? (*He nods*) How did you break it? Tell me.

WOODROW: I was sawing something.

DONNA: *What* were you sawing, Woodrow? (WOODROW *pulls away, frightened.*) Come now, Woodrow, you must tell me. What did you saw?

WOODROW: My mommy's tree.

DONNA: Your mommy's tree? (*He nods.*)

MRS. SHELDON (*Shocked*): I can't believe it!

DONNA: Tell me why, Woodrow. (*He whispers.*) I see. (*To the others*) He wanted the money he'd get for the tree to buy some candy.

MRS. SHELDON: But he knows that sugar is bad for him. I've told him so many times.

DONNA: At his age, that's hard to believe. And not having any candy may make him want it all the more.

MRS. SHELDON: You may be right.

PERKINS (*Pointing to* MACK): It wasn't this other fellow at all, then.

MACK: I bought the tree from Woodrow, but I didn't know where it came from.

MRS. SHELDON (*Pointing to* FREDDY): What is Santa going to think? (WOODROW *hangs his head, ashamed.*)

MACK: May I say something? (*Takes* WOODROW *by the hand*) This other fellow and I . . . (*Indicating* FREDDY) we're just Santa's helpers. But I think the real Santa will say, "Woody was bad, but he told the truth about it." (*To* MRS. SHELDON) That's important, isn't it?

PERKINS: I'll say it is!

MRS. SHELDON: Why . . . why, yes, I guess you're right. And I'm sorry about all this. (*To* PERKINS) I hope you'll excuse the fuss I made.

PERKINS (*Smiling*): I will.

MRS. SHELDON: Come now, Woodrow. (*Takes him by the hand, and they exit right, as* WOODROW *waves.*)

PERKINS: Listen, kids, when I get off duty, I'll bring my

niece to see Santa. I hope there'll be one this time —
not two! (*Waves and exits*)

DONNA: Wow! That was a close call. Mack, you're quite
a guy, to take the blame for what that little boy did.

MACK: It was nothing.

BETSY: Front and center, everyone! Our schedule is
jammed with kids, and they all want to have their pictures taken with Santa. Which of you is it going to be?

FREDDY: Not me! I'll blow it again.

DONNA: O.K. Mack, you're elected. (*Sound of knock on
door is heard*) That's our next appointment! Let's get
going. (BETSY *pushes* FREDDY *off left*. MACK *sits in
Santa's chair*. DONNA *admits* MRS. AVERY, SHARON,
PARENTS *and* CHILDREN.)

SHARON: Hello, Santa Claus!

MRS. AVERY: I hope we're not too early.

DONNA: Not at all. You're right on time. (*She guides*
SHARON *to sit on* MACK's *lap*.)

MACK: Ho, ho, ho! Tell old Santa what you want for
Christmas!

MRS. AVERY: Isn't that cute? Let's sing a Christmas
carol. (*She starts to sing "Jingle Bells," joined by
other* PARENTS *and* CHILDREN.)

DONNA *and* BETSY (*Ad lib*): Stop! Wait! Don't sing
that song! (*Etc.*)

FREDDY (*Bursting in, left*): You rang? (*He rings bells.*
MRS. AVERY *and others look from* FREDDY *to* MACK *in
confusion*.)

BETSY (*Pushing* FREDDY *out left*): Freddy, that's a no-no!

DONNA (*Shrugging*): This year, you get twice as much for
your money. Santa Claus is twins! (*Quick curtain*)

THE END

The North Pole Computer Caper

Frank V. Priore

Santa proves that real Christmas spirit can't be programmed. . . .

Characters

SANTA CLAUS
MRS. SANTA CLAUS
SANTA, JR.
THREE ELVES
KUMQUAT, *voice*

SCENE 1

SETTING: *Santa's living room at the North Pole. Desk is left of center; armchair and small end table are right of center. A large day-by-day calendar is on upstage wall. Exit up center leads outside. Exit up left leads to workshop. Exit up right leads to kitchen.*

AT RISE: *Calendar reads "December 19." SANTA is at desk. He is wearing glasses and going through some letters.* MRS. SANTA CLAUS *is sitting in armchair, sewing; sewing basket is beside chair.*

SANTA *(Looking at a letter):* Let's see . . . little Johnny Jones wants a new stereo for Christmas. *(Pauses)* Well, he's been a good boy all year. I'll stamp his letter "Request Approved." *(Looking around desk)* I will, that is, as soon as I find my rubber stamp.

MRS. SANTA: It's in the upper left-hand drawer of your desk.

SANTA *(Opening drawer):* Aha, there it is. Now if I could only find the stamp pad. . . .

MRS. SANTA *(Matter-of-factly):* Lower right-hand drawer.

SANTA *(Taking pad from drawer):* So it is—so it is. Thanks again, dear.

MRS. SANTA: That's why I'm here, Santa. Beside every successful jolly old elf, there's a loving wife who reminds him to hitch the reindeer to the sleigh every Christmas Eve.

SANTA: Ho, ho, ho! I guess that's true. *(Absent-mindedly)* By the way, dear . . . er, exactly when is. . .

MRS. SANTA: Christmas Eve is next Wednesday.

SANTA *(Smiling):* I don't know what I'd do without you, dear. *(A few off-key guitar chords are heard offstage.)*

SANTA, JR. *(Singing offstage):* "Bury me 'neath the cherry tree. My life is the pits without you. . . ."

SANTA *(Groaning):* Oh, no! There's Junior with that cat—erwauling again!

MRS. SANTA: Now, be patient, Santa. (SANTA, JR. *enters with guitar. He wears garish, shiny, sequin-covered western outfit with hat and boots.)*

SANTA, JR. *(In an exaggerated country accent):* Howdy, y'all!

SANTA: Good grief! Son, you glitter more than the Christmas tree!

SANTA, JR.: Well, golly, gee whiz, Big Daddy . . . (SANTA

turns to audience and mouths, "Big Daddy?") All the top country-western singing stars dress like this.

SANTA *(Sarcastically):* What does that have to do with you? You're no star. Although, I must admit you twinkle like one.

SANTA, JR.: I know I'm not a star yet, but I'll make it—just wait and see. All it takes is hard work and lots of practice. *(Begins to strum guitar, but* SANTA *puts hands over frets, stopping him)*

SANTA: Son, I realize practice makes perfect, but do me a favor, and practice somewhere else.

SANTA, JR.: But I need to practice in front of a live audience.

SANTA: Try the toy workshop. You can serenade the elves.

SANTA, JR.: What a great idea! They can be the first to hear my new song: "You're the Crazy Glue That Mends My Broken Heart." *(Exits left)*

SANTA *(Chuckling):* The head elf probably won't talk to me for a week.

MRS. SANTA: You shouldn't be making fun of Junior's ambition. I'm glad he's taking an interest in music.

SANTA: I'd hardly call that noise music.

MRS. SANTA: Well, he has to practice a bit more.

SANTA: That boy could practice until the cows come home, and the only thing he'd accomplish is turning their milk sour. *(Sighs)* And I had such big hopes for our son. After all, sooner or later, I'll be retiring, and I always thought he'd take over for me.

MRS. SANTA: Why couldn't he? It takes only one night a year to be Santa. The rest of the time he could concentrate on his music.

SANTA: Image, dear, image. When people see Santa flying by in his sleigh, they're looking for someone a little more . . . traditional. You know—the red suit, white beard, black boots—the whole bit.

MRS. SANTA: Junior wears black boots.

SANTA: But Santa's boots don't have spurs on them! And if Junior ever tried to shake like a bowlful of jelly, that tight-fitting cowboy suit would probably split down the seams! I don't know what I'm going to do with that boy!. . . *(Scratching his head)* Do . . . do. Hm-m-m, I was about to do something when he came in. What was it?

MRS. SANTA: You were going to add the new names to your list.

SANTA: Ah, yes. The list. *(Looks around)* I checked it twice . . . and now I've lost the silly thing. (MRS. SANTA *rises, goes to* SANTA, *lifts his hat. A long roll of adding machine paper falls out and unrolls.)* Now I remember! I put it under my hat so I wouldn't forget where it was. *(Bends over and picks up paper)*

MRS. SANTA: An idea that obviously didn't work.

SANTA: Ho, ho, ho! Next time, I'll tie a string around my finger.

MRS. SANTA *(Shaking her head):* Santa, Santa, Santa. How do you remember which toys go to which children every year? You've never even been able to remember so much as the reindeer's names.

SANTA *(Happily):* Delivering toys is something I do instinctively. That's all part of being Santa Claus. Memory has nothing to do with it.

MRS. SANTA: I see.

SANTA *(Miffed):* I *do* remember the reindeer's names. There's Dasher and Dancer and Prancer and, ah . . . the other five.

MRS. SANTA: Right. I think I ought to give you your Christmas present a little early. You can use it to organize things.

SANTA: What did you get me—another file cabinet?

MRS. SANTA: No, dear. I got you a Kumquat.

SANTA: Ho, ho, ho! That'll certainly make a nice snack, but I don't see how it will help me remember things. Unless, of course, you think I work better on a full stomach.

MRS. SANTA *(Moving right):* I wasn't referring to a kumquat you can eat, silly. *(She exits, then quickly re-enters, rolling a table on wheels. The table has a personal computer on it.* NOTE: *See Production Notes.)* This is a Kumquat Personal Computer. *(She rolls table in front of* SANTA's *desk. Screen faces up right so audience can't see it.)*

SANTA *(Surprised):* A computer! Why, my dear, I don't know what to say.

MRS. SANTA: It's programmed to help you make everything run more smoothly here at the North Pole. Just plug it in, and you'll see.

SANTA: I'll do that, dear. *(Takes plug, inserts it into outlet on floor near desk;* MRS. SANTA *taps out a few instructions on the keyboard.)*

KUMQUAT *(Speaking in a robot-like, mechanical voice):* Hello. I am Kumquat, your personal computer.

SANTA: My goodness! It speaks!

MRS. SANTA: Of course. I ordered the deluxe model.

SANTA: It's—er . . . very nice, dear. I'll fiddle around with it after Christmas. Right now, I have too much to do to spend time playing with a video game.

MRS. SANTA: This isn't a game. It's a machine that's going to solve all your problems. Listen. *(Punches a few more buttons on computer)*

KUMQUAT: I am programmed to keep track of every child's letter to Santa Claus. I cross-reference all toy requests to existing inventory and issue appropriate work orders to the elves. In addition, I am capable of recording all good and bad deeds done by little boys and girls.

MRS. SANTA: Isn't that nice? You won't have to rely on your memory any more.

SANTA: But I've always done it that way. It's traditional!

MRS. SANTA: Nonsense. It's time to enter the computer age. Watch this. *(Punches more buttons)*

KUMQUAT: I can compute the most efficient route for Santa Claus to follow on Christmas Eve.

MRS. SANTA *(Excitedly):* How about that, Santa? No more worrying about which route to take. Your new computer will figure out the fastest way. It'll have you back here before midnight.

SANTA *(Aside, to audience):* The only night I get to go out all year, and this infernal machine wants to cut it short!

MRS. SANTA: And that's not all it can do. If we hook it up to the heating system, it will automatically regulate the temperature in the house, workshop, and stable. Oh, and I almost forgot—look at this program. *(She picks up a computer disk from table and hands it to* SANTA.)

SANTA *(Reading from disk label): Feed-o-Fawn,* a scientifically-balanced diet program for the proper nutrition of your reindeer.

MRS. SANTA: Isn't that great? *(Takes disk from* SANTA *and inserts it into computer)*

KUMQUAT: Please punch in the number of reindeer you wish to feed.

MRS. SANTA *(As she punches it into keyboard)*: Eight.

KUMQUAT: Enter height and weight of each reindeer, please.

MRS. SANTA: We'll have to measure and weigh each of them. *(Takes tape measure from sewing basket, hands it to* SANTA) Here's a tape measure for the height. You can use the bathroom scale for the weight.

SANTA: How do you expect me to get all four hooves on a tiny bathroom scale?

MRS. SANTA: Use two scales.

SANTA: Do we have two?

MRS. SANTA: Yes, dear. For you—remember?

SANTA *(Patting his belly):* Ho, ho, ho! That's right. I forgot. *(Absent-mindedly puts tape measure down on desk)*

MRS. SANTA: You'll never forget anything again, Santa. Not with Kumquat, here. *(Pats computer)* Now, you just run along and measure those reindeer. I have some brownies in the oven. *(She exits right.)*

SANTA *(Shaking head):* Weighing reindeer! I never heard of anything so ridiculous in my entire life. And who needs special diet plans for them? They've always eaten a bucket of mush every day. I've never had any complaints. *(Starts to exit center)*

KUMQUAT: Don't forget the tape measure.

SANTA *(Turning):* What?

KUMQUAT: The tape measure. You left it on your desk.

SANTA: So I did, so I did. *(Takes tape measure)* It's bad enough having my wife constantly reminding me to do things. Now, she has a machine to help her! *(Starts for door)*

KUMQUAT: Don't forget the scales.

SANTA *(Turning, annoyed):* Machine, I'm known for my good nature. They don't call me a jolly old elf for nothing. But don't push me. You may wind up with a lump of coal in your memory bank. *(Curtain)*

* * * * *

SCENE 2

TIME: *Christmas Eve.*

SETTING: *Same as Scene 1.*

AT RISE: *The computer is still in the room. Calendar shows "24." MRS. SANTA sits, sewing. SANTA enters right, carrying big can of wax. He heads for center exit.*

MRS. SANTA: Where are you going, dear?

SANTA: I thought I'd wax the runners on the sleigh.

KUMQUAT: Not necessary.

SANTA: Of course it's necessary. I wax the runners every Christmas Eve.

KUMQUAT: It was taken care of yesterday. I included that in the pre-flight checklist I issued to the elves.

SANTA: But I like to do that myself.

KUMQUAT: Inefficient. Elves can accomplish that task far more effectively than you can. (THREE ELVES *enter left, each carrying a fishing pole over his shoulder.*)

SANTA *(Upset):* Where are you elves going? Did you forget this is Christmas Eve? There are always last-minute toy requests on Christmas Eve.

1ST ELF: We finished everything last night. Your computer figured out all sorts of ways to make the operation run more efficiently.

2ND ELF: The toys are made, and your sled is all loaded and ready to go.

3RD ELF: We're going ice fishing. See you later. *(They exit center.)*

SANTA: Hm-m-m. This machine has it all figured out, doesn't it?

KUMQUAT: Correct. Right down to the last tin soldier, doll, and video game.

MRS. SANTA: Things run much more smoothly now,

thanks to Kumquat.

SANTA: But it's not right! How can you replace all the traditions of Christmas Eve with computer programs? Why, the next thing you know, this computer will figure out a way to do without Santa Claus altogether!

KUMQUAT: Actually, the deliveries *could* be handled more efficiently by express mail.

SANTA *(Angrily):* I give up! If you want me, I'll be out ice-fishing with the elves! *(Exits. After a few moments, off-key guitar music is heard, then* SANTA, JR. *enters from left.)*

SANTA, JR.: Howdy, Mom.

MRS. SANTA: Er—howdy, son.

SANTA, JR. *(Sitting on edge of desk, crossing legs and strumming guitar):* You're about to get a genuine A-one treat, Mom. I'm going to sing my new song for you. It's about a truck driver who comes to Alaska to prospect for gold. It's called, "Dog sleds are fine, but forty paws can't hold a candle to eighteen wheels."

MRS. SANTA *(Rising abruptly):* I thought your father told you to go practice in the workshop, dear.

SANTA, JR.: I did, but the head elf kicked me out.

MRS. SANTA: Well, what about the stables?

SANTA, JR.: I tried there. The head reindeer actually kicked me.

MRS. SANTA: You know, there's a nice glacier a few miles from here. . . .

SANTA, JR.: I was there, too. The head walrus out-barked me. So, I have to practice right here.

MRS. SANTA *(Sighing):* Very well. *(Moves right)*

SANTA, JR.: Where are you going, Mom? Don't you want to hear my song?

MRS. SANTA: Some other time, dear. I have some brownies in the oven. *(She exits.)*

SANTA, JR. *(To audience):* She *always* seems to have brownies in the oven! *(Rises)* Shucks, if nobody wants to listen to me play, I'll never know whether my music is any good.

KUMQUAT: Take it from me, kid. It stinks.

SANTA, JR. *(Looking around; puzzled):* Who said that?

KUMQUAT: I did.

SANTA, JR. *(Spotting computer):* Well, golly, gosh, gee willikers. This here's a genuine computatin' machine.

KUMQUAT: Do you want to translate that into English?

SANTA, JR. *(Walking around, examining computer):* It has a speech synthesizer. *(Sits at computer, prepares to punch some keys)*

KUMQUAT: Don't touch anything. You might break me.

SANTA, JR.: Not a chance. Playing country music isn't the only thing I'm terrific at. I got an A+ in my computer programming course at school. *(Sits down at keyboard)* Now, let's see. I'll do this *(Punches some keys)* . . . and this *(Punches keys)* . . . and this. *(Punches keys)*

KUMQUAT: Just what do you think you're doing?

SANTA, JR.: Reprogramming you. When I'm through, you'll be able to appreciate some of the finer things in life.

KUMQUAT: Like what?

SANTA, JR.: Why, country-western music, of course.

KUMQUAT: Oh, give me a break, kid!

SANTA, JR.: Just keep your micro-circuits cool. I'll have this set up in no time at all.

KUMQUAT: Stop! Don't push those buttons! What are you . . . (SANTA, JR., *undaunted, continues at the keyboard as the curtain falls.*)

* * * * *

Scene 3

TIME: *Christmas Eve, early evening.*

SETTING: *Same.*

AT RISE: *The computer has a western-style red bandanna tied around its monitor screen, and a cowboy hat on top of the monitor.*

KUMQUAT (*Singing*): Don't bury my transistors on the lone prairie. . . (MRS. SANTA *enters right, carrying a tray with hot cocoa and a plate of brownies.*)

MRS. SANTA: Santa, have some nice hot cocoa and brownies. (*Looks around*) Oh, dear. He must have left already to deliver the toys. (*Puts tray on table, spots hat and bandanna on computer*) Now, who did that? (*Goes to computer*)

KUMQUAT (*With country accent*): Well, hi there, little lady!

MRS. SANTA: Little lady?

KUMQUAT: Would you care for a little tune?

MRS. SANTA: What's happened to that computer? (1ST ELF *enters left, carrying large stack of computer printout paper.*)

1ST ELF: Santa! Santa!

MRS. SANTA: I think he's left already.

1ST ELF: Oh, no! Then I'm too late.

MRS. SANTA: What's wrong?

1ST ELF: When I got back from fishing, I thought I'd check the workshop to make sure the lights were all out. When I got there, I saw this on the printer. (*Hands her the paper*)

MRS. SANTA (*Looking through it*): Why, all the children's toy orders have been changed. The girls are getting nothing but cowgirl outfits, and all the boys are getting guitars and cowboy boots. (SANTA *enters center, carry-*

ing a computer printout.) Santa! I thought you'd already left.

SANTA *(Angrily)*: I did, but once I took a look at the flight plan this infernal contraption printed out, I turned around and came right back. *(Shows printout to* MRS. SANTA*)*

MRS. SANTA *(Surprised):* All the stops are in Nashville!

SANTA: Exactly. I'm going back to my old *handwritten* route *(Looks around)* . . . if I can find it.

MRS. SANTA: Lower right desk drawer.

SANTA: Ah, yes.

MRS. SANTA: Before you leave, Santa, I think you'd better have the elves repack your bag. *(Shows printout to him)*

SANTA *(Looking at it)*: Cowgirl outfits! Guitars! Cowboy boots! Who did this?

MRS. SANTA: I'm afraid the computer did. (2ND ELF *enters quickly from center.)*

2ND ELF: Santa! Santa! *(Runs to* SANTA*)* I've just come from the stables. Something's gone haywire with the computer diet plan for the reindeer. It's scheduled to feed them nothing but grits and wilted greens.

KUMQUAT: Yes, siree, good old-fashioned country-western grub.

SANTA *(Furiously):* That machine has got to go! *(Moves to computer)*

KUMQUAT: Now, hold on there, pardner. What are you . . . (SANTA *pulls plug, and computer's voice runs down.)* do-oo-ing.

SANTA: That settles that.

MRS. SANTA: I'm sorry, Santa.

SANTA: Quite all right, my dear. The elves and I will fix everything in time.

1ST ELF: I'll get the gang together right away. We'll have you ready to go in no time. *(To* 2ND ELF*)* Come on.

(They exit center.)

MRS. SANTA: Will you still be able to make all the deliveries tonight?

SANTA: Of course. I haven't missed one Christmas Eve yet, have I?

MRS. SANTA: No, you haven't, Santa. But I wonder what happened to the computer?

SANTA: Who cares? If you ask me, too many people nowadays believe in machines, and not enough believe in Santa Claus.

MRS. SANTA *(Thinking):* That is true, but still, it was working so well this afternoon. Why, when I left Junior and the computer alone to tend to my brownies . . .

SANTA: Junior? (SANTA, JR. *enters left, still carrying his guitar.)*

SANTA, JR.: Somebody call me?

SANTA: Son, were you fooling around with the computer?

SANTA, JR.: I wasn't "fooling around," Dad. I know exactly what I'm doing when I reprogram a computer.

MRS. SANTA: Reprogram! So, it was you!

SANTA *(Quickly):* Now, now, Mama. Boys will be boys. *(Pats SANTA, JR. on back)* Heh, heh. Neat little trick, son.

SANTA, JR.: Why, thank you, Dad.

SANTA: Say, would you like to make the trip with me tonight?

SANTA, JR.: Wow! Can I?

SANTA: Of course. *(They head for exit, center. SANTA stops.)* Leave the guitar home, son.

SANTA, JR.: Sure thing, Dad. *(Hands guitar to MRS. SANTA)*

SANTA *(Aside to MRS. SANTA):* Deep six it while we're gone. *(She nods; to SANTA, JR.)* And one other thing. *(Takes off SANTA, JR.'s cowboy hat, tosses it aside;*

takes out a "Santa" hat from his pocket) Try this on for size.

SANTA, JR. *(Putting it on)*: A perfect fit. *(As they start to exit)* Where did you get it?

SANTA *(Putting his arm around* SANTA, JR.*'s shoulder)*: I had it made the day you were born, son! *(They exit center as curtain falls.)*

THE END

We Interrupt This Program . . .

by Claire Boiko

An unidentified flying object is heading for the North Pole, and scientists predict it will arrive on Christmas Eve!

Characters

MASTER OF CEREMONIES
SUSAN JAMISON, *pianist*
J. HOLLY BARBERRY, *anchorman*
MESSENGER
TWO CAMERAMEN
IVY GREEN, *commentator*
GENERAL REVEL
THREE SCIENTISTS
ROBBIE SMITH
TWO AIDES
TWO GRENADIERS
COMPUTER TECHNICIAN
ASSISTANT
TWO ELVES
SANTA CLAUS
MRS. SANTA CLAUS
CAROLERS
CHILDREN OF THE WORLD

SCENE 1

BEFORE RISE: MASTER OF CEREMONIES *enters through curtain, as if to begin Christmas assembly program.*

MASTER OF CEREMONIES: Good afternoon! A happy holiday season to you all. We will now present a special program of Christmas music, and to begin, we'll hear a medley of favorite carols played by Susan Jamison on the piano. (MASTER OF CEREMONIES *exits right, as* SUSAN JAMISON *enters, takes place at piano and begins to play a Christmas song. After several bars are played,* MASTER OF CEREMONIES *rushes onstage from right, a sheet of paper in hand, crosses to* SUSAN *and whispers into her ear.*)

SUSAN (*Excited*): What! Unidentified? Over the *North Pole?* Oh, my goodness! (SUSAN *picks up music and exits right, shaking head.*)

MASTER OF CEREMONIES (*To audience*): Boys and girls, I've just been handed a news bulletin from television station N-O-E-L. (*Reads*) "An unidentified flying object has been sighted above the Earth flying toward the North Pole." This is all the information we have at present, but we are going to switch you directly to the studios of station N-O-E-L. (*He exits through curtains. A broadcast news desk, decorated with small Christmas tree, is rolled out. Front of desk has banner in red and green which reads,* YOUR HOLIDAY STATION — N-O-E-L. J. HOLLY BARBERRY, *wearing a neck microphone, enters and sits at desk.* 1ST CAMERAMAN *enters with television camera and follows action onstage. Sound of newsroom ticker is heard.*)

J. HOLLY BARBERRY: Greetings, boys and girls, this is your television anchorman, J. Holly Barberry, with a fast-breaking story about an unidentified flying object headed directly for our North Pole. Where has it come

from? We don't know. What is its mission? That, too,
is a mystery, but we will keep you informed as bulletins sizzle off the news wires. . . . (MESSENGER *runs in
from down left, carrying sheet of paper.*)

MESSENGER: Here's some hot copy, chief! (MESSENGER
runs to BARBERRY, *gives him bulletin, then races offstage.*)

J. HOLLY BARBERRY (*Reading bulletin*): Boys and girls,
the skywatchers at the space laboratories on Christmas
Island have issued this bulletin: the object in the sky is
definitely a rocket. I repeat, a rocket. But why is a
rocket streaking across the heavens toward the North
Pole?

MESSENGER (*Running back onstage with paper*): Another
scorcher, chief! (*Drops paper on desk, then runs off.*)

J. HOLLY BARBERRY: The mystery deepens, folks! (*Reads,
looks up*) Now we can tell you where the rocket came
from. Listen to this — the tracking stations say that
the rocket was launched from a small backyard in a
middle-sized town somewhere in the center of the
United States. How about that, folks! Stand by as we
switch you to the center of these new developments.
Take it away, Ivy Green, at the space laboratories on
Christmas Island. (*Recording of Christmas music
played on electronic instruments is heard as desk and
camera are rolled offstage.* 1ST CAMERAMAN *and* J.
HOLLY BARBERRY *exit right as curtains open.*)

*   *   *

SETTING: *Interior of a space laboratory with astronomical
charts on walls, and large computer console upstage,
with a music stand beside it. Up left is a door marked*
PRIVATE, TOP SECRET. *Down left is a table with three
red and green telephones, labeled* OPERATION YULE-

WATCH. *At right is another table with lab equipment.*
AT RISE: GENERAL REVEL *and* 1ST AIDE *sit at table at
left, consulting large maps.* TWO GRENADIERS *stand
guard at door.* THREE SCIENTISTS *sit working intently
at table at right.* 1ST SCIENTIST *pours liquid from test
tube into beaker.* 2ND SCIENTIST *listens through pair of
earphones.* 3RD SCIENTIST *peers through microscope.*
COMPUTER TECHNICIAN *works at console.* IVY GREEN,
*wearing neck microphone and carrying a hand micro-
phone, stands at center.* 2ND CAMERAMAN, *with portable television camera, stands down right, following
action.*

IVY GREEN: Boys and girls, this is Ivy Green, your on-
the-spot reporter, here in the main laboratories of the
space research station on Christmas Island. To your
left, you will see the special guardian of the holiday
season, General Revel, and his staff, preparing to defend Santa's Workshop at the North Pole from the
mysterious rocket. Over here, at the other table, are
three world-famous scientists now about to compute
the results of their research on the rocket. (ASSISTANT
enters right. THREE SCIENTISTS *hold out data sheets.*)

THREE SCIENTISTS (*Together*): Compute, please! (ASSIS-
TANT *collects sheets, handing them with a bow to* COM-
PUTER TECHNICIAN, *who places them on music rack,
rubs his hands, then plays on computer keys like an
organist.* ASSISTANT *turns pages. Recording of Christmas carol performed on electronic instruments is
heard, followed by excited computer chatter, then loud
cymbal clash.* ASSISTANT *removes from computer three
punch-out cards, handing them with flourish to* THREE
SCIENTISTS.)

1ST SCIENTIST (*Shocked*): Unbelievable!
2ND SCIENTIST: Inconceivable!

3RD SCIENTIST (*Mystified*): Absolutely incomprehensible!

1ST SCIENTIST: The rocket is made of tin whistles!

2ND SCIENTIST: The rocket is propelled by fizzy soda.

3RD SCIENTIST (*Amazed*): The rocket is guided by a compass — a little, itsy-bitsy pocket compass!

IVY GREEN (*Impatiently*): But the cargo — the freight. What is *inside* the rocket?

1ST SCIENTIST: Odds and ends . . .

2ND SCIENTIST: This and that . . .

3RD SCIENTIST: Trifles and trinkets . . . (*Music to "The Twelve Days of Christmas" is heard, and* THREE SCIENTISTS *sing following lines to that tune.*)

1ST SCIENTIST (*Singing*):
  Down in the rocket
  The strangest things you'll see —

2ND SCIENTIST (*Singing*):
  Twelve ginger cupcakes,

3RD SCIENTIST (*Singing*):
  Eleven candy kisses,

1ST SCIENTIST (*Singing*):
  Ten braided bookmarks,

2ND SCIENTIST (*Singing*):
  Nine fancy pillows,

3RD SCIENTIST (*Singing*):
  Eight homemade bookends,

1ST SCIENTIST (*Singing*):
  Seven lacy doilies,

2ND SCIENTIST (*Singing*):
  Six scarves of cashmere,

3RD SCIENTIST (*Singing*):
  Five . . . Spanish . . . shawls,

1ST SCIENTIST (*Singing*):
  Four calling cards,

2ND SCIENTIST (*Singing*):
  Three French pens,

3RD SCIENTIST (*Singing*):
Two furry gloves,
1ST SCIENTIST (*Singing*):
And a nightcap on a shoe tree.
2ND SCIENTIST (*Sitting abruptly down at table, shaking head in bafflement*): Unbelievable!
1ST SCIENTIST (*Also sitting down*): Inconceivable!
3RD SCIENTIST: Absolutely incomprehensible! (*Several telephones ring at once.* GENERAL REVEL *speaks into each phone in rapid succession.*)
GENERAL REVEL (*Into first phone*): Hello . . . General Revel here. . . . What? You've found the fellow who built the rocket? Splendid. Fly him here by double-swift high-speed jet. (*He hangs up. Into second phone*) General Revel here. . . . What? He's here? The fellow who built the rocket has landed at Christmas Island? . . . Splendid. Rush him here by special-delivery helicopter. (*He hangs up, answers third phone*) Hello? . . . The fellow who built the rocket is here at the space laboratory? . . . (*Looks at watch*) Well, what kept him? (*To* 1ST AIDE) Aide, bring in the fellow who built the rocket! I have a lot of important questions to ask him.
1ST AIDE: Yes, sir. (*As* 1ST AIDE *crosses to door and exits,* IVY GREEN *continues her narration.*)
IVY GREEN: Boys and girls, things are really popping now! In one moment we will see and hear the genius who built the rocket which is now streaking toward the North Pole. (1ST AIDE *re-enters, followed by* 2ND AIDE *and* ROBBIE SMITH. *They take a step into the room but are stopped by* GRENADIERS, *who cross swords and hold them in front of* 2ND AIDE *and* ROBBIE.)
1ST AIDE: Advance and be recognized. What is the pass word?

2ND AIDE: Marzipan!

1ST AIDE: Correct. (GRENADIERS *lower swords.* ROBBIE *and* 2ND AIDE *advance to* GENERAL REVEL.)

GENERAL REVEL (*Bewildered*): Here now! Who is this? (*Points to* ROBBIE) Where is the fellow who built the rocket?

ROBBIE (*Embarrassed*): I think you mean me. I'm Robbie Smith. (*Proudly*) I built the rocket. I launched it too, from my own backyard!

GENERAL REVEL (*Astonished*): *You* — a tadpole like you — built and launched a rocket? (*All ad lib surprise.*)

ROBBIE (*Modestly*): I had help. Lots of help and technical advice.

GENERAL REVEL (*Knowingly*): Aha. I suspected as much. Now, don't be afraid, my boy. Who helped you?

ROBBIE: I'm not afraid to tell you. (*He fishes in his pocket, and brings out a bubble gum wrapper.*) Here's a list of my technical assistants. Sorry that it's written on a bubble gum wrapper, but it was the handiest paper I had.

GENERAL REVEL (*Snatching paper and reading it aloud*): Taro Watanabe — Tokyo, Japan. Sven Pedersen — Oslo, Norway. Juan Sanchez — Lima, Peru. (*Triumphantly*) Aha, secret agents, eh, Robbie?

ROBBIE (*Surprised*): Oh, no, sir. They're *children.* Children from all over the world. That list is only part of them. The rocket was their idea as much as mine.

GENERAL REVEL (*Mystified*): But why? Why in the name of all the happy holidays did you build a rocket? What is in it — and why is it headed for the North Pole?

ROBBIE (*Apologetically*): I can't tell you. Not until midnight tonight — Christmas Eve! That's when the rocket lands. Then you'll know everything.

GENERAL REVEL (*Sternly*): But you must tell me now,

Robbie. The safety of Christmas and all other holidays is in my hands. I must know what is in that rocket and why it is going to the North Pole.

ROBBIE (*Bravely*): But I promised the other children I wouldn't tell.

GENERAL REVEL (*Wheedling*): Not even for a triple-dip banana split?

ROBBIE (*Wavering*): A triple-dip banana split! Mm-m-m.

GENERAL REVEL: With nuts!

ROBBIE: With nuts? (*He shakes his head stubbornly.*) No, sir. My lips are sealed.

IVY GREEN (*To camera and audience*): What a dramatic development! Robbie Smith, builder of the rocket, refuses to tell General Revel the mission of the rocket. What will the General do now, I wonder?

GENERAL REVEL (*Into phone*): Get me the jet patrol. . . . General Revel, here. (*Importantly*) Send me a high-speed jet. . . . When? Immediately, of course! (*Gives bubble gum wrapper to* 1ST AIDE) Here — have jets sent to every city on this list. Pick up each and every one of these children.

1ST AIDE: Yes, sir. But, sir — where shall I dispatch the jets? What is their destination?

GENERAL REVEL (*Airily*): Why — the North Pole, of course. (*With a sweeping gesture*) That's where we're going — where we're *all* going. To the North Pole! (*Determined*) I'll find out the secret of that rocket if it's the last thing I do!

IVY GREEN: Boys and girls, keep your television sets tuned to this station. Stand by for a remote transmission from the North Pole. (*Curtains begin to close.*) Meanwhile, we invite you to enjoy a program of seasonal music as we switch you now to our regularly scheduled broadcast. (*Curtain closes.* CAROLERS *enter before curtain and sing a medley of Christmas carols. At conclusion of music,* CAROLERS *exit, and curtains open.*)

* * * *

SCENE 2

TIME: *Immediately following.*

SETTING: *North Pole. Backdrop shows northern lights and Santa's workshop.*

AT RISE: GENERAL REVEL, ROBBIE, TWO AIDES, THREE SCIENTISTS, COMPUTER TECHNICIAN, *and* ASSISTANT *are seated on benches at left.* TWO GRENADIERS *stand behind them. At right are more benches.* IVY GREEN *stands center.* 2ND CAMERAMAN *is down right, following action with camera.*

IVY GREEN (*To camera and audience*): Here we are at the actual North Pole, boys and girls. There is a beautiful display of northern lights over Santa's workshop in the distance. (CHILDREN *are heard offstage singing "Here We Come A-Wassailing."*) Listen! I hear children's voices. . . . The jet planes have landed, bringing boys and girls from all over the world to the North Pole. (CHILDREN *enter, carrying flags.*) What a sight! There are children from North America, South America, Europe, Asia, Africa and Australia. I think they have a song to sing. (CHILDREN *stand center. They sing "Here We Come A-Wassailing" or other song. After ending song, they sit on benches. Jingle bells are heard offstage.*)

IVY GREEN: Did you hear that? Jingle bells — coming from Santa's workshop! Boys and girls, we're going to have a television first. A visit from Santa Claus before Christmas! (*Bells ring louder.* TWO ELVES, *doing cartwheels or somersaults, enter right.* IVY GREEN *crosses left and sits with* GENERAL REVEL'*s party.* TWO ELVES *cross to center.*)

TWO ELVES (*Together*): Make way! Make way for their royal jollinesses, Mr. and Mrs. Santa Claus! (*All applaud and cheer.* SANTA CLAUS *and* MRS. CLAUS, *very bewildered, enter right, crossing to center.* TWO ELVES *sit cross-legged in front of benches where* CHILDREN *are seated.*)

SANTA CLAUS (*Mystified*): What in the name of aurora borealis is *this?*

MRS. SANTA CLAUS (*Startled*): Oh, my goodness, gracious me. Visitors! I didn't invite any visitors. Did you, Santa?

SANTA CLAUS: Certainly not. We never invite visitors during our busy season.

MRS. SANTA CLAUS: Look, Santa. There are children here. (*Distressed*) Oh, my goodness, gracious me. There shouldn't be children at the North Pole on Christmas Eve!

SANTA CLAUS (*To* CHILDREN): Now, children, I want you all to go home. (CHILDREN *giggle.*) It's the middle of the night! A very special night. . . . Go home now, little ones. Shoo! Scat! Go home to bed before — (*Chimes sounding twelve are heard from offstage.*)

MRS. SANTA CLAUS: Oh, my goodness, gracious me! It's midnight! (*Loud whistling sound is heard from offstage.*)

ALL (*Ad lib; shading eyes and looking up*): Look, the rocket! The rocket is here! (*Etc.*)

SANTA CLAUS (*Bewildered*): Rocket? What rocket? I didn't order a rocket — did you, my dear?

MRS. SANTA CLAUS (*Shaking head*): Oh, no, my dear. *I* didn't order a rocket. Did you order a rocket, elves?

1ST ELF: I ordered a locket and a socket, but not a rocket.

2ND ELF: I ordered a sprocket and a pocket, but not a rocket.

SANTA CLAUS: Well, my dear, if you didn't and I didn't and the elves didn't — who *did* order that rocket?

ROBBIE (*Proudly*): *We* did!

CHILDREN (*Together*): We ordered the rocket.

SANTA CLAUS (*Confused*): You did? But, why? (*Sound of a loud bump is heard at back of auditorium, and there is a flash of light. All onstage point toward source of noise.*)

ROBBIE (*Excitedly*): Look! The rocket has landed. (CHILDREN *applaud and cheer.*) Now we can finally tell you why we built the rocket.

GENERAL REVEL (*Impatiently*): Wait! I want to know what is in that rocket. Guards — bring the cargo here. (TWO GRENADIERS *run offstage and return carrying a large sack of wrapped Christmas gifts which they bring to center and open.*)

1ST GRENADIER (*In surprise*): Well, well, well!

1ST *and* 2ND GRENADIERS (*Together*): Christmas presents! (*They begin taking wrapped packages from sack.*)

CHILDREN (*Together*): Surprise! Surprise!

ROBBIE (*Gratefully*): Mr. and Mrs. Santa Claus, for years and years you have filled our stockings and our shoes, and left us gifts beside our fireplaces or beneath our Christmas trees. You've never asked us for anything — not even so much as a thank you. (*Proudly*) This year, things are different. This year it's *our* turn. This year, *we* want to wish *you* a Merry Christmas! (*Music to "Jolly Old St. Nicholas" is heard.* CHILDREN *sing following lines to that tune, as* TWO GRENADIERS *carry presents to* SANTA CLAUS *and* MRS. SANTA CLAUS.)

CHILDREN (*Singing*):
    Jolly old St. Nicholas, lean your ear this way,
    Here is what we've brought to you,
    On this Christmas day.
GERMAN SOLO:
    Gingerbread from Dusseldorf,
    Kisses from Dundee,
DUTCH SOLO:
    Bookmarks made in Rotterdam,
    Near the Zuider Zee.
MOROCCAN SOLO:
    Pillows stitched in Marrakesh,
PERUVIAN SOLO:
    Bookends from Peru,
IRISH SOLO:
    Doilies made of Dublin lace,
NEPAL SOLO:
    Scarves from Katmandu.
JAPANESE SOLO:
    Calling cards from Tokyo,
FRENCH SOLO:
    Pens from gay Paree,
ESKIMO SOLO:
    Furry gloves from Anchorage,
WELSH SOLO:
    And a Welsh shoe tree. (CHILDREN *all bow.* SANTA
    CLAUS *begins opening packages.*)
MRS. SANTA CLAUS (*Amazed*): Oh, goodness, gracious
    me. It's our very finest Christmas!
SANTA CLAUS (*Pleased; holding up nightcap and shoe
    tree*): Bless my soul! A nightcap and a shoe tree. Just
    what I always wanted! Thank you, thank you, my dear
    little children. (*Chime sounding one is heard offstage.*)

MRS. SANTA CLAUS (*Dismayed*): Santa — it's one o'clock. We're late.

SANTA CLAUS (*Quickly*): Elves — hitch up the reindeer. (TWO ELVES *rush off right.*) Come, now, children. You really must go home to your beds now. (CHILDREN *nod. To* MRS. SANTA CLAUS) Come, my dear. We have work to do. (*He puts finger beside his nose and winks at* CHILDREN.) Important work. Ho, ho, ho! (SANTA CLAUS *and* MRS. SANTA CLAUS *cross up right, turn and wave to* CHILDREN.)

ROBBIE: Three cheers for Mr. and Mrs. Santa Claus!

ALL (*Together*): Hip, hip, hooray! Hip, hip, hooray! Hip, hip, hooray! (*All sing "We Wish You a Merry Christmas" as* SANTA CLAUS *and* MRS. CLAUS *exit.*)

IVY GREEN (*Crossing center*): This concludes our broadcast from the North Pole. But before we go, perhaps we can catch a final farewell from Santa Claus. Listen . . . (*She holds up hand mike.*)

SANTA CLAUS (*Offstage, trailing off as jingle bells ring*): Merry Christmas to all, and to all a good . . . night. . . .

IVY GREEN: We now return you to your school assembly. (*Curtain.* CAROLERS *return and sing "Up on the Housetop" or a familiar carol.*)

THE END

Long Live Christmas

by Islay Benson

The Christmas that almost wasn't! . .

Characters

GRANDFATHER LORENZ
PETER
BARBARA
ALEC, *a boy*
LISELLA, *his sister*
HERMAN, *town decorator*
GEORGE, *his assistant*
MR. HUMBOLDT
MRS. HUMBOLDT
AMBROSE
BERT
TEENA, *young girl*
KING'S CHAMBERLAIN
KING ULRIC
MR. JASON
MRS. JASON
TWO GUARDS

CHRISTMAS FAIRY
PEACE
LOVE
KINDNESS
FAITH   } *Spirits of Christmas*
CHILDHOOD
HOPE
FUN
FIVE PAGES
OTHER TOWNSPEOPLE
OFFSTAGE VOICE

SETTING: *Public square. Stage is bare, except for arch up center and benches at left and far right.*

AT RISE: PETER, BARBARA, *and* GRANDFATHER LORENZ *enter left, and stroll across stage.*

GRANDFATHER: Hurry up, children; let's go home. It feels like snow.

PETER: Snow! Oh, I hope so. Snow means Christmas.

BARBARA: How long is it until Christmas, Grandfather?

GRANDFATHER: Let's see, this is December fifth, so it's twenty days until Christmas.

BARBARA: Twenty days! That's forever. What a long time to wait!

PETER: Yes, I feel as if Christmas will never come.

BARBARA (*Quickly*): Don't say that, Peter! It will come, won't it, Grandfather?

PETER: Don't be silly, Barbara. Of course it will. Christmas always comes.

GRANDFATHER: I remember a story about a Christmas that almost didn't come.

PETER: Almost didn't come!

BARBARA: Grandfather! Tell us the story. . . .

GRANDFATHER (*Dreamily*): It was long, long ago and far

away, miles across the sea, in the little Kingdom of Camerovia. . . . *(Lights dim to indicate passage of time. Pause. Lights come up on center stage as* 1ST *and* 2ND PAGES *enter behind arch, carrying large scroll wound on two sticks.* PAGES *come down front side by side, then walk in opposite directions, opening the scroll and revealing the words, "This is the Kingdom of Camerovia." Then they exit.)* It was almost Christmas, and one day a young boy named Alec and his sister Lisella walked through the public square in the capital of the little kingdom. (ALEC *and* LISELLA *enter from left.)*

LISELLA: Just think, Alec, it's almost Christmas!

ALEC: Yes, isn't it exciting!

LISELLA: I can feel it in the air. I just love Christmas! I love everything about it—the way the shops look, and the Christmas trees, and everyone laughing and dashing around full of—full of—

ALEC: Turkey?

LISELLA: No! Just full of—Christmas. Let's sit here and watch it all. *(They sit on bench at left.* HERMAN *and* GEORGE *enter with wreaths and other Christmas decorations, which they start hanging on arch.)*

ALEC *(To* HERMAN): What are you doing?

HERMAN: We're getting the town ready for Christmas.

LISELLA: The wreaths are beautiful.

GEORGE: Yes. We should have a merry Christmas this year.

HERMAN *(Putting up wreath; then stepping back)*: There! We're all finished.

LISELLA *and* ALEC: Merry Christmas!

GEORGE: Merry Christmas to you! (HERMAN *and* GEORGE *exit.* MRS. HUMBOLDT *enters carrying small parcel and holding a long Christmas list. She is fol-*

lowed by MR. HUMBOLDT, *who carries tower of packages. They stop;* MRS. HUMBOLDT *hands parcel to* MR. HUMBOLDT.)

MRS. HUMBOLDT: Here, dear, *you* carry this. I need both hands for my list. (*As they start walking again,* AMBROSE *runs on and bumps into* MR. HUMBOLDT, *who drops all the packages.*)

AMBROSE: I'm sorry, sir.

MR. HUMBOLDT: Oh, that's all right.

AMBROSE: You mean you're not angry?

MR. HUMBOLDT: Why no, my boy. I know you didn't mean to do it. And I just can't get angry around Christmastime.

AMBROSE: Well, at least I can help you pick them up.

MR. HUMBOLDT: Thank you. (*They pick packages up.*)

AMBROSE: Thank *you* sir, and a very Merry Christmas!

MRS. HUMBOLDT: Merry Christmas to you. (MR. *and* MRS. HUMBOLDT *and* AMBROSE *exit.* BERT *enters and walks around stage, then stands to one side, looking out at audience.*)

TEENA (*Rushing on*): Hello, Lisella. Hello, Alec.

LISELLA *and* ALEC: Hello, Teena. Merry Christmas!

TEENA: Oh, what pretty decorations! (*She runs about looking, singing "Good King Wenceslas" in a loud voice.* 3RD *and* 4TH PAGES *enter through arch and blow trumpets.*)

PAGES: Make way for the King's Chamberlain! Make way for the King's Chamberlain! (TOWNSPEOPLE *rush on.* CHAMBERLAIN *enters through arch;* 5TH PAGE *follows closely, carrying large scroll on tray.*)

CHAMBERLAIN: Hear ye! Hear ye! By order of His Majesty the King!

TOWNSPEOPLE (*Loudly*): The King! The King! Long live the King!

CHAMBERLAIN: Proclamation issued by His Majesty the King.

TOWNSPEOPLE: The King! The King! Long live the King!

CHAMBERLAIN *(Looking around for scroll):* The Proclamation! Where is the Proclamation? How can I proclaim without a Proclamation? (5TH PAGE *quickly hands scroll to* CHAMBERLAIN, *who unrolls it.)* Ahem! "Whereas, His Majesty the King—"

TOWNSPEOPLE: The King! The King! Long live the King!

CHAMBERLAIN *(Reading):* "Whereas His Majesty the King wishes to state that it is drawing close to that season of the year popularly known as Christmas, and whereas he is dismayed by the amount of money being spent on Christmas, and upset because the people are paying more attention to Christmas than they are to him, he hereby decrees that there is to be no Christmas this year in the Kingdom of Camerovia."

TOWNSPEOPLE *(Ad lib):* What! No Christmas? That's terrible! *(Etc.)*

CHAMBERLAIN *(Still reading):* "There shall be no Christmas trees, no decorations, no bell ringing, no carol singing."

TEENA: No carol singing?

CHAMBERLAIN: Silence! *(Continues to read)* "No Christmas presents, no feasting on turkey and plum pudding, mince pies or eggnog. Anyone not obeying this proclamation will be punished severely. . ." *(Pauses, looks up at crowd, then continues reading)* "and banished forever from the Kingdom of Camerovia. By Order of His Majesty the King." (TOWNSPEOPLE *are silent.)* I said: By order of His Majesty the King.

TOWNSPEOPLE *(Quietly, with no enthusiasm):* The King. The King. Long live the King. (CHAMBERLAIN *exits, followed by* PAGES. *Immediately,* TWO GUARDS *enter*

*and grimly remove Christmas decorations. They
change the sign "Christmas Turkeys," on* BERT's *sandwich board, to "Stew Beef." They take away* MR.
HUMBOLDT's *Christmas packages.* TOWNSPEOPLE *exit
unhappily, except for* LISELLA *and* ALEC, *who remain
on bench.)*

LISELLA: No Christmas! No Christmas!

ALEC: It's terrible, isn't it?

LISELLA: I can't believe it! *(She starts to cry.)*

ALEC *(Soothingly):* Don't cry Lisella. Let's go home.
*(They rise and exit left. Lights dim on main stage. Spot
up on bench right.)*

BARBARA: That's terrible, Grandfather!

PETER: No Christmas! I can't imagine it.

BARBARA: What did the townspeople do? Was there
really no Christmas that year?

GRANDFATHER: Well, now, let me go on. . . . A few days
after the proclamation, a strange thing happened. . . .
(Spot out. Lights come up center stage, as ALEC *and*
LISELLA *enter sadly.)*

ALEC: Everyone has been so unhappy since the King's
proclamation.

LISELLA: No one laughs or smiles any more. (CHRISTMAS
FAIRY *enters and taps* ALEC *on shoulder.)*

FAIRY: Hello! I'm the Christmas Fairy.

ALEC: The Christmas Fairy? What's that?

FAIRY: A little more respect, young man. I am not a
"what." I'm a "who."

ALEC: I beg your pardon. What I really meant was what
are you doing here?

FAIRY: I'm starting my Christmas checkup. I always
make my rounds at this time of the year. *(Motioning
with arms)* I have to make sure people are preparing for
Christmas, getting the right spirit. I have to see that
everything's going smoothly for this important holiday.

LISELLA *(Sadly):* Well, you've certainly come to the wrong place for that.

ALEC: Yes, you won't have to stay here long.

FAIRY: What do you mean?

ALEC: There isn't going to be any Christmas here.

FAIRY: No Christmas! How can that be?

ALEC: The King has decreed that there is to be no Christmas at all in Camerovia this year.

FAIRY: But he can't do that!

LISELLA: He has done it.

FAIRY *(Angrily):* Oh he has, has he? We'll see about that. *(Music is heard as she goes left and lifts her arms.)* Spirits of Christmas! Come! *(She goes right.)* Spirits of Christmas! Come! Your queen is calling you! (PEACE, LOVE, KINDNESS, *and* FAITH *dance in from right, as* HOPE *and* CHILDHOOD *dance in from left, followed by* FUN, *who enters, cartwheeling.)*

LISELLA: Who are all these lively creatures?

FAIRY: These are the Spirits of Christmas: Peace, Love, Kindness, Faith, Hope, Childhood, and Fun. *(As their names are called, they come forward and bow, except for* FUN, *who turns another cartwheel, and* CHILDHOOD, *who throws ball in the air and catches it.)* Without these seven, there would be no Christmas, and with them you cannot help but have Christmas.

PEACE: You called us, dear Queen.

LOVE: We came as quickly as we could.

KINDNESS: What is your bidding?

FAIRY: I have something important to tell you. The King of Camerovia has decreed that there is to be no Christmas in his kingdom. *(Spirits laugh.)*

LISELLA: Why do they laugh at such a shocking thing?

FAIRY: Tell them why you laugh, Faith.

FAITH: Because if the King wants to get rid of Christmas, he'll have to get rid of us first.

HOPE: And that's pretty hard to do. Others have tried it.

CHILDHOOD: And sometimes they seem to succeed, but not for long.

FUN: No, we're more than a match for the King of Camerovia, or any other king.

LOVE: Or all kings put together.

FAIRY: Yes, but we must keep our wits and work hard. *(She turns to* LISELLA *and* ALEC.*)* Go home to bed now, children, and leave the matter in our hands. The next time you see these spirits—well, you won't *see* them, for they'll be invisible to mortal eyes. But they'll be there, and you'll soon know it. *(They exit.)*

ALEC *and* LISELLA: Goodbye!

FAIRY: Now come with me, my spirits, and I will tell you what we must do. (FAIRY *and Spirits exit. Lights dim. Spot up on bench right.)*

BARBARA: And what happened next?

PETER: Yes, go on!

GRANDFATHER: Well, as I remember the story, . . . on Christmas Eve, the King's Chamberlain called all the townspeople together. . . . *(Spot out. Lights come up as* 1ST *and* 2ND PAGES *enter with scroll, as before. It reads, "Christmas Eve in Camerovia." *3RD *and* 4TH PAGES *enter and blow trumpets.)*

3RD *and* 4TH PAGES: Make way for the King's Chamberlain! Make way for the King's Chamberlain! (ALEC, LISELLA, TEENA, *and* TOWNSPEOPLE *enter slowly, looking unhappy.* CHAMBERLAIN *enters through arch, followed by* 5TH PAGE.*)*

CHAMBERLAIN: Hear ye! Hear ye! By Order of His Majesty the King. (TOWNSPEOPLE *remain silent.)* I said, by Order of His Majesty the King.

TOWNSPEOPLE *(With no enthusiasm):* The King. The King. Long live the King.

CHAMBERLAIN: Herewith a proclamation by His Majesty the King. (TOWNSPEOPLE *remain silent.*) I said, a proclamation by His Majesty the King.

TOWNSPEOPLE *(Dully):* The King. The King. Long live the King.

CHAMBERLAIN *(Reading):* "Whereas His Majesty wants to remind the people of the importance of his decree, he has caused the following to be read in the public square. Whereas this is the 24th of December, formerly known as Christmas Eve—"

TEENA *(Bursting out in song):* "Good King Wenceslas—"

CHAMBERLAIN *(Shouting):* Silence! *(Reading)* ". . . formerly known as Christmas Eve, His Majesty wishes to remind the people that this evening is to be like any other evening and tomorrow is to be like any other day." (TOWNSPEOPLE *murmur unhappily, shaking their heads.* TEENA *wails).* Quiet! I'm proclaiming. *(Reading)* "There will be no show of Christmas whatsoever." *(He rolls up scroll.)* And now I have a surprise for you, a splendid, delightful surprise. Out of the great goodness of his heart, His Majesty is coming here to make sure his people understand his decree. (AMBROSE *rushes in.)*

AMBROSE *(Waving his arms):* The King! The King's coming!

TOWNSPEOPLE *(Ad lib):* Oh! What shall we do? The King! Coming here! *(Etc.)*

CHAMBERLAIN: Down! Down! Everybody down on your knees! *(All kneel except* TEENA, *who remains standing.* 3RD *and* 4TH PAGES *sound the trumpets.)*

3RD *and* 4TH PAGES: His Royal Majesty, the King of Camerovia, Gracious Lord of the Hills, Mighty Ruler of the Seas, and Monarch of all the People. Ulric the First. (KING *enters slowly, stands in archway and looks out at* TOWNSPEOPLE. *He sees that* TEENA *is not kneeling.*

KING *(Pointing):* Why does she not kneel before the King?

CHAMBERLAIN *(To* TEENA, *in threatening tone):* All subjects must kneel in the presence of the King!

TEENA: But then I won't be able to see anything.

CHAMBERLAIN: There's nothing to *see,* you silly child. *(With loud gasp, he turns to* KING.) Oh, Your Majesty! Your Majesty! Forgive me. I had no intention of. . . .

KING *(Interrupting him):* Stop bumbling, Oscar. The child's point is well taken. *(To* TEENA) You may stand. *(To* TOWNSPEOPLE)Have any of you questions to ask?

TOWNSPEOPLE *(Ad lib):* No, Your Majesty.

TEENA *(Running to* KING): I have, Your Majesty.

CHAMBERLAIN *(Seizing her and shooing her back into crowd):* Get away from the King, you little imp!

TEENA: I'm not a little imp, I'm a people. And *I* have a question.

KING *(To* TEENA): Come here child. You may speak. What is your question?

TEENA: Thank you, Your Majesty. *(Curtsying)* Sire, is it really true that there will be no Christmas this year?

KING: Absolutely true. No Christmas.

TEENA: No presents?

KING: No presents.

TEENA: No turkey?

KING: No turkey.

TEENA: No carol singing?

KING *(Firmly):* No carol singing.

TEENA *(Wistfully):* Not even "Good King Wenceslas"? *(*KING *shakes his head.)*

OFFSTAGE VOICE: Merry Christmas, everybody! *(*KING *looks offstage left, in direction of voice.)*

KING *(Angrily):* Who dares to say "Merry Christmas"? Find me the culprit who would defy my order! *(Pointing in direction of voice off left)* Arrest him at once and throw him in the dungeon. (CHAMBERLAIN *and* PAGES *rush off left.*) Now, I shall return to the tranquility of my palace. (KING *exits quickly through arch.* TEENA, *upset, runs off right.* ALEC, LISELLA, *and* TOWNSPEOPLE *rise from their knees and exit sadly. Lights dim. Spot up on bench right.*)

BARBARA: What a wicked, wicked King!

PETER: Did he really put people in the dungeon?

GRANDFATHER: Now, now. If you'll just give me a chance, I'll tell you. . . . *(Spot out. Lights come up and* ALEC *and* LISELLA *enter sadly, left, and sit on bench.)*

ALEC: In spite of what the Christmas Fairy said, there's no Christmas!

LISELLA: Maybe the King was too much for the Spirits of Christmas. (FAITH *runs in, dances around* ALEC. *She is now invisible to him. She touches him with her wand and runs off.*)

ALEC: No, wait a minute. There *is.* There *is* a Christmas. There must be, there always has been. Not even a king can do away with Christmas.

LISELLA: Oh, but Alec, he's taken away all our Christmas decorations and celebrations, so what's left?

ALEC: Christmas is left! I *know* it. *(As he speaks,* HOPE *runs on and touches* LISELLA, *then runs off.)*

LISELLA: Oh, Alec, do you think so? Truly? You almost make me believe it. You give me hope again.

ALEC: Let's try to find the Christmas Fairy. Maybe she can do something about it, if we can find her again. *(They exit left.* MR. *and* MRS. JASON *enter from right and sit on bench without speaking.* MR. HUMBOLDT *enters carrying mop, pail, and several bulky packages.*

From opposite direction, AMBROSE *enters briskly, his head deep in a newspaper.* AMBROSE *and* MR. HUMBOLDT *collide, and packages fall.)*

MR. HUMBOLDT *(Irritated):* Why don't you look where you're going?

AMBROSE: Why don't you!

MR. HUMBOLDT: You clumsy oaf!

AMBROSE: Clumsy yourself! (KINDNESS *runs on quickly, touches them both with her wand, and runs off.)*

MR. HUMBOLDT *(Shaking his head):* Oh, why am I talking like an old grouch? You didn't do it on purpose.

AMBROSE: No, I didn't. But just the same, it was careless of me. I'm sorry.

MR. HUMBOLDT: That's all right. Accidents will happen.

AMBROSE: I can help you pick them up, at any rate. *(He does so, and they exit.)*

MRS. JASON: You're a fine companion, I must say.

MR. JASON *(Angrily):* What do you mean?

MRS. JASON: Never a smile, never a word, just sit there, as glum as a caterpillar with corns.

MR. JASON: Well, that's the way I feel. What about you, anyway? You're no better.

MRS. JASON: Oh, I know. This was supposed to be Christmas Eve, and we should be home trimming the tree and getting the children's surprises ready. (LOVE *tiptoes in and touches* MRS. JASON *with wand.* MRS. JASON *straightens up and smiles.)* Still, I suppose that's no reason for us to be so gloomy. Even without the tree and the presents, we *do* have a lot of things to be thankful for.

MR. JASON: What, for instance? (LOVE *touches him and runs off, as* CHILDHOOD *enters, bouncing ball.* CHILDHOOD *touches them both with ball gently and exits.)*

MRS. JASON *(Brightening):* Well, we have each other and

the children. That's a lot, isn't it? Even without anything else.

MR. JASON: Yes, I guess you're right. We still have the children and each other. We do have a lot to be thankful for. (FUN *enters, smiling impishly.* FUN *tiptoes over to* MRS. JASON *and touches her with jester's stick.* MRS. JASON *starts to laugh out loud.*) What are you laughing at?

MRS. JASON: I was thinking how funny that man looked when he dropped all his packages.

MR. JASON *(Smiling):* Yes, it was funny, wasn't it? *(They laugh together.)*

MRS. JASON: I guess little things can still amuse us, Christmas or no Christmas.

MR. JASON: I suddenly feel as I used to on Christmas Eve. I don't know why. Merry Christmas, my dear! (MR. HUMBOLDT *enters.*)

MRS. JASON: Merry Christmas.

MR. HUMBOLDT: That's just the way I feel. Merry Christmas! (MRS. HUMBOLDT *and other* TOWNSPEOPLE *enter, in good spirits.* ALEC *and* LISELLA *enter right.*)

LISELLA: Alec, look at the people! They must feel as good as we do.

ALEC: Yes, they have their Christmas spirit back too.

LISELLA: Oh, how wonderful! (TEENA *runs on and greets* ALEC *and* LISELLA. CHAMBERLAIN *enters hastily, through arch.*)

CHAMBERLAIN *(Gruffly):* What's going on here? What's all this?

TOWNSPEOPLE: Merry Christmas, your honor!

CHAMBERLAIN: What! *(Angrily)* Do you defy the King?

ALEC: Does it look as if we do?

CHAMBERLAIN: What does that impudent remark mean?

MRS. JASON: Do you see any Christmas trees or decorations?

LISELLA: Or any sign of feasting?

MRS. HUMBOLDT: Or present giving?

MR. JASON: Or bell ringing? (CHAMBERLAIN *is silent.*)

ALL: Well, do you?

CHAMBERLAIN: No . . . but you were all saying "Merry Christmas."

ALEC: Well, it *is* a Merry Christmas. (KING *enters through arch.* TOWNSPEOPLE *do not kneel.*)

KING *(Angrily):* What was that! Who dared to say "Merry Christmas"?

ALEC: *I* did, Your Majesty.

MR. HUMBOLDT: We all did, Your Majesty.

KING *(Menacingly):* What! All of you? You dare to disobey me?

MR. HUMBOLDT: No, Your Majesty. We have obeyed you. There are no trees or decorations, Your Majesty.

MRS. HUMBOLDT: And no presents, Your Majesty.

MRS. JASON: And no feasting, Your Majesty.

TEENA: Not even any carol singing. Other kings would allow carol singing—King Wenceslas was even *in* a carol and everybody loves him for it. But nobody will ever love you . . . because you're trying to take Christmas away from us!

KING *(Furiously):* Silence, child! *(To* CHAMBERLAIN*)* Take her away!

CHAMBERLAIN *(Starting to* TEENA*):* To the dungeon with you! *(As he takes her arm and starts to pull her off,* ALEC *dashes forward and holds her protectively.)*

ALEC *(To* KING*):* Your Majesty, please forgive her! Don't hurt her. She's only a little girl. If you punish her, you'll have to punish every one of us.

MR. JASON: The boy's right, Your Majesty. We've obeyed you, but we still have Christmas. You see, Christmas is not feasting or decorations or presents.

MRS. JASON: No, Your Majesty. You can abolish all those things, and it will still be Christmas.

MRS. HUMBOLDT: Always, because Christmas is a state of mind.

MR. HUMBOLDT: And a state of heart. *(Spirits enter.)*

PEACE: Christmas is peace.

LOVE: Christmas is love.

KINDNESS: Christmas is kindness.

FAITH: Christmas is faith.

CHILDHOOD: Christmas is childhood.

HOPE: Christmas is hope.

FUN: Christmas is fun. (CHRISTMAS FAIRY *enters.*)

FAIRY: Yes, all those things make up Christmas, and when you have them, you don't need decorations and feasting. You have Christmas, and you'll always have it. No king, nothing, and no one can ever take it from you. *(She runs over to* CHAMBERLAIN *and to* KING *and touches them with her wand.)*

MR. HUMBOLDT *(Going to* KING *and dropping on one knee):* Forgive us, Your Majesty. We *must* keep Christmas in our hearts.

KING: Rise, my good man. *(To all)* It is your king who must ask his people's forgiveness. I will never again try to take Christmas from you.

ALL: The King! Long live the King! Long live good King Ulric! Christmas! Christmas! Long live Christmas! *(Curtain)*

THE END

Randy the Red-Horned Rainmoose

by Rick Kilcup

What happens when Rudolph's nose is on the blink. . . .

Characters

RANDY THE RAINMOOSE
SANTA
RUDOLPH
HUSTLE ⎫
BUSTLE ⎬ *Santa's messy elves*
FRED ⎭
WEATHER ELF
TISSUE ELF
DASHER
DANCER
PRANCER
VIXEN
COMET
CUPID

DONNER
BLITZEN
RALPH
MATILDA

TIME: *Christmas Eve.*

SETTING: *Santa's workshop. There is a workbench covered with tools, boxes, and wrapping paper; large can of "Sleigh Wax" and tool chest are at rear. Toys, boxes, long sheets of paper are scattered about stage.*

AT RISE: RANDY THE RAINMOOSE *is sweeping the floor, looking discouraged.*

RANDY *(Singing to the tune of "Row Your Boat"):*
Scrub, scrub, scrub, and sweep,
Polish every day.
When will all this hard work end
So I can stop and play?
(Stops sweeping, leans on broom and mops brow; to audience) Hi, I'm Randy, the rainmoose. I used to live in the rain forest, where it rains so much that moss grows on everything—even antlers. *(Points to his antlers)* Then one day, I saw an ad for a job that promised excitement and a chance to work with Santa and Rudolph. *(Starts sweeping)* I was so tired of the drip and splash of everyday life in the rain forest that I took the job. Unfortunately, I didn't read the fine print. What Santa needed was a cleaner-upper! So now it's *(Sighs)*
Scrub, scrub, scrub, and sweep,
Polish every day.
When will all this hard work end
So I can stop and play?
The job's not that bad—don't get me wrong. I like working with Santa, and Rudolph's my all-time hero.

It's those pesky elves, Hustle, Bustle, and Fred that get me down. They're so messy! Every time I get the place cleaned up, they mess it up again! (HUSTLE, BUSTLE, *and* FRED *enter.* FRED *carries clipboard, others hold stacks of computer paper.*) Oh, no! Look who's here!

FRED: All right, Hustle and Bustle. It's almost time for Santa to take off, so we'd better go over our preflight checklist.

HUSTLE *and* BUSTLE: Right, Fred! (FRED *calls out items, and others tear off sheets of paper as they answer, then throw them on floor.*)

FRED: All wooden toys boxes painted?

HUSTLE *and* BUSTLE: Check.

FRED: Wind-up toys wound up?

HUSTLE *and* BUSTLE: Yes.

FRED: Packages wrapped and labeled?

HUSTLE *and* BUSTLE: Right.

FRED: So far, so good!

HUSTLE *(Pointing):* Say, there's Randy, the rainmoose. Hi, Randy. What's the matter? You sure look down in the dumps.

BUSTLE *(Patting* RANDY *on back):* Come on, cheer up! You shouldn't be so gloomy on Christmas Eve!

FRED: That's right—smile! *(Looks around)* Uh—I hate to mention it, Randy, but this place is a mess.

RANDY *(Exasperated):* Well, I've been trying to . . .

FRED *(Interrupting):* By the way, Randy, don't forget to wax the sleigh and brush the reindeer. (RANDY *shakes his head angrily.*)

HUSTLE *(Suddenly):* The reindeer! We forgot to put them through their warmup exercises!

BUSTLE: Yikes! We'd better get to it, Hustle. We can't have the reindeer getting pulled muscles.

FRED: Let's go! *(Elves run off.)*

RANDY *(To audience):* See what I mean about those messy elves? Maybe I should just pack up my galoshes and umbrella and head back to the rain forest. *(Begins cleaning.* SANTA *and* RUDOLPH *enter.* TISSUE ELF *follows, pulling wagon with wastebasket and boxes of tissue.)* Hi, Santa! Hi, Rudolph!

SANTA: Randy, I want you to know that you're doing a great job. Without you, those messy elves would never get anything done!

RANDY: Thanks, Santa! *(To audience)* On second thought, I don't think I'll pack after all.

RUDOLPH: A—choo! The sleigh's almost loaded, Santa. *(Takes tissue from wagon, blows nose, then throws tissue into wastebasket)* A—choo!

SANTA: Bless you, Rudolph! *(Concerned)* Is your cold getting worse?

RUDOLPH: I'm afraid so. My nose is all stuffed up and my throat's sore. *(Coughs into tissue, throws it away)*

TISSUE ELF *(Shaking empty tissue box):* Rudolph's used seven boxes of tissue already today, Santa!

SANTA *(Wringing his hands):* I sure hope you're not too sick to lead my sleigh tonight, Rudolph.

RUDOLPH: Don't worry, I'll make it. . . . a—choo! . . . somehow.

SANTA: Let's hope for clear weather tonight. Then you won't need to lead the sleigh, and you can stay home in bed! (WEATHER ELF *enters, wearing Hawaiian shirt, sunglasses, shorts, sandals, straw hat. He carries clipboard and can of soda. Beach towel is draped over his shoulder; bottle of suntan lotion sticks out of his pocket.)* Speaking of weather, here's the Weather Elf with the latest report.

WEATHER ELF: I've got good news, Santa! *(Checks clipboard)* The skies are clear, and the air is warm all around the world. Should be a perfect night for your flight.

SANTA: Great! (RUDOLPH *sneezes.*)

WEATHER ELF: Gee, Rudolph, you sound awful, and you look even worse! Santa, you'd better take his temperature while I go check the radar.

SANTA (*Feeling* RUDOLPH's *forehead*): Good idea. Come on, Rudolph, let's go find a thermometer. (*All exit except* RANDY.)

RANDY (*Picking up can of sleigh wax*): I'd better go wax the sleigh and brush the reindeer. (HUSTLE, BUSTLE, *and* FRED *enter, followed by* DASHER, DANCER, PRANCER, VIXEN, COMET, CUPID, DONNER, BLITZEN, RALPH, *and* MATILDA.)

FRED (*Trying to keep reindeer in line*): All right, you reindeer, keep those knees up! (*Reindeer form line facing front;* RALPH *and* MATILDA *are at end of line, out of step.*)

BUSTLE: All right, let's get going! (*Elves lead Reindeer through warm-ups—toe touches, jumping jacks, etc.— while singing to tune of "Jingle Bells."*)
Let's warm up!
Let's warm up!
Soon it's time to fly!
Oh, what fun it is to soar
With Santa in the sky!

Run in place,
Stretch and twist.
Soon it's time to go.
Oh, what fun it is to fly
With Santa—ho, ho, ho!

HUSTLE: Now it's time for swooping and soaring practice.

RANDY (*Panicking*): No! No! Not swooping and soaring!

BUSTLE: Ready, set, go! *(Reindeer swoop and soar around set, kicking items off table and making a mess as* RANDY *looks defeated.* RALPH *and* MATILDA *are still not in step.)*

FRED: O.K., hold it! *(All stop.)* Great job! Now, let's head back to the stables for a hearty meal of hayburgers, oatshakes, and candy cane juice before takeoff! *(Reindeer cheer, jog off as names are called.)* On Dasher and Dancer, on Prancer and Vixen!

HUSTLE: Now Comet and Cupid, now Donner and Blitzen!

BUSTLE: On Ralph and Matilda! (RALPH *and* MATILDA *don't move.)* Hey, come on, you two! *(They jump to attention and begin to jog off in wrong direction, then turn around and exit clumsily, following other Reindeer.)*

RANDY: Ralph and Matilda? I've never heard of those two.

BUSTLE: They're new—extra help hired for the holiday rush.

FRED *(Looking around):* You know, Randy, this place is still a wreck! Get with it, will you? *(Elves exit.)*

RANDY: Well, here I go again. *(Begins cleaning up as* SANTA, RUDOLPH, *and* TISSUE ELF *enter.* RUDOLPH *holds ice pack on his head.)*

RUDOLPH: Santa, my throat feels terrible, and I'm starting to lose my voice.

SANTA: Oh, Rudolph, if you lose your voice, we'll be in big trouble! Thanks to your nose, you're the only one who can see through bad weather to lead the sleigh, and if you can't shout directions to the other reindeer, they might take a wrong turn! We could get stuck in a tree or tangled up in some telephone wires! Let's hope the weather stays clear so you won't have to shout.

(WEATHER ELF *rushes in, looking worried and wearing raincoat, rain hat, galoshes. He carries clipboard and umbrella.*)

WEATHER ELF: Here's the latest forecast! *(Waves clipboard)* There's a storm front moving in! Heavy rain is headed our way!

SANTA: Oh, no! Rudolph, you'll have to shout after all!

RUDOLPH *(Hoarsely):* I'll do my best, boss, but even if I don't lose my voice, I'm not sure I can fly and sneeze at the same time. A-choo! *(Grabs tissue)*

SANTA *(Shaking his head):* Things are going from bad to worse. Come on, Rudolph, we'd better hook up the sleigh's windshield wipers.

WEATHER ELF: I'm off to the weather center, Santa. I'll let you know if there's any change in the forecast.(WEATHER ELF *hurries off.* SANTA *and* RUDOLPH *exit, looking grim.*)

RANDY *(Still cleaning):* Wow, if Rudolph does lose his voice, how can Santa deliver the presents? Christmas could be in big trouble! *(Looks around)* Well, the workshop's all cleaned up—once again. Now, where's that big can of sleigh wax? *(Looks around, picks up can of wax)* Ah, here it is. (HUSTLE, BUSTLE, *and* FRED *enter.* FRED *has clipboard, others have computer paper.*) Oh, no.

FRED: Is Santa's rain gear packed?

HUSTLE *and* BUSTLE: Check! *(Papers are thrown around room, as before.)*

FRED: Reindeer rain hats ready to go?

HUSTLE *and* BUSTLE: You've got it!

FRED: Lists of naughty and nice kids packed?

HUSTLE *and* BUSTLE *(Looking at papers, then at each other, in shock):* Oh, no!

HUSTLE: Where can those lists be? We had them this morning.

BUSTLE *(Snapping fingers):* I know! We left them on the workbench! *(Points to neatly arranged table)*

FRED: We'd better find them, and fast! *(They dig through papers, throwing them in the air.)*

HUSTLE *(Holding up long sheets of paper):* Here they are!

BUSTLE: Whew! That was a close call!

FRED *(Shaking finger at RANDY):* Randy, if we'd lost these lists, it would have been your fault. You let the workshop become such a mess that we can't find anything. Come on, Hustle and Bustle! Let's get these lists loaded. *(They exit.)*

RANDY *(Starting to pick up papers):* Sometimes I wonder why I even bother! *(Coughing is heard offstage. SANTA, RUDOLPH, and TISSUE ELF enter.)*

TISSUE ELF: It's pouring out there, Santa. (RUDOLPH *grabs tissue, blows his nose.)* That's twelve boxes, boss. (WEATHER ELF *enters, wearing snow boots, ski jacket, ski cap, mittens, and earmuffs. He carries clipboard.)*

WEATHER ELF: Santa, I've got some good news and some bad news. The good news is that the rain is going to stop before takeoff.

SANTA *(Happily):* That's great!

WEATHER ELF: The bad news is that there's a new storm blowing in. A real blizzard with lots of snow and fog. I'll let you know if there are any changes, but the way I see it, there's no avoiding this one! *(Rushes out)*

SANTA *(Discouraged):* This is terrible! Rudolph, your voice just has to last!

RUDOLPH *(In faltering voice):* Maybe some cough drops would help. *(Coughs, then tries to talk, but no words come out. He points to his mouth in panic.)*

TISSUE ELF: His voice is gone! Christmas is doomed!

RANDY: I wish I could do something to help!

SANTA *(Pleading):* Speak to me, Rudolph! Say something, anything! *(Elves enter.)*

FRED: What's the matter, Santa?

SANTA: Rudolph has lost his voice. He won't be able to guide my sleigh tonight!

HUSTLE: Don't worry, Santa! We'll have him fixed up in no time! (HUSTLE, BUSTLE, *and* FRED *rush to* RUDOLPH.)

SANTA *(Doubtfully):* Are you sure you know what you're doing?

BUSTLE: Sure! If we can build walking, talking dolls and home-work machines, we can fix a faulty reindeer voice. (FRED *pulls sheet, three white smocks, and three sets of white gloves from under table.)*

FRED: Here Santa. *(Hands* SANTA *sheet)* Have Rudolph sit down on the workbench and cover him with this sheet while Doctors Hustle, Bustle, and Fred get ready to see the patient. (SANTA *helps* RUDOLPH *to table;* RUDOLPH *lies down, and* SANTA *covers him with sheet. Elves put on smocks and gloves.)*

SANTA: Well, I hope this works. There are only two more hours till takeoff.

FRED: Don't worry. We'll have Rudolph's voice back in no time. Bustle, bring the doctor's kit!

BUSTLE: Right, Fred. *(Graps tool kit, sets it on table with loud clank)*

TISSUE ELF *(Worriedly):* That's not a doctor's kit—it's a tool kit!

HUSTLE: It sure is. We elves always come prepared.

TISSUE ELF *(Concerned):* Santa, are you sure these elves know what they're doing?

SANTA: Let's hope so. Christmas is at stake!

FRED: Now, Rudolph, this is going to hurt you more than it is us . . . er . . . I mean . . . Oh, never mind. (RUDOLPH *looks upset.)* Open wide. (RUDOLPH *opens his mouth,* FRED *pantomimes using screwdriver, as tongue depressor.)* That's right. Now say "ah." *(No sound)* Say "ah!" *(No sound; angrily)* How do you expect me to help you if you won't even say "ah"?

HUSTLE: Uh, Fred. He can't say "ah"—he's lost his voice, remember?

FRED *(Embarrassed):* Oh, yeah.

BUSTLE: Here, let me take a look. *(Pulls flashlight and pliers from kit, peers down* RUDOLPH'S *throat)* I've got it! His battery is worn out! *(Pulls battery from kit)* I'll just plop in a new one and his voice will be as good as new. *(He looks for a place to insert battery.)* Where do you put this in, anyway?

HUSTLE *(Exasperated):* Bustle! Rudolph's not a toy! He doesn't use batteries.

BUSTLE *(Embarrassed):* Oh, that's right.

HUSTLE: Give me that flashlight! *(Looks down* RUDOLPH'S *throat, feels his forehead; in serious tone)* Well, Santa, I've got the cure for Rudolph.

ALL *(Eagerly; ad lib):* You do? What is it? *(Etc.)*

HUSTLE: Have him drink plenty of fluid, give him two aspirin, and put him in bed for a good night's sleep. Call me in the morning. His voice should be fine by then.

TISSUE ELF: But we need him to lead the sleigh tonight!

SANTA *(Gravely):* I think Hustle's advice is the best so far. Fred, take that sheet off Rudolph. *(To* RUDOLPH*)* Let's go and get you a big glass of orange juice and two aspirin. *(*FRED *removes sheet from* RUDOLPH *and tosses it onto* RANDY'S *antlers.)*

FRED: Here, Randy, fold this sheet. *(*RANDY *struggles, pulls off sheet, revealing bright red antlers. See Production Notes.)*

SANTA: Hey, where's that red glow coming from?

HUSTLE *(Pointing):* Look! It's coming from Randy's antlers!

FRED: Randy! What's happened to your horns?

RANDY *(Shocked):* I don't know. They've always been covered with moss, so I never knew they glowed! I guess the moss came off when I pulled the sheet off my head.

BUSTLE *(Excitedly):* Santa, Randy's the answer to your problems. He and his flashy antlers can guide your sleigh!

ALL *(Ad lib)*: Great idea! Christmas is saved! *(Etc.)*

SANTA: How about it, Randy? Will you light the way and save Christmas?

RANDY: I'd love to, but I can't fly.

FRED: No problem. *(Reaches into tool kit and pulls out can)* One little dose of Momma Elf's Magical, Multi-Purpose Oven Cleaner and Reindeer Flying Elixir and you'll be doing barrel rolls and loop the loops in no time!

RANDY: Gee, I've always wanted to fly, but there's one other problem.

SANTA: What's that?

RANDY: I still have a lot of work to do. The sleigh hasn't been waxed and the workshop's a mess.

SANTA: Don't worry about that, Randy. I've got the perfect replacements for you *(Looks at Elves)*—three of them!

BUSTLE: Oh, no! I hate sleigh waxing and workshop cleaning!

FRED: Santa, couldn't we discuss this? (SANTA *shakes his head emphatically.)* I was afraid of that.

TISSUE ELF: Congratulations, Randy! You saved Christmas! Three cheers for Randy, the red-horned rainmoose! *(As* TISSUE ELF, HUSTLE, BUSTLE, FRED, *and* SANTA *give three cheers,* REINDEER *and* WEATHER ELF *enter.)*

ALL *(Singing to the tune of "Rudolph the Red-Nosed Reindeer"):*
Randy, the red-horned rainmoose,
Has two very shiny horns.
And until Santa saw them,
He was really quite forlorn.
Then that foggy Christmas Eve,
Santa came to say:
"Randy with your horns so bright,
How'd you like to fly tonight?"

Then how we reindeer loved him
As we shouted out—all right!
Randy, the red-horned rainmoose,
You will lead us through the night!

(To audience) Merry Christmoose to all and to all a good night! *(Curtain)*

THE END

Christmas at the Cratchits

Adapted from Charles Dickens' "A Christmas Carol"

by *Deborah Newman*

Tiny Tim's poor but happy family celebrates Christmas with warmth and love. . . .

Characters

BOB CRATCHIT
MRS. CRATCHIT
PETER
BELINDA
MARTHA
TINY TIM
TWO YOUNG CRATCHITS, *boy and girl*

TIME: *Christmas Day.*
SETTING: *The Cratchit home in London.*
AT RISE: PETER *stands by the fireplace poking a long fork into a large saucepan.* MRS. CRATCHIT *and* BELINDA *are setting the table.*

MRS. CRATCHIT (*Handing* BELINDA *the plates*): Here, Belinda, put the plates on the side near the fire. You children might as well be as warm as you can.
PETER: Couldn't I make a bigger fire, Mother?

MRS. CRATCHIT (*Busy at the table*): I should say not. With Mr. Scrooge paying your poor father only fifteen bob a week, we'll have to make this fire do.

BELINDA (*Pouting as she puts down the plates*): Oh, Mr. Scrooge! Who wants to think about Mr. Scrooge on Christmas Day?

MRS. CRATCHIT: Then *don't* think about Mr. Scrooge. Goodness knows Mr. Scrooge doesn't think about Christmas—or about the Cratchits.

BELINDA: Shall I put Tiny Tim next to Father?

MRS. CRATCHIT (*Stopping for a moment and sighing*): Yes —poor boy. He's never happy unless he's near your father. (*Shaking her head, then bustling quickly around table*) Peter! Mind you don't get gravy on your father's collar. Your poor father doesn't have enough clean collars as it is. (*The two young Cratchits rush in.*)

BOY (*Running to fireplace*): Oh, it *is* our goose that smells so good!

GIRL: We smelled it all the way down by the baker's, and we knew it must be *our* Christmas goose.

PETER (*Poking at it proudly*): There's not a finer goose in all of Camden Town.

GIRL: Not a finer goose in all of London.

BOY: Even Mr. Scrooge won't have such a fine goose.

BELINDA (*Scornfully*): Mr. Scrooge probably won't even have a goose. *He'll* spend Christmas Day counting his money.

BOY: Isn't our dinner ready yet?

MRS. CRATCHIT: It's almost done. But where is your father with Tiny Tim? And Martha wasn't as late last Christmas Day by half an hour.

MARTHA (*Entering quickly*): Here's Martha, Mother. (*The two young Cratchits run up to her.*)

BOY: Merry Christmas, Martha. Come look at our goose.

GIRL: There never was such a goose!

MRS. CRATCHIT (*Patting* MARTHA): Why, bless your heart, dear, how late you are.

MARTHA (*Taking off her shawl*): We had a lot of work to finish up last night and we had to clear away this morning, Mother.

MRS. CRATCHIT: Well, never mind, so long as you've come. Sit down before the fire and get warm. I'll go out and look at the pudding. (*She exits.*)

MARTHA (*Sitting down and stretching*): Oh, tomorrow morning I mean to lie in bed for a good long rest.

BELINDA: Poor Martha. You must be very tired.

MARTHA: Not poor Martha—not on Christmas Day. Lucky Martha, that's who I am.

GIRL: We're lucky, too—with all that goose and potatoes and apple sauce.

BOY: I'm going to eat and eat and eat.

BELINDA: And then you'll get sick and a fine merry Christmas you'll have.

PETER (*Imitates Scrooge*): Christmas? Bah! Humbug!

BOY (*Delighted*): Peter, imitate Mr. Scrooge for Martha.

GIRL: Yes, do. We listened through the keyhole and heard Father telling Mother what Mr. Scrooge said—and Peter can sound just like Mr. Scrooge.

PETER (*Coming forward and waving the fork menacingly*): Christmas? Bah! Humbug! What a world of fools! Merry Christmas? Away with Merry Christmas! What's Christmas time to you but a time for paying bills without money; a time for finding yourself a year older, and not an hour richer; a time for balancing your books and having every item in 'em through a round dozen of months presented dead against you? If I could work my will, every idiot who goes about with "Merry Christmas" on his lips should be boiled with his own pudding and buried with a stake of holly through his heart. (*All laugh as* MARTHA *applauds and* PETER *bows.*)

MARTHA: Peter, you're a wonder!

GIRL (*Looking out window*): Here's Father coming with Tiny Tim.

BOY (*Excited*): Hide, Martha, hide! (MARTHA *ducks behind screen as* BOB CRATCHIT *and* TINY TIM *enter.* BOB *is singing a carol.* TINY TIM *limps and carries a crutch.*)

BOB (*Looking around*): Why, where's our Martha? Isn't she here yet?

BELINDA: She's not coming.

BOB (*Sitting down heavily*): Not coming? Not coming on Christmas Day?

MARTHA (*Running out from screen*): It was a joke, Father! Of course I'm here. (*She hugs her father and* TINY TIM.) Merry Christmas.

TINY TIM: Merry Christmas, Martha. Have you seen our goose?

GIRL: You haven't seen our pudding, Tim.

BOY: I can tell it's delicious just by looking at it. Come and take a look, Tim. (*The* BOY *and* GIRL *exit with* TINY TIM.)

MARTHA: How did little Tim behave in church today?

BOB (*Removing his long scarf*): As good as gold and better. Somehow he gets thoughtful, sitting by himself so much, and he thinks the strangest things you ever heard. He told me, coming home, that he hoped people saw him in church because he was a cripple, and it might be pleasant to them to remember upon Christmas Day who made lame beggars walk and blind men see. (*He sighs and shakes his head sadly.*)

MARTHA: He is so sweet and patient for such a little boy.

BOB: And so light to carry. How do you think he looks, Martha?

MARTHA: His cheeks look feverish—but that may be only the damp air.

BOB (*Shaking his head*): No, I fear it is more than that. He needs good care and good food and sunshine—and all those things take money.

MARTHA: But Tim seems happy.

BOB (*Sighing*): Because it is Christmas, and he loves Christmas. (*Shaking his head*) I cannot bear to think of coming home, and seeing that little seat in the chimney-corner empty, his crutch leaning against the fireplace—without an owner. I do not mind working long hours and doing without myself—if *only* Tiny Tim will live.

MARTHA (*Taking* BOB's *scarf*): He *will* live! I know he will. Somehow—in some way—Tiny Tim will get the care he needs.

BOB: That would take a miracle.

MARTHA: And miracles have been known to happen on Christmas Day. Who knows? Perhaps, at this very moment, someone, somewhere, may be planning to help Tiny Tim. Have faith in the Christmas spirit, Father. I do! (*She smiles so enthusiastically at* BOB *that he manages to smile back at her as the two young Cratchits enter with* TINY TIM.)

BOY: Mother says we are to sit down at the table. She's gone to the baker's.

GIRL: The pudding is all done.

TINY TIM: It's the most beautiful pudding I've ever seen. (*They start to sit down.* PETER, BELINDA *and* MARTHA *put the goose on a platter with the potatoes and bring it to the table.*)

PETER: Did you leave the pudding out there all by itself?

BOY: Mother said to leave it in the wash-house. She'll bring it in.

PETER (*In mock horror*): But suppose—just suppose somebody should jump over the wall of the backyard and steal it?

GIRL (*Dismayed*): Steal it? Steal our Christmas pudding?

BOY: They couldn't. I mean to eat almost all of it myself.

TINY TIM: No one would steal a Christmas pudding—would they?

BOB: Peter, I'm ashamed of you. Of course no one would think of stealing our very special Christmas pudding. (*They are all seated at the table when* MRS. CRATCHIT *enters with the pudding.*) Ah! Here it is! (MRS. CRATCHIT *puts the pudding on the table.*)

MARTHA: What's that smell—like washing day?

GIRL: That's the cloth!

BOY: Oh, it smells like an eating house and a pastry cook's—right next door to each other!

TINY TIM: Can we have some pudding right now?

BELINDA: Pudding before goose?

BOB: I don't see why not. Sit down, my dear, and let's start our Christmas dinner with the pudding. (MRS. CRATCHIT *serves it. As each member of the family is served, he immediately tastes it and exclaims over it.*)

TINY TIM: What a wonderful, wonderful pudding.

BOY: It's the best Christmas pudding we've ever had.

GIRL: I wish we had three more. It's not a very big pudding.

BELINDA: It's a huge pudding!

PETER: There's more than enough for all of us.

BOB: Mrs. Cratchit, I might say that I regard this pudding as the greatest success you have achieved since our marriage.

MRS. CRATCHIT (*Relieved*): Umm—it *is* good.

MARTHA: It's perfect!

MRS. CRATCHIT: I must confess I had my doubts about the flour.

BOB: And now let's begin on the goose. (*He serves everyone, helped by* BELINDA *and* MARTHA.)

PETER (*The following dialogue goes on as the family eats*): I've just thought of a new game we can play.

BOY: Is it like Blindman's Buff, or can we play it right now?

PETER: We can play it right now. It's called—"Yes and No."

GIRL: "Yes and No." Oh, tell us how to play it, Peter.

PETER: This is what we do. I'm thinking of something. . . .

TINY TIM: What are you thinking of?

PETER: That's what you must find out. You ask me questions.

GIRL: Is it red or green?

PETER: I can't tell you. All I can say is "Yes" or "No." That's why I called the game "Yes and No."

BOB: Are you thinking of an animal?

PETER: Yes.

MARTHA: Is it a live animal?

PETER: Yes.

TINY TIM: Is it a nice animal—like our cat?

PETER: No—it's a *very* disagreeable animal.

BELINDA: Does it make any sounds?

PETER: Oh, yes.

MRS. CRATCHIT: Does it bark?

PETER: It barks—and sometimes it talks.

GIRL: Oh, Peter, you said you could answer only yes and no!

BOB: That's right, Peter. Stick to your rules. Let's see—
we have a very disagreeable live animal that barks and
sometimes talks.

MARTHA: Does it live in London?

PETER: Yes.

GIRL: It must belong to a menagerie! Does it, Peter?

PETER: No.

TINY TIM: Is it a horse?

PETER: No!

GIRL: Is it a—a bear?

PETER (*Laughing*): No.

MRS. CRATCHIT: Well, is it a pig?

PETER: No.

BOB: Does it belong to someone? Does someone lead it
around the streets?

PETER: It walks around the streets all by itself.

TINY TIM: It walks around all alone?

PETER: Yes—all alone.

BELINDA (*Jumping up*): I know! I know what it is!

PETER: You don't.

BELINDA (*Excited*): Yes, I do. It's Mr. Scrooge!

PETER (*Nodding*): You guessed. (*All laugh heartily.*)

GIRL: Oh, Peter, you should have said "yes" when I asked
you if it was a bear!

MRS. CRATCHIT: That's Ebenezer Scrooge, all right—
mean rich old animal that he is. What I wouldn't do
with one-quarter of his money!

BELINDA: Mr. Scrooge is very rich, isn't he?

BOB: What of it? His wealth is of no use to him. He
doesn't do any good with it. He doesn't make himself
comfortable with it. Who suffers by his ill whims? Himself, always!

MRS. CRATCHIT: That's well enough for you to say. You

slave for him in that cold dark office and then he thinks himself ill-used because he pays you for Christmas Day. A poor excuse for picking a man's pocket every twenty-fifth of December, is it? I'll poor excuse him!

BOB (*Gently*): Mr. Scrooge is a business man, my dear.

MRS. CRATCHIT (*Hotly*): Business! Mankind is his business. The common welfare is his business.

MARTHA (*Softly*): But just think—Mr. Scrooge is spending Christmas Day in that old, dreary, ugly room of his, all by himself. And here we are, warm, happy and well-fed—together.

BOB: Right you are, Martha. *We* know how to keep Christmas, even if Mr. Scrooge doesn't. And that calls for a toast. (*All murmur "A toast."*) Belinda, the glasses, please.

BELINDA (*Rising and going to mantel*): But we don't have enough glasses.

MRS. CRATCHIT: Bring the two tumblers and the custard cup without the handle.

BOB: That's it. They'll do just as well as golden goblets. Peter, the jug. (BELINDA *brings the glasses,* PETER, *the jug.* BOB *pours from the jug.*)

TINY TIM: I want some, too.

BOB: And you shall have some, Tim. (*Hands him cup. Everyone holds his glass.* BOB *raises his.*) And now I give you Mr. Scrooge. A toast to Mr. Scrooge, the Founder of the Feast.

MRS. CRATCHIT (*Setting her drink down*): The Founder of the Feast, indeed! I wish I had him here. I'd give him a piece of my mind to feast upon, and I hope he'd have a good appetite for it.

BOB (*Gently*): My dear—the children. Christmas Day.

MRS. CRATCHIT: It should be Christmas Day, I am sure, on

which one drinks the health of such an odious, stingy, hard, unfeeling man as Mr. Scrooge. You know he is, Robert! Nobody knows it better than you do.

BOB: My dear—Christmas Day.

MRS. CRATCHIT (*Picking up her glass*): I'll drink his health for your sake and the Day's then—not for his. Long life to him. A merry Christmas and a happy New Year. He'll be very merry and very happy, I have no doubt.

MARTHA (*Raising her glass*): Then to Mr. Scrooge—may he learn the meaning of merry Christmas. (*All murmur "Mr. Scrooge," and sip. Singing is heard offstage.*)

GIRL: Listen! The carol singers are coming.

BELINDA: I'll open the window so we can hear them as they pass. (*She goes to window and opens it, then returns to table. The carol singers may be seen framed in the window, or their singing may be heard from offstage. They sing one or two Christmas carols—preferably old English songs—while the Cratchits sit and listen in silence. The Cratchits join in the singing at the end of the song as the voices of the carolers fade away. When the singing is finished,* BOB *rises.*)

BOB: And now I propose a toast to my very favorite family —the Cratchits. A merry Christmas to us all, my dears. God bless us!

ALL (*Rising and holding up glasses*): Merry Christmas— and God bless us.

TINY TIM: God bless us—every one. (*They hold this pose as the curtain falls.*)

THE END

Puppet Play

Santa's Magic Hat

by *Jane Foster Thornton*

A puppet play about the spirit of Christmas . . .

Characters

HENRY
ELF
SANTA CLAUS
SNOW FAIRY
SNOW BOY
SNOW ELF
LITTLE GIRL
COOKIE LADY
WIZARD

SCENE 1

SETTING: *Henry's house.*

AT RISE: HENRY, *surrounded by Christmas wrappings, is looking into a box.*

HENRY: Here it is the day before Christmas, and I've found all the presents that were hidden in the house! I wonder what Santa Claus is going to bring me? It wouldn't feel like Christmas if I didn't get *everything* I

253

asked for. I wish every day could be Christmas! (ELF *appears.* HENRY, *startled, drops box*.) Who are you?

ELF: I'm a friend—just about the best friend you've ever had, as you'll soon find out. We're going to be partners!

HENRY: Partners? What do you mean?

ELF: I came in answer to your wish. You wished that every day of the year might be Christmas so that you could get more and more and *more* presents. It was the greediest wish I ever heard. You shall have your wish.

HENRY *(Gleefully):* Christmas every day? Lots and lots more toys—all for me? But how?

ELF: I know the secret of Christmas! A long time ago I was one of Santa's toymakers, but I lost my job because Santa said I kept all the best toys for myself. That made me so angry, I decided I'd get even with Santa one day. And I can do it, because I know his secret.

HENRY: What's the secret?

ELF: Santa wears a magic hat, you see, and whoever can get it will be in charge of Christmas. When we have it, there won't be any more of this nonsense of *giving* presents to people. We'll keep everything for ourselves!

HENRY: But how can we get the hat?

ELF: You'll see. First, with the help of my magic powder, we're off for the North Pole. But we must hurry. We can't let Santa go off in his sleigh, or the toys will be scattered all over the world.

HENRY: You're right! I'm ready. Let's go!

ELF *(Tossing powder in air):*
Magic powder in my pocket,
Make us take off like a rocket!
Off we go without a pause
To snatch the cap of Santa Claus!
(They exit. Curtain or blackout.)

* * * * *

SCENE 2

SETTING: *The North Pole.*

AT RISE: HENRY *and* ELF *enter.*

HENRY: It sure is cold here at the North Pole. When we're in charge of Christmas, will we have to live here all the time?

ELF: Of course not! We can live anywhere we like. But first we have to get that hat. *(Pointing off)* Look, here comes Santa now. You go out and wait for me. I'll follow him and wait for a chance to grab it. (HENRY *exits.* SANTA *enters. During his speech,* ELF *follows* SANTA, *unseen by him, and snatches unsuccessfully at hat.)*

SANTA *(Moving back and forth across stage):* What a busy day I've had! I can hardly keep up with the latest trends in toys. Why, I had to transfer a whole division of elves out of wind-up toys and put them into the transformer and robot division. We don't get much call for wooden rocking horses any more. Even trains aren't very popular. Now it's all monsters, outer-space villains, and space ships. But I move with the times. It's my job to make the children happy, and that's the best job in the world. *(Sits)* Now I think I'll take a little nap before it's time to load up the sleigh and start with presents for all the children of the world. (SANTA *dozes and* ELF *snatches hat.* SANTA *is unobtrusively moved offstage.* ELF *jumps around waving hat.)*

ELF *(Excitedly):* I have Santa's hat, now I'm in charge of Christmas! Won't the children be surprised to wake up and find their stockings empty on Christmas morning! *(Laughs meanly)* I'll have more presents than anybody

in the whole wide world! Merry Christmas to *me*!
(HENRY *enters.*)

HENRY: Hey! What about me? We're partners, remember? You're supposed to make *my* wishes come
true! I want those presents, too.

ELF: I've changed my mind. The North Pole's not big
enough for both of us. You hurry on home.

HENRY *(Upset):* But I don't know how to get home. And I
want my share of Christmas! Give me that hat! Give it
to me! *(They fight for hat and tear it in half.)*

ELF: Now look what you've done! The magic hat is torn!
Oh well, I have the bigger half, and I'm going to use it
right away.
Magic hat, magic hat,
Give me what I wish!
Give me lots of games and toys
And a bowl of golden fish!
(Nothing happens.)

HENRY *(Excitedly):* You have the big half, but it doesn't
work! The magic must all be in my half!
Magic hat, magic hat,
Hear my wish today!
Give me all the children's toys
In Santa's magic sleigh!
(Nothing happens.)

ELF: It doesn't work! You broke the spell!

HENRY: No, *you* broke it! It's all *your* fault! *(They fight
again. Suddenly, SNOW FAIRY appears and taps each
with her wand. Amazed, they stop.)*

ELF: The Snow Fairy!

SNOW FAIRY: You should both be ashamed of yourselves!
Not only have you been selfish and greedy, but you
have taken and destroyed something that does not belong to you. Now you must be punished.

HENRY: Oh, Snow Fairy, I'm sorry! Please let me go home. I promise I'll never be selfish or greedy again.

SNOW FAIRY: It won't be as easy as that. When I wave my magic wand, you will both be turned into snow. If you do not find the magic words to break the spell, by sunrise on Christmas morning, you will be melted away. You may go where you like now, ask whom you will, but remember—sunrise tomorrow is the deadline. Goodbye. (SNOW FAIRY *waves wand and exits.* ELF *and* HENRY *sink out.* SNOW ELF *and* SNOW BOY, *really* ELF *and* HENRY, *enter.*)

SNOW ELF: She did it! She turned us into snow!

SNOW BOY *(Shivering):* I'm really and truly freezing!

SNOW ELF: If my magic powder still works, it will take us to a town where we'll find people to ask about those magic words so we can break her spell. *(Tosses powder in air)*

Magic powder made of snow,

Take us where we want to go.

Take us up or take us down,

But take us to a friendly town.

(To SNOW BOY*)* Here we go!

(They exit. Curtain or blackout)

* * * * *

SCENE 3

SETTING: *A village square.*

AT RISE: SNOW ELF *and* SNOW BOY *enter.*

SNOW BOY: Oh, I hope we can find someone to tell us the magic words.

SNOW ELF (*Pointing off*): Here comes a lady now. She looks friendly. Maybe she can help us. (COOKIE LADY *enters. She carries a stack of boxes wrapped in Christmas paper.*)

COOKIE LADY: Oh, dear, it's almost time for the Girl Scout Christmas party. How will I ever get all these boxes of cookies there? Oh, they're falling! (SNOW ELF *and* SNOW BOY *grab packages as they fall.*) Thank you, thank you! You've saved all my cookies from being smashed. Are you boys all right? You're as white as snowmen!

SNOW BOY: We're fine, ma'am. We'll help you carry your boxes.

COOKIE LADY: That's very kind of you. I'll give you a box of cookies. (*Gives him box*)

SNOW ELF: Thank you. Er—my friend and I were wondering . . . that is . . . I know it sounds silly, but . . .

SNOW BOY: What he means is, we wondered if you know any magic words. We've been put under a spell by the Snow Fairy.

COOKIE LADY: A spell! And on Christmas Eve, too! Now let me think—magic words, let's see. The only magic words I know right offhand are "Please" and "Thank you." I always tell my own children, "please" and "thank you" are the only magic words they'll ever need. Just remember them, and you'll be all right. Why, here we are! Thank you for helping me, and Merry Christmas to you! (*She takes back boxes, hands one to* SNOW ELF, *and exits.*)

SNOW BOY: "Please" and "thank you." Could those be the words the Snow Fairy means?

SNOW ELF: I don't know. (*Sighs*) We'd better find someone else to ask, just in case. (LITTLE GIRL *enters, crying.*)

SNOW BOY: Look, there's a little girl, crying. Let's see what's the matter.

SNOW ELF: We don't have time to help people! It's getting late. *(Pauses)* Well, all right. Maybe she knows some magic words!

SNOW BOY: Why are you crying, little girl?

LITTLE GIRL *(Sobbing):* I was helping Mother with our Christmas shopping, and the stores were so crowded. I wanted to buy a present for Mother, but I didn't have enough money. Now the stores are closed, and I can't find my mother anywhere. She'll be so worried about me! And I don't even have a Christmas present for her or Daddy! *(Sobs)*

SNOW BOY: Maybe your mother thought you'd gone home and went there to look for you.

LITTLE GIRL: I live on Maple Street, but I'm not supposed to cross the street by myself.

SNOW ELF: I guess we can help you cross the street. *(They walk along.)*

LITTLE GIRL: Oh, thank you! It's terrible to be all alone on Christmas Eve. I wish I had a present for Mother and Daddy. I hope they'll understand. Mother always says it's not the presents that count on Christmas anyway.

SNOW BOY: Yes, we've just begun to find that out!

LITTLE GIRL: They know I love them, and that's the important thing. Once I was very naughty, and I was going to run away from home, but then I remembered the magic words.

SNOW ELF: Magic words?

LITTLE GIRL: Yes, the Wizard told me once that any time I felt like running away, I should just say, "East or West, home is best," and I wouldn't want to run away anymore.

SNOW ELF: The Wizard—where does he live?

LITTLE GIRL: Why, we're right in front of his house, and that's my house down the street. Thank you for helping me.

SNOW BOY: Here, take this box of cookies and give it to your parents for a Christmas present. I think we'll visit the Wizard. There's something we have to ask him.

LITTLE GIRL: Oh, thank you! And Merry Christmas to you! (LITTLE GIRL *exits with cookie box*.)

SNOW ELF: East or West, home is best. Now we know more magic words! Maybe the Wizard can tell us if they're the right ones.

SNOW BOY: Let's knock on the door right now! (*They pantomime knocking on door. A sign pops up reading,* CLOSED FOR THE HOLIDAYS.)

SNOW ELF: Closed! But it can't be! He's got to help us! (*They knock again.* WIZARD *appears behind sign.*)

WIZARD (*Crossly*): Don't you see my sign? I'm closed for the holidays. No potions, incantations, or advice. Come back in a couple of days. Good night! (WIZARD *exits.*)

SNOW BOY (*Calling*): Oh, please, Mr. Wizard, we *can't* come back! It'll be too late! We need help right now! (WIZARD *reappears.*)

WIZARD: Help? Well, if you need help, that's a different story. What's your problem?

SNOW ELF: We've been changed into snowmen by the Snow Fairy because we were selfish and greedy and wanted Christmas all for ourselves. But we're really *very* sorry. Now we have to find the magic words to break the spell before the sun rises on Christmas morning, or we'll melt away!

WIZARD: Well, well! That's a real problem, all right. Let me find my *Encyclopedia of Useful Magic Phrases for*

All Occasions. (Exits and reappears with large book)
Here we are. *(Opens book)* Snowballs, snow business,
snowfalls, snowmen, *snow spells! (Reads)*
The magic words you need to know
To change you back from boys of snow
Are: "Please" and "thank you," "home is best,"
And four more words; make up the rest. *(Closes book)*

SNOW ELF: That's all it says? Just four more words? But
what words?

WIZARD: Sorry, that's all the book has to say. You must
both try very hard to think what four words you've
heard many times lately. It shouldn't be too hard. Good
luck, and Merry Christmas to you! *(He exits.)*

SNOW BOY: We'll *never* find those other four words! If the
Wizard can't tell us, no one can! I'll never see my
family again, and they'll never know what happened to
me, and we've torn Santa's magic hat so there won't be
any Christmas for anyone ever again, and *(Starts to
cry)* . . . and I never even told my mother and father
"Merry Christmas to you!" (SNOW FAIRY *appears.*)

SNOW FAIRY: Well, it's about time! I was beginning to
think you'd *never* find those last four magic words!

SNOW ELF: But we didn't. We found "please" and "thank
you," and "East or West, home is best," but we didn't
find the rest!

SNOW FAIRY: Yes, you did, although you didn't know it.
Your friend just said them. The last four words are—
Merry Christmas to you! You had to learn to think of
others instead of yourselves, not only at Christmas but
all the time. And that is the true meaning of Christmas.

SNOW ELF: But what about the hat? Santa's magic hat?
It's torn, and now there won't be any Christmas for
anyone!

SNOW FAIRY: You silly elf! The magic of Christmas isn't

small enough or weak enough to be hidden in one little hat. That was just your own foolish idea. Santa is on his way this very minute, delivering toys all over the world to good boys and girls. *(Waves wand)*
Be no longer made of snow!
Boy and Elf, back home you go!
(SNOW BOY *and* SNOW ELF *exit, and reappear as* HENRY *and* ELF.)
HENRY *and* ELF: Hooray! Hooray!
HENRY: I can't wait to give Mother and Dad their presents and wish them the merriest Christmas they ever had!
SNOW FAIRY: If you hurry, Henry, you can be fast asleep in your own bed before Santa climbs down your chimney. *(To* ELF) As for you, if you've really learned your lesson, you may report to Santa's workshop and be a toymaker again!
ELF: Wonderful! I can't wait to start making toys again— and for the children, not for myself!
SNOW FAIRY *(To audience):*
Now everyone's happy, we've broken the spell,
And there's nothing left of our story to tell.
But we hope you'll remember these magic words, too.
And we all want to say . . .
ALL: Merry Christmas to you! *(Curtain)*

THE END

Curtain Raiser

The Christmas Doubters

by Charles Baker

Is there a Santa in the house? . . .

Characters

CHERYL JAMESON, *12*
KAREN JAMESON, *10*
JAKE JAMESON ⎫
HELEN JAMESON ⎬ *their parents*
NICK, *a visitor*
AL ⎫
ARTIE ⎬ *elves*
JOAN ⎭
HARRY SMITHERS, *neighbor*

TIME: *Christmas Eve.*
SETTING: *The Jameson living room, traditionally furnished and festively decorated for Christmas. Christmas tree left has no presents under it. At center is a large brick fireplace. Door right leads outside, and*

staircase down right leads upstairs. NICK, AL, ARTIE
and JOAN *hide behind couch.*

AT RISE: KAREN *and* CHERYL, *dressed in bathrobes, are
center.* JAKE *and* HELEN *are sitting on couch.*

CHERYL: Not this again, Dad. Karen and I are long past
the age of believing in Santa Claus.

HELEN: Really, Jake, I do think the girls are old enough
now that we can stop all this Santa Claus business.

JAKE: I still believe in Santa Claus. He's the one who puts
gifts under the tree while visions of sugar plums dance
in my head.

CHERYL *(Matter-of-factly):* Dad, we're too old for dancing sugar plums.

JAKE: I just want to warn you that nonbelievers will
someday learn.

KAREN: Mom, will you reason with him? Can't we get the
gifts and put them under the tree as every other normal
family does on Christmas Eve?

HELEN *(Pleading):* Well, Jake, are you going to concede?

JAKE: O.K. Put the presents under the tree, but promise
that you won't do it until I'm out of sight. That way
somebody in the house will still have something to
believe in.

CHERYL: All right, Dad. Good night, and don't let too
many sugar plums dance in your head. (*To* KAREN)
Come on, Karen, let's go upstairs.

KAREN: O.K. Good night. Say hello to St. Nick for us,
Dad. *(Girls exit.)*

JAKE *(Quietly):* I've got the greatest Christmas Eve plan
ever. This time I'm really going to convince them.

HELEN: Jake, the girls are too old for this Santa nonsense. They recognize you in that old red suit every
year.

JAKE: But I won't be in it this time.

HELEN: You're not going to do anything foolish, are you?

JAKE: Trust me, and maybe even you'll be a believer before the night is over.

HELEN: I'll try my best. *(They exit. After a few moments, KAREN and CHERYL enter, carrying gift boxes.)*

KAREN: If somebody finds out that we're putting presents under a tree just so Dad will think that Santa Claus put them there, I'll die. How embarrassing!

NICK *(Peeking over back of sofa):* Oh, don't be embarrassed. Many people . . . *(Girls, startled, throw gifts into air and run to stairs. NICK raises his arms, and sound of bell is heard. Girls stop and turn toward NICK, who stands. He is dressed in everyday clothes, with touches of green and red.)*

KAREN *(Calling softly):* Mom! Dad! We have company.

NICK *(Grinning):* It won't do you any good to call them. They can't hear you. At this very moment your father has visions of sugar plums dancing in his head. Go ahead and see for yourself. (KAREN *runs upstairs.* CHERYL *moves cautiously toward* NICK.)

CHERYL: We don't want any trouble. Take anything you want and leave. We won't call the police. . . .

NICK: They won't respond. Spirits aren't their line of work.

CHERYL: Spirits?

NICK: Right—spirits. That's what I am—a Christmas spirit. (CHERYL *stares at him quizzically.*) St. Nick, Kris Kringle, Santa Claus, but you can call me Nick if you like.

KAREN *(Entering; stunned):* I couldn't wake Dad. He's just lying in bed, with that silly cap he wears every Christmas Eve and a big grin on his face, muttering about something.

NICK: Dancing sugar plums, right?

KAREN: How did you know?

NICK: Magic. I do it like this. *(He waves his hand, and bells sound.)*

CHERYL: I don't believe it.

NICK: Really? How about this? *(He waves his hands. Bells are heard, and then a Christmas song blares out. He shouts above the music.)* Pretty good, eh? *(Girls look around.* NICK *waves his hands. Bells sound, and music stops.)* It won't do you any good to look. It's magic.

CHERYL *(Suddenly):* Wait a minute! I get it now! My father hired you, didn't he? *(To* KAREN*)* Karen, Dad's up to his old tricks. Remember, he told us to go ahead and bring down these gifts. He warned us that some day we would believe in Santa. Well, this is his way of "proving" it.

KAREN *(To* NICK*):* Hey, mister, you really had me believing in you for a minute. Especially the way you had Mom and Dad pretend to be asleep. When we see Dad tomorrow morning, we'll tell him that we learned our lesson.

NICK: And what lesson was that?

KAREN: Oh, whatever you want us to say.

NICK: I've still missed the point with you two.

CHERYL *(Disappointed):* Don't tell me there's more.

NICK: I need some help. *(He waves his hand. Bell is heard, and* AL, ARTIE, *and* JOAN *pop up behind couch. They wear everyday dress, with touches of green and red. They are about the same age as* CHERYL *and* KAREN.*)* Would your father have thought this up?

CHERYL: What's so great about kids from some other neighborhood?

JOAN *(Kindly):* Excuse me, but we're not kids, we're elves.

NICK: That's Al, Artie, and Joan. *(Elves nod their heads as they're introduced.)*

CHERYL: Al, Artie, and Joan don't sound like elfin names.

JOAN: They're just temporary. You'd never be able to pronounce our real elfin names.

KAREN: If you're elves, where are your long elfin hats, elfin tights, and elfin shoes?

ARTIE: We left those at the North Pole. These clothes are part of our new image. Santa says more kids will believe in us if we dress the way they do.

CHERYL *(Irritated):* This isn't funny any more.

AL: We know. We're in big trouble.

KAREN: I'll say.

NICK: Nobody believes in us any more.

CHERYL: How can you expect us to believe that you're Santa Claus and they're elves when you're not even dressed correctly?

KAREN: At least you could have rented some costumes.

NICK: This is a costume.

JOAN *(To* NICK*):* I told you this modern approach wouldn't work. Let's get out your old red suit.

CHERYL: Listen! You're all very good actors. We get the message, and now, why don't you go home and enjoy the rest of the holiday with your families.

NICK: Just a minute, please, Cheryl. *(To elves)* How about showing the girls a little of your elfin magic?

AL: O.K. But will it work under these conditions?

ARTIE: Sure it will. We've done this old trick a million times. Stand back, everyone, and watch two master elves at work.

AL: Rope, please. (ARTIE *hands rope to* AL.) We will now perform the great elfin escape trick. *(Begins tying* AR-TIE *with rope)* Not only will the elf escape from these bonds, but he will disappear right before your very eyes. *(He removes handkerchief from pocket and ties it around* ARTIE's *mouth.)* O.K., Artie, see you at the North Pole later tonight. "Keep your eyes peeled, have no fear! Watch this elfin disappear." *(Nothing happens.* ARTIE *struggles to free himself.* AL *chants again.)* "Keep your eyes peeled, have no fear! Watch this elfin disappear." (ARTIE *continues to struggle with ropes.* AL *addresses* NICK; *sheepishly)* It doesn't work, Nick. *(Unties* ARTIE, *while* CHERYL *and* KAREN *shake their heads)*

ARTIE: What went wrong?

NICK: It has to be the clothes. There's no elfin magic in them.

CHERYL: That's not much of an excuse.

NICK: This is discouraging. I wish we could convince you. You see, we've tried everything over the years to keep our following—books, songs, movies, even television specials—but hardly anyone believes in Santa any more. *(Sadly)* I guess this isn't going to work, either.

CHERYL: I'm sorry, mister. You have put on a good act for us, though.

NICK (*To elves*): Let's go, friends. We're finished here. We have a long night ahead of us. (AL *heads for fireplace, puts foot inside.* CHERYL *grabs his arm.)*

CHERYL: Please use the front door. You might get hurt trying to climb up there.

AL: You don't understand. I can go up there without any trouble.

CHERYL: You don't have to go on with this show any longer. You've earned your money.

JOAN, ARTIE, *and* AL *(Ad lib):* All right. Good night. *(They exit.* NICK *follows them, then turns at door.)*

NICK *(Reaching inside his shirt pocket):* These are for you. *(He gives each girl a candy plum.)*

KAREN *(Holding it by the tip):* What is it?

NICK: It's a sugar plum. You don't see them much any more.

KAREN *(Twirling plum by stem):* What do you do with these things?

NICK: Ask your dad. He'll know. Good night. *(Exits)*

CHERYL *(Closing door quickly; relieved):* Thank goodness they've gone. I thought they'd never leave.

KAREN: They really were quite good, don't you think? *(Holding up plum)* And what about this thing?

CHERYL: Who knows? Ask Dad about it in the morning. I'm sure he'll be glad to discuss it.

KAREN: How did that guy manage all those sound effects?

CHERYL: Will you drop it? Let's put these presents under the tree and go to bed. *(They start to pick up boxes. Suddenly, jingle bells are heard offstage.)*

SMITHERS *(Offstage):* Ho! Ho! Ho! *(The front door bursts open, and SMITHERS, dressed as Santa Claus, enters, shaking strings of bells. He shouts.)* Merry Christmas! Merry Christmas!

CHERYL: Oh, no, not again.

SMITHERS: Merry Christmas! Merry Christmas! I'll bet you girls didn't expect to see Santa, did you? *(JAKE, dressed in long nightshirt and cap, and HELEN, in robe, enter.)*

JAKE *(Pretending to be surprised):* Well, I'll be. It's Santa Claus.

CHERYL: Hardly, Dad. This is apparently act two of the same play.

JAKE: What are you talking about?

CHERYL: We just said good night to this guy a few minutes ago. You should have made him wear a costume in the first place. *(Crosses to SMITHERS)* This is—*(She pulls off* SMITHERS's *beard; shocked*) Mr. Smithers? What are you doing here?

KAREN *(Shocked):* Mr. Smithers? Then who was the other guy?

HELEN: Jake, look at these poor girls. You'd better explain.

SMITHERS: Sorry, Jake. I guess I messed up your plan. They must've recognized my voice.

JAKE *(Disappointed):* That's O.K., Harry. They're just too old to go for the Santa Claus idea, and it's about time I accepted the fact. *(To girls)* I asked Mr. Smithers to play Santa Claus because I wanted to give you a little reminder of what it was like when you still believed.

KAREN: But who was the other Santa Claus?

JAKE: What "other" Santa?

CHERYL: The one with the elves in modern dress.

JAKE: What are you talking about?

CHERYL: Oh, Dad, don't play dumb.

SMITHERS *(Looking at girls; perplexed):* If you don't mind, I'm going home. I'm getting confused. *(To* JAKE*)* If you need a Santa again, call someone else, would you? *(He exits.)*

CHERYL: Dad, there was a man here tonight, dressed in regular clothing, and he said he was Santa trying out a new image. He had a bunch of kids with him who claimed to be elves.

JAKE *(Smiling):* I get it. You two are turning the tables on me by telling me that Santa was here and that you talked to him. *(Hugging them)* How about that, Helen? Just like their dad! Listen, girls, next time he shows up, wake me.

KAREN: But I tried to wake you.

JAKE: You did?

KAREN *(Puzzled):* He did some magic with bells.

JAKE *(Glowing):* You don't say.

CHERYL: And they tried a rope trick, but it didn't work, so they *(Hesitates)* tried to go up the chimney.

HELEN: The chimney? Why didn't they?

KAREN: Cheryl told them to use the front door.

CHERYL *(Slowly):* Karen, are you thinking what I'm thinking?

KAREN *(Nodding):* They were very convincing.

CHERYL *(Shaking her head):* It's impossible.

KAREN *(To* JAKE*):* He gave me this. *(Holds out sugar plum)* He told me to ask you about it.

JAKE *(Surprised):* It's a sugar plum. *(Takes plum and examines it)* How in the world did he know about sugar plums?

HELEN: I don't know anything about sugar plums, but I think it's about time you girls got into bed. This will all make sense in the morning. Maybe you just had a bad dream.

CHERYL: Why would we have the same dream?

HELEN: Well, the only other explanation is that it really happened.

CHERYL: I guess you're right, Mom. It must have been a dream, and I'm going upstairs right now before anything else happens. *(To* KAREN*)* Don't ever tell a soul at school about this, Karen. Let's go to bed. (CHERYL *exits, followed by* KAREN, *who stops and turns at foot of stairs.*)

KAREN: You don't really think that . . .

HELEN: I'm sure your father will explain it all in the morning.

KAREN: Well, it's O.K. with me if he doesn't. Good night. *(She exits.)*

HELEN: Jake, just what went on here tonight?

JAKE *(Staring at sugar plum):* I'm not certain myself

(Looks up), but I guess it's time to get back to bed. Good night. Merry Christmas! *(He exits. The front door opens slightly, and* NICK *peeks in.)*

NICK: Psst! Mrs. Jameson?

HELEN *(Turning):* Oh, Nick, come in. Watch out, though, or they'll hear you.

NICK *(Entering):* How'd we do?

HELEN: Splendidly! That was a very convincing perform-ance. They all fell for it. They'll never figure out just what happened on this Christmas Eve.

NICK: Then we've made believers of them?

HELEN: Yes, I think so.

NICK: Terrific.

HELEN: Say, I didn't expect you to bring along actors and special effects. How much do I owe you?

NICK: There were no actors and special effects.

HELEN *(Confused):* What? *(Suddenly)* Hey, how did you know about the dancing sugar plums? Jake's always talking about them, but I never told you about that.

NICK: Helen, the Christmas Spirit works in many ways. *(He exits quickly.)*

HELEN: Wait a minute. *(She races to the door and opens it, shouting)* Nick! Nick! *(Puzzled; to herself)* Now where did he go? *(Turns to face audience)* No. He couldn't be . . . *(Shakes her head)* That's impossible, isn't it? *(Offstage, a hearty laugh is heard, followed by sound of bells. Christmas tree lights go off.)*

NICK *(Offstate; calling):* Merry Christmas, Helen! Enjoy those dancing sugar plums! *(Curtain)*

THE END

Dramatized Christmas Classics

A Christmas Carol

by Charles Dickens
Adapted by Adele Thane

Miserly Ebenezer Scrooge sat alone and friendless on Christmas Eve, when a ghost from his past appeared with a dire warning. . . .

Characters

EBENEZER SCROOGE
BOB CRATCHIT, *his clerk*
FRED, *Scrooge's nephew*
COLLECTOR FOR CHARITY
MARLEY'S GHOST
GHOST OF CHRISTMAS PAST
EBENEZER SCROOGE, *as a schoolboy*
FAN, *his sister*
YOUNG SCROOGE, *as an apprentice*
DICK WILKINS, *a fellow apprentice*
MR. FEZZIWIG, *their boss*
MRS. FEZZIWIG
BELLE, *young Scrooge's fiancée*
GHOST OF CHRISTMAS PRESENT
MRS. CRATCHIT, *Bob's wife*

PETER
BELINDA
MARTHA
NED
SALLY
TINY TIM
} *Cratchit children*

GHOST OF CHRISTMAS YET TO COME
FIDDLER
BOY
CAROLERS, *extras*

SCENE 1

TIME: *Christmas Eve, in the 19th century.*

SETTING: *London. The business office of Scrooge and Marley. In the right wall is the door that opens to the street. Upstage of the door there is a clothes tree, holding Bob Cratchit's hat, and Scrooge's muffler, hat and overcoat. At center is a flat-topped desk for Scrooge, with a stool behind it. On the desk is a pile of ledgers, pen and inkstand, a ruler, a metal cash box with money in it, and a lighted candle. Set against the wall is Bob Cratchit's high clerk's desk and stool. This desk also has a lighted candle, ledgers, pen and inkstand. A casement window is downstage of clerk's desk, and potbellied stove is upstage between the two desks. Coal hod and shovel are beside stove.*

AT RISE: SCROOGE *and* BOB CRATCHIT *are working at their desks.* BOB *has long white muffler wound around his neck.* CAROLERS *offstage start singing, "God Rest Ye Merry, Gentlemen."* SCROOGE *rises impatiently, goes to street door and flings it open.*

SCROOGE (*Shouting off right*): Hey! Stop that singing! Stop it, I say! Keep quiet out there! (CAROLERS *stop singing.* SCROOGE *closes door and returns to desk, mut-*

tering.) Police ought to shut those people up. Singing around in the street as if they had no proper business. (*Counts money in cash box, standing with his back to* BOB, *who gets down off stool, blowing on his hands and rubbing them together*)

BOB: Weather seems to be getting colder.

SCROOGE (*Without turning around*): Cold? Humbug! It doesn't feel cold to mc. (BOB *goes to coal hod and lifts out shovel, making a grating noise.* SCROOGE *whirls on on him.*) What are you doing with that shovel?

BOB (*Timidly*): I thought I'd put another coal on the fire — if it's all right.

SCROOGE: It's not all right, and you know it. If you persist in burning up my coal like tinder, you will have to find another position!

BOB: But my hand is so cold I can hardly write.

SCROOGE: Warm it at the candle. (*Closes and locks cash box.* BOB *replaces shovel in coal hod, sits at desk and holds hands over candle. Door bursts open and* FRED *enters briskly.*)

FRED (*Cheerfully, removing his hat*): Merry Christmas, Uncle! God save you!

SCROOGE: Bah! Humbug!

FRED (*Laughing*): Christmas a humbug, Uncle? Surely you don't mean that.

SCROOGE: I do! (*Scornfully*) Merry Christmas! What reason have you to be merry? You're poor enough.

FRED: Come, then. What reason have you to be sad? You're rich enough.

SCROOGE: Bah! Humbug!

FRED (*Coaxingly*): Don't be cross, Uncle.

SCROOGE: What else can I be, when I live in such a world of fools? A pox upon Merry Christmas! What's Christmas to *you* but a time for paying bills without money;

a time for finding yourself a year older, but not an hour richer. If I had my way, every idiot who goes about with "Merry Christmas" on his lips should be boiled in his own pudding, and buried with a stake of holly through his heart.

FRED: Oh, really, Uncle!

SCROOGE (*Mockingly*): Oh, really, nephew! Keep Christmas in your own way, and let me keep it in mine.

FRED: Keep it! But you don't keep it at all.

SCROOGE: Let me leave it alone, then. What good has Christmas ever done *you*?

FRED: Why, Uncle, it has done me a lot of good. It is the only time I know when men and women seem to open their shut-up hearts freely — and though it has never put a scrap of gold or silver in my pocket, I believe it *has* done me good, and *will* do me good, and I say (*Thumping* SCROOGE's *desk*) — *God bless it!*

BOB (*Applauding*): Splendid, sir, splendid!

SCROOGE (*Turning to* BOB *with a vengeance*): Let me hear another sound out of *you*, Bob Cratchit, and you'll keep *your* Christmas by losing your situation! (*Sarcastically, to* FRED) You're quite a powerful speaker, Fred. I wonder why you don't go into Parliament.

FRED (*Soothingly*): Don't be angry, Uncle. Come, dine with us tomorrow.

SCROOGE (*Angrily*): I'll dine with the devil first.

FRED: I want nothing from you; I ask nothing of you. Why can't we be friends?

SCROOGE (*Returning to his work*): Good afternoon.

FRED: I am sorry, with all my heart, to find you so resolute. But I have made this visit in honor of Christmas, and I'll keep my Christmas humor to the last. So a Merry Christmas, Uncle! And a Happy New Year!

SCROOGE (*Thundering*): Good afternoon!

FRED (*Waving to* BOB *with his hat*): Merry Christmas to you, Bob!

BOB: The same to you, sir! God bless you! (FRED *opens door to exit;* COLLECTOR FOR CHARITY *is standing outside, consulting notebook.*)

COLLECTOR: How do you do, sir? Scrooge and Marley, I believe? (FRED *nods and gestures toward* SCROOGE. COLLECTOR *enters.* FRED *exits, closing door.* COLLECTOR *speaks to* SCROOGE.) Have I the pleasure of addressing Mr. Scrooge or Mr. Marley?

SCROOGE (*Impatiently*): Mr. Marley has been dead these seven years. He died seven years ago this very night.

COLLECTOR: I have no doubt his generosity is well represented in his surviving partner. My credentials, sir. (*Lays card on desk;* SCROOGE *brushes it aside without looking at it.*) Mr. Scrooge, at this festive season of the year, we all want to make some slight provision for the poor and destitute. Many thousands are in want of common necessities; hundreds of thousands are in want of common comforts.

SCROOGE (*Putting down pen*): Are there no prisons?

COLLECTOR: Plenty of prisons.

SCROOGE: What about the union workhouses and treadmill? Are they still in operation?

COLLECTOR: They are. I wish I could say they were not.

SCROOGE: Good. I was afraid from what you said that something had stopped them in their useful work.

COLLECTOR: I would hardly call them useful! As I say, Mr. Scrooge, a few of us are trying to raise a fund to buy meat and drink for the poor. We chose this time because it is the time when want is felt most keenly. (*Picking up pen from desk*) What shall I put you down for?

SCROOGE (*Snatching pen from* COLLECTOR's *hand*): Nothing.

COLLECTOR: You wish to be anonymous?

SCROOGE (*Slamming pen down on desk*): I wish to be left alone! (*Rising*) I don't make myself merry at Christmas, and I can't afford to make a lot of idle people merry. I help support the prisons and poorhouses — they cost enough. Those who are badly off must go there.

COLLECTOR: Many would rather die than go there.

SCROOGE: If they would rather die, they had better do it and decrease the surplus population. Besides, this has nothing to do with my business. (*Turns to desk*)

COLLECTOR (*Reproachfully*): You ought to make it your business to help your fellow man.

SCROOGE (*Testily*): It's enough for a man to understand his own business and not interfere with other people's. Mine occupies me constantly. Good afternoon. (*Sits at desk*)

COLLECTOR (*Going to door, then turning*): If Mr. Marley felt as you do, I fear his ghost is not resting in peace. Good afternoon. (*Exits*)

SCROOGE: Bah! Humbug! (*Looks at watch and speaks grudgingly to* BOB) You might as well go, it's five minutes past time. Get along.

BOB: Yes, sir. (*Closes ledgers, blows out candle, goes to clothes tree for hat, then stands twirling it nervously in his hands.*)

SCROOGE: Well, what are you waiting for?

BOB: About tomorrow, sir.

SCROOGE: You'll want all day tomorrow, I suppose?

BOB: Yes, sir, if it's quite convenient.

SCROOGE (*Rising, banging ruler on desk*): It's *not* convenient, and it's not fair! If I were to deduct something from your salary, you'd think yourself ill-used. And yet, you don't think *me* ill-used when I pay a day's wages for no work.

BOB (*Pleadingly*): Christmas is only once a year, sir.

SCROOGE: A poor excuse for picking a man's pocket every twenty-fifth of December! Very well, take the day off — but be here all the earlier the next morning.

BOB (*Eagerly, as he goes toward exit*): Oh, I *will*, sir! Good night Mr. Scrooge — and a Merry Christmas to you! (*Hurries out, closing door*)

SCROOGE (*Crossing to lock door*): There's another one, Bob Cratchit, with fifteen shillings a week, and a wife and family, talking about a Merry Christmas. They'll drive me to distraction. (CAROLERS *start singing "The First Noël" offstage.*) Carolers, carolers! Will they never leave a man in peace? (*Sits at desk and resumes work.* CAROLERS *fade. Candle flickers, lights dim. Sound of clanking chains is heard off right, faint at first, then growing louder.* SCROOGE *looks up, listening, then shakes head.*) Humbug! (*Suddenly door flies open.* MARLEY'S GHOST *appears in the doorway, pale, heavily bound with chains that drag behind him.* SCROOGE *gives a start, looks toward door, then quickly shakes his head.*) Humbug, I say! That door is locked! (MARLEY'S GHOST *enters dragging chains, and as* SCROOGE *turns again to look he advances to clothes tree, where spotlight comes upon him.* SCROOGE *slides off stool and slowly approaches* GHOST. *In a nervous voice*) Who — who are you?

MARLEY'S GHOST (*Speaking in a deep, forbidding voice*): Ask me who I *was*.

SCROOGE: Who *were* you, then?

MARLEY'S GHOST: In life I was your partner, Jacob Marley.

SCROOGE (*Drawing away*): Jacob Marley! What do you want with me?

MARLEY'S GHOST: Much. (*Pause*) Don't you believe in me?

SCROOGE (*Boastfully*): I don't.

MARLEY'S GHOST: You can see me, can't you?

SCROOGE: I think I can.

MARLEY'S GHOST: Why do you doubt your own senses?

SCROOGE: Because a little thing affects my senses — a slight disorder of the stomach — a bit of undigested beef, a blot of mustard, a crumb of cheese. (*Cackling at his own joke*) There's more of gravy than of the grave about you, whatever you are. (MARLEY'S GHOST *raises a frightful cry and shakes his chains.*)

MARLEY'S GHOST: Silence! (SCROOGE, *suddenly terrified, falls on his knees.*)

SCROOGE: Mercy, oh mercy!

MARLEY'S GHOST (*In a booming voice*): Do you believe in me or not?

SCROOGE (*Terrified*): I do, I must! But why do you walk on earth? And why do you come to me?

MARLEY'S GHOST: It is required of every man that the spirit within him should walk abroad among his fellow men. If that spirit does not go out in life, it is condemned to do so after death. It is doomed to wander through the world. Oh, woe is me! (*Wails dismally, lifting chains high and flinging them heavily to the floor*)

SCROOGE (*Rising fearfully*): You are chained — tell me why.

MARLEY'S GHOST: I wear the chain I forged in life. I made it link by link. I girded it on of my own free will. Is its pattern strange to you?

SCROOGE: I've never seen anything like it before.

MARLEY'S GHOST: That's strange. You wear such a chain yourself. (SCROOGE *looks anxiously about him on the floor.*) It was as long as this chain of mine seven Christmas Eves ago. You've made it longer since.

SCROOGE (*Clasping his hands in supplication*): Oh, no! Jacob, say something to comfort me.

MARLEY'S GHOST: I have no comfort for you.

SCROOGE: But you were always a good man of business, Jacob.

MARLEY'S GHOST: Business! Mankind was my business. I did nothing to help my fellow man. Oh, woe is me! (*Wails again and shakes his chains*)

SCROOGE: Is something hurting you?

MARLEY'S GHOST: I suffer most at Christmas time. Hear me, Ebenezer. My time is nearly gone. I am here to warn you. You may yet have a chance to escape my fate.

SCROOGE: You were always a good friend to me, Jacob.

MARLEY'S GHOST (*Relentlessly*): You will be haunted by three Spirits.

SCROOGE (*Faltering*): Is that the chance you mentioned, Jacob?

MARLEY'S GHOST: It is.

SCROOGE: Then I think I'd better not take that chance.

MARLEY'S GHOST: You have no choice. (*Starts walking backward, step by step, toward door*) Expect the Ghost of Christmas Past when the bell tolls one. Expect the Ghost of Christmas Present when the bell tolls two. Expect the Ghost of Christmas Yet to Come when the bell tolls three. (*Pauses in doorway*) For your own sake, Scrooge, remember what has passed between us. Farewell. (MARLEY'S GHOST *disappears in the darkness off right, dragging his chains.*)

SCROOGE (*Rushing to doorway*): Jacob, wait! Help me! Jacob! (*Falls on knees. Bell tolls one. Live or recorded music of "Lo, How A Rose E'er Blooming" is heard offstage, and continues under following dialogue. Spotlight comes up on* GHOST OF CHRISTMAS PAST, *a ruddy-faced youth wearing white tunic with golden belt, a shining crown, and carrying holly branch, standing left center.* SCROOGE *rises, sees* GHOST, *and walks hesitantly toward him.*) Are you the spirit whose coming was foretold to me?

1ST GHOST (*Softly, gently*): I am.

SCROOGE: Who and what are you?

1ST GHOST: I am the Ghost of Christmas Past.

SCROOGE: Long past?

1ST GHOST: No, your past. Come and walk with me.

SCROOGE (*Shrinking back*): No, no, I can't!

1ST GHOST: It is your only hope of being saved. (*Taking* SCROOGE *by the arm*) Come, we have far to go.

SCROOGE (*Remonstrating*): It's bitter cold outside.

1ST GHOST: What does it matter? Nothing can wither your cold spirit. We will move swiftly through the air. (*Points to casement window, left, and as he points, it opens magically.* NOTE: *Shutters are pushed open from offstage.*)

SCROOGE (*Pulling away*): Through the air? I am mortal, I will fall!

1ST GHOST: Bear but a touch of my hand there (*Touching* SCROOGE's *heart*), and you shall be upheld in more than this. Come! (*As* 1ST GHOST *and* SCROOGE *start walking toward window, lights dim to blackout. Curtain closes to sound of whistling wind.*)

*   *   *   *

SCENE 2

SETTING: *This scene is played in front of curtain. Schoolroom. School desk and bench are center.*

AT RISE: *Sound of whistling wind fades as spotlight comes up on* 1ST GHOST *and* SCROOGE, *down left.* SCROOGE *is on his knees, clinging to* 1ST GHOST.

SCROOGE: Help, help, I'm falling!

1ST GHOST: Stand up! You're on the ground now. You haven't lost your feet. Stand up, I say!

SCROOGE (*Getting up, looking around, then walking about, nervously*): Where are we?

1ST GHOST: You've been here many times before. (*Spotlight comes up on* EBENEZER SCROOGE *as a schoolboy, seated at desk, his head on his arms, sobbing softly. He does not notice others.*)

SCROOGE: Why, it's my old school. Everybody has gone home for the Christmas holidays.

1ST GHOST: Not everybody. A solitary boy is left there still.

SCROOGE: I know him all too well — my lonely self. Poor boy!

FAN (*Off right, calling*): Hello! Is anybody here? (*Enters, calling*) I'm looking for my brother, Ebenezer Scrooge.

EBENEZER (*Rising*): Fan!

FAN (*Seeing him*): Ebenezer! (*Runs to him and hugs him*) I've come to take you home!

EBENEZER: Home? Is Father dead?

FAN: No, he sent me in a carriage to get you. He's much kinder than he used to be. We're to be together all the Christmas long. (*Taking his hand*) Hurry, let's go! I'm so excited I can hardly talk! (*They run off, right. Spotlight fades out on schoolroom, up on* SCROOGE *and* 1ST GHOST, *down left. During following dialogue, desk and bench are moved to right, representing* FEZZI-WIG'S *warehouse.*)

SCROOGE: That was the only happy Christmas I ever had at home. My sister died several years later.

1ST GHOST: She left a child, didn't she? Your nephew, Fred. What have you done for him? Have you loved him dearly for your sister's sake?

SCROOGE (*Ashamed*): Take me away, I don't want to remember any more.

1ST GHOST: You have no choice. I am here to show you the Christmas Past. (*Lights come up full.* YOUNG SCROOGE *and* DICK WILKINS, *both in shirtsleeves, are seated at desk, writing in ledgers.*) Do you know this place?

SCROOGE: Know it! Of course, I do. It's Fezziwig's warehouse — I was apprenticed here. (FEZZIWIG *enters, carrying small Christmas tree and stand.*)

FEZZIWIG (*Jovially, to* YOUNG SCROOGE *and* DICK): Yo ho, there, Ebenezer Scrooge — Dick Wilkins! No more work tonight. It's Christmas Eve. Clear away, my lads, and let's have lots of room here!

SCROOGE (*Excitedly*): It's old Fezziwig! Bless his heart, it's Fezziwig alive again! And there's Dick Wilkins. He was very much attached to me, was Dick. (YOUNG SCROOGE *and* DICK *move desk off right, but leave bench on stage.* FEZZIWIG *sets Christmas tree left stage.* MRS. FEZZIWIG *enters, right, with holly wreath which she hangs on stage curtain.*)

MRS. FEZZIWIG: Merry Christmas, Mr. Fezziwig.

FEZZIWIG: Ho, there, Mrs. Fezziwig! Christmas comes only once a year. Worth waiting for — worth celebrating — worth remembering. (YOUNG SCROOGE *and* DICK *re-enter, struggling into their coats.* CAROLERS *come down aisles of auditorium, singing "Deck the Halls," and go onstage.* FIDDLER *enters, right, with fiddle and bow, stands on bench and begins to play appropriate dance tune. Recorded music may be used.* CAROLERS *dance, as* YOUNG SCROOGE *and* DICK *clap their hands, and* MR. *and* MRS. FEZZIWIG *link arms and dance in circle.* SCROOGE *watches with apparent pleasure, clapping his hands and tapping his foot in*

time to music. The dance ends with CAROLERS, YOUNG
SCROOGE, DICK, MR. *and* MRS. FEZZIWIG *and* FIDDLER
dancing up aisles and out at rear of auditorium.)

SCROOGE: Those were happy times, spirit. And how grateful we all were to old Fezziwig for those Christmas Eves.

1ST GHOST: Yet Mr. Fezziwig didn't spend more than a
few pounds on the whole party.

SCROOGE: What difference does that make? The happiness he gave us was quite as great as if he had spent
a fortune.

1ST GHOST: How did you ever forget these things in your
later years? (*Pause*) My time grows short. One shadow
more from your past. (*Spotlight comes up on* BELLE,
standing center.)

SCROOGE (*Crying out*): Belle! The girl I was to marry!

1ST GHOST: Listen again to the words she spoke on that
fateful Christmas Day when she released you from
your promise of marriage.

BELLE (*Removing ring from finger*): I return your ring,
Ebenezer. Another idol has displaced me, a golden
one. I've seen your love of gold grow like a mighty
passion until nothing else matters to you. Our contract
is an old one, made when we were both poor. I release you from it, with a full heart, for the love of
him you once were. May you be happy in the life you
have chosen. (*Spotlight on* BELLE *fades out.*)

SCROOGE: Spirit, why do you delight in torturing me?
Show me no more!

1ST GHOST: Listen. (*Bell tolls twice.*) My time is up.
Another spirit comes. Farewell. (1ST GHOST *exits left.
Spotlight comes up right, revealing* GHOST OF CHRIST-
MAS PRESENT, *who wears simple green robe, a holly
wreath on his head, and carries a horn of plenty as a
torch.*)

2ND GHOST (*Cheerily, in a hearty voice*): Look upon me, and know me better, man! I am the Ghost of Christmas Present. Will you come forth with me, Ebenezer Scrooge?

SCROOGE (*Crossing to* 2ND GHOST *meekly*): Spirit, conduct me where you will. If you have anything to teach me, let me benefit by it.

2ND GHOST: Come then, let us visit Bob Cratchit's home. (2ND GHOST *gestures toward stage curtain with his torch; glitter falls from torch, and sound of tinkling bells is heard from offstage. Curtain opens, and* 2ND GHOST *and* SCROOGE *stand down right to watch the action.*)

* * * * *

SCENE 3

SETTING: *The kitchen of the Cratchit home. Setting is same as Scene 1, except that office window frame down left has been removed to make an exit. A fireplace is left. Center is large table covered with red-checked tablecloth, plates, glasses, etc. Chairs and stools for eight are placed around the table.*

AT RISE: MRS. CRATCHIT *and* BELINDA *are putting the finishing touches to the table, which is set for dinner.* PETER *is at the fireplace, blowing up the fire with bellows.*

MRS. CRATCHIT (*Looking at clock on mantel*): Whatever is keeping your dear father and Tiny Tim? And Martha wasn't as late as this last Christmas Day. (*Door flies open, and* NED *and* SALLY *rush in, followed by* MARTHA, *wearing bonnet and shawl.*)

SALLY: Mother, here's Martha!

NED: There's *such* a goose for dinner, Martha! Hurrah! (NED *and* SALLY *rush back out.*)

MRS. CRATCHIT (*kissing* MARTHA): Bless your heart, Martha, how late you are!

MARTHA (*Hanging bonnet and shawl on clothes tree*): We had a lot of work to finish at the shop last night, Mother, and then we had to clean it this morning.

MRS. CRATCHIT: Sit down, my dear, and rest. (MARTHA *starts to sit in chair at table but stops as* NED *and* SALLY *run in from outside.*)

SALLY: Hide, Martha, hide!

NED: Father's coming with Tiny Tim! Let's surprise him!

SALLY: Hide in the pantry! (NED, SALLY *and* MARTHA *hurry out, down left.* BOB CRATCHIT *enters, galloping, with* TINY TIM *on his back, holding a crutch.*)

BOB: Clear the way for the fastest horse in London town!

TIM: Whoa there, whoa!

BOB (*Lowering* TIM *to floor and glancing about room*): Why, where's our Martha?

MRS. CRATCHIT: She's not coming, Bob. (PETER *and* BELINDA, *at fireplace, nudge each other and giggle.*)

BOB: Not coming — on Christmas Day! (*Disappointed*) It just won't be Christmas without Martha.

MARTHA (*Entering, running to* BOB, *and hugging him*): Here I am, Father! I was only hiding. We wanted to tease you. (*Hugging* TIM) Why, Tim! How is my little brother?

TIM: I threw a snowball as far as Peter — almost.

PETER: Come and smell our pudding, Tim. (PETER *and* BELINDA *exit down left with* TIM.)

MRS. CRATCHIT: How did Tim behave in church, Bob?

BOB (*Hanging hat and muffler on clothes tree*): As good as gold, and better. Coming home, he told me that he hoped all the people in church saw him, because he was a cripple. He thought it might help them to remember on Christmas Day who it was that made lame beggars walk and blind men see.

MRS. CRATCHIT: Bless his heart, he does think of the strangest things. (*Calling off left*) Children, come to dinner! (*Cratchit children race in,* PETER *carrying bowl of punch, which he sets at* BOB's *place, right end of table. There is much talking and moving of chairs as everyone gets into place around table.* BOB *ladles out punch into mugs and glasses.*)

BOB: I propose a toast. (*Raising his glass*) To Mr. Scrooge, the founder of the feast.

MRS. CRATCHIT (*Putting down her glass*): Founder of the feast, indeed! I wish I had him here! I'd give him a piece of my mind to feast upon, and I hope he'd have a good appetite for it!

BOB: My dear, the children! It's Christmas Day.

MRS. CRATCHIT: It should be Christmas Day, I'm sure, when one drinks the health of such an odious, stingy, hard, unfeeling man as Mr. Scrooge.

BOB (*Mildly*): My dear, Christmas Day.

MRS. CRATCHIT: I'll drink his health, Robert, for your sake and the day's, but not for his! (*Raising glass*) Long life to him! A Merry Christmas and a Happy New Year! He'll be very merry and very happy, I have no doubt!

BOB: A Merry Christmas to us all, my dears. God bless us!

TIM: God bless us, every one!

BOB (*Picking up carving knife*): And now — the goose! (*All cheer. Blackout. Curtain closes. Spotlight comes up on* SCROOGE *and* 2ND GHOST, *down right.*)

SCROOGE: Spirit, tell me — will Tiny Tim live?

2ND GHOST: I see a vacant chair in that poor room — a crutch without an owner, carefully preserved. If these shadows remain unaltered by the future, Tiny Tim will die.

SCROOGE: No, no! He must *not* die!

2ND GHOST: You can do nothing to change the past, nothing to alter the present. But there is still the future; perhaps in it lie your hope and salvation. I must leave you now. My life upon this globe is very brief. I go, but another spirit comes. (*Bell tolls three times.* 2ND GHOST *exits, right, as spotlight comes up on* GHOST OF CHRISTMAS YET TO COME, *wearing a black robe with a hood hiding his face, down left.* SCROOGE *crosses to him. Spotlight right stage fades out.*)

SCROOGE (*Awed, clasping his hands*): Am I in the presence of the Ghost of Christmas Yet to Come? (3RD GHOST *nods slowly.*) Ghost of the future, I fear you more than any other specter I have seen. But I know you intend to do me good, so I'll bear your company and do it with a thankful heart. Spirit, if you can see the future, show me what has happened to Tiny Tim. (*Live or recorded Christmas hymn is heard.* 3RD GHOST *points to right stage where spotlight comes up on Cratchits.* MRS. CRATCHIT *sits in armchair, hand to brow, weeping.* MARTHA *sits beside her on arm of chair.* PETER, *on stool, is reading from large book.* BELINDA *stands behind him, looking over his shoulder.* NED *and* SALLY *are seated on floor.*)

MARTHA (*Comforting her*): Don't cry, Mother. Our Tim is happy now. He won't ever need his crutch again.

PETER (*Closing book*): Father is late tonight. I think he walks a little slower than he used to.

MRS. CRATCHIT (*Wiping away tears*): I have known him to walk very fast indeed with Tiny Tim on his shoulder. But then, Tim was very light to carry, and his father loved him so, that it was no trouble — no trouble at all.

BELINDA: Here's Father now. (BOB *enters, giving hat to*

MARTHA. MRS. CRATCHIT *rises and motions for him to sit in armchair.*)

BOB: I have visited Tim's grave today. (*To* MRS. CRATCHIT) I wish you could have gone. It would have done you good to see how green a place it is. But you'll see it often. I promised Tim that we would walk there every Sunday. (BOB *speaks gently to children.*) Children, we mustn't grieve — Tim would not want it so. We shall be closer than ever before. When we remember how patient and mild Tim was, I know that we shall not quarrel among ourselves.

ALL (*Ad lib*): No, never, Father. (*Etc.*)

BOB: Then I am very happy — for him, and for us all. (*Spotlight fades out on Cratchits.*)

SCROOGE: Spirit, are these the shadows of things that will be, or is it possible to change the future? Why show me these things if I am past all hope? (3RD GHOST *turns away.*) Spirit, hear me! I am not the man I was. I will honor Christmas in my heart and try to keep it all the year. I will live in the past, the present, and the future. I will not shut out the lessons they teach. (SCROOGE *kneels and clutches* 3RD GHOST'*s robe.*) Oh, speak to me! Give me some hope. Tell me that I may still have time to change. Speak to me! Speak to me! (*Fast fade to blackout.*)

* * * *

SCENE 4

TIME: *Christmas day.*

AT RISE: *Ringing of church bells is heard from offstage. SCROOGE is alone in his office, kneeling near his desk, violently shaking his stool.*

SCROOGE: Speak to me! Tell me it is not too late! (SCROOGE *looks about incredulously and slowly gets to his feet.*) Why, this is my stool! (*Sets it down*) And this is my office! How did I get here? Am I dreaming? (*Dancing a few steps*) I feel as light as a feather — as merry as a schoolboy! (*Hears bells ringing outside*) Church bells! What day is this? I must find out what day it is. (*Opens street door and calls out*) Hello, out there! Come in here a minute! Don't be afraid — come in! (BOY *enters hesitantly.*) What's today, my fine fellow?

BOY: Today? Why, it's Christmas Day!

SCROOGE: Christmas Day! (*Leaping into the air*) Hurrah! I haven't missed it after all! My fine fellow, do you know the grocer's down the street?

BOY: I should hope so.

SCROOGE (*Grabbing* BOY's *hand and shaking it*): An intelligent, a remarkable boy! Do you know whether they've sold the prize turkey that was hanging in the window?

BOY: The one that's as big as I am? It's hanging there now.

SCROOGE: Then go and buy it. (BOY *looks incredulous.*) No, no, I'm serious. Here's the money. (*Gives* BOY *several coins from cash box, then scribbles on piece of paper*) Deliver it to this address in Camden Town. It will be too heavy to carry, so take a cab. And you're not to say where that turkey came from — not a word.

BOY: I won't, sir, thank you, sir. Merry Christmas! (*Runs out*)

SCROOGE (*Calling after him*): Merry Christmas! (*Rubbing his hands together gleefully*) Won't Bob Cratchit be surprised to get that turkey! It's twice the size of Tiny Tim. And he won't know who sent it. How surprised they'll be! (*Church bells peal again.*) Just listen to those bells! Makes me feel good just to hear them. (*Calls through open door*) Merry Christmas!

COLLECTOR (*Coming to door*): Are you speaking to me, sir?

SCROOGE: Of course I'm speaking to you. Come in, come in! (COLLECTOR *enters and* SCROOGE *shakes his hand vigorously.*) How are you? I hope you succeeded yesterday in collecting money for the poor. I'm afraid you don't remember me with much pleasure. Allow me to ask your pardon. (*Getting roll of bank notes from cash box and handing it to* COLLECTOR) Will you have the goodness to accept this?

COLLECTOR: Bless me! Are you serious, Mr. Scrooge?

SCROOGE: If you please, not a farthing less. A great many back payments are included in it, I assure you. Come and see me any time you need help. Will you do that?

COLLECTOR: I will indeed, sir.

SCROOGE: Thank you — thank you a hundred times. Bless you.

COLLECTOR: Bless *you*, Mr. Scrooge, and a very Merry Christmas. (COLLECTOR *exits.*)

SCROOGE (*Skipping to clothes tree*): Merry Christmas, Ebenezer, you old humbug! I'm going to have dinner with my nephew, Fred. He invited me, yes, he did! (*Sings "God Rest Ye Merry, Gentlemen" as he puts on muffler, coat and hat. Exits, singing and dancing. Curtain closes.*)

* * * * *

SCENE 5

TIME: *The next morning.*

SETTING: *Same as Scene 1.*

AT RISE: SCROOGE *is peeking out the half-open street door.*

SCROOGE (*Looking at his watch*): Eighteen and a half minutes past nine. (*Chuckling*) He's late! The day after

Christmas, and Bob Cratchit is late for work. Ah, here he comes now. (SCROOGE *closes door, scurries to desk and busies himself, writing.* BOB *enters hurriedly, whips off his hat, tossing it onto clothes tree, and starts across to his desk nervously.* SCROOGE *looks up, scowling.*) What do you mean by coming to work at this time of day, Bob Cratchit?

BOB: I'm very sorry, sir. I *am* behind my time. It won't happen again.

SCROOGE (*Rising with pretended exasperation*): Now, I'll tell you what, my man. I'm not going to stand this sort of thing any longer. And so (*Clapping* BOB *on the back and laughing*) — I am going to raise your salary! (BOB *staggers, gaping in astonishment.*) A merry Christmas, Bob! A merrier Christmas, my good fellow, than I have given you for many a year! I'll raise your salary and endeavor to assist your struggling family. Tiny Tim shall have the best doctors in London. (*Putting arm around* BOB*'s shoulder*) We'll discuss your affairs this very afternoon, over a Christmas bowl of mulled wine. And I promise you that from this day forth, I will be as good a friend, as good a master, and as good a man as this old city will ever know. May it always be said of me that if any man alive knew how to keep Christmas well, that man was Ebenezer Scrooge.

BOB: May that be truly said of all of us, Mr. Scrooge. (*Clasping his hand gratefully*) God bless you. As Tiny Tim always says, God bless us, every one! (*Live or recorded music of "Joy to the World" is heard from offstage. Curtain closes.*)

THE END

Sherlock Holmes' Christmas Goose

by Sir Arthur Conan Doyle
Adapted by Paul T. Nolan

The famous sleuth uses ingenious means to trap a jewel thief. . . .

Characters

SHERLOCK HOLMES, *the famous detective*
DR. JOHN WATSON, *his friend*
COMMISSIONER PETERSON, *a police official*
HENRY BAKER, *a suspect*
MR. BRECKINRIDGE, *a goose merchant*
JAMES RYDER, *a witness*

SCENE 1

TIME: *The Christmas season in London, in the 1880's.*
SETTING: *Sherlock Holmes's study/living room. Up center is a large sofa. Up right of it is a library table*

covered with papers and books. Down right and left of
the sofa are chairs. Down left is a small table on which
sit a large magnifying glass and a large hat. Doors are
down right and left.

AT RISE: *Christmas music is heard offstage.* HOLMES, *in*
a dressing gown, is stretched out on sofa. Door left
opens, the music stops, and DR. WATSON, *dressed for*
winter, enters.

WATSON *(Full of good cheer)*: Season's greetings,
Holmes. Season's greetings. (*Looks at* HOLMES) Oh,
are you asleep? Sorry.

HOLMES: No. Come in. Come in.

WATSON: Are you thinking?

HOLMES: Always. Even when I'm sleeping.

WATSON: Perhaps I interrupt you.

HOLMES: Not at all. I'm glad to see you. I have a case I'd
like to discuss with you.

WATSON: Another crime?

HOLMES: It is a puzzle, a striking and bizarre one—but
no crime. A perfectly trivial matter, really. *(Jerks*
thumb in direction of hat on table) But interesting.

WATSON *(Removing coat and hat)*: Does it have anything
to do with that old hat?

HOLMES *(Smiling)*: Very good, Watson. Very observant.
(Pauses) You know Commissioner Peterson, of course.

WATSON: Yes. Is it his hat?

HOLMES: No, no, he found it. Its owner is unknown.

WATSON *(Going to table and picking up hat)*: How did
you get it? *(Sits, with hat on his lap)*

HOLMES: It arrived on Christmas morning in the company of a good fat goose.

WATSON: Where's the goose?

HOLMES: At this moment I assume it is roasting in front
of Peterson's fire. But back to the hat. Early Christmas

morning, Peterson was returning from a party, making his way homeward down Tottenham Court Road. In front of him he saw in the gaslight a tall man, walking with a slight stagger, carrying a white goose slung over his shoulder. Then suddenly, a group of young ruffians came out of the shadows and made for the man. The man raised his stick to defend himself and broke a store window back of him.

WATSON: How unfortunate.

HOLMES: Peterson rushed to his aid. But when the man saw Peterson coming, he dropped the goose, his hat fell off, and he ran off.

WATSON: He probably feared he would be arrested for breaking the store window.

HOLMES: Most probably. The mystery now is to find the owner and return the hat.

WATSON *(Looking at hat):* Half of the derelicts in London must have such a hat. I fear this mystery will remain unsolved.

HOLMES: There's no such thing for me as leaving a case unsolved. The man is probably a Mr. Henry Baker. At least that is the name that was on the card tied to the bird's leg. "For Henry Baker." Unfortunately, there are hundreds of Henry Bakers in London.

WATSON: But the goose may not have belonged to the man who dropped the hat.

HOLMES: It probably did. If you will look inside the band, you will see the initials "H.B." Henry Baker, of course. Peterson wants me to find the owner. He would have returned the goose, too, but unfortunately a goose does not keep forever, even in cold weather. So Henry Baker, whoever he is, has lost his Christmas dinner.

WATSON: What do you propose to do, Holmes?

HOLMES: Observe, my dear Watson, observe.

WATSON: What is there to observe? *(Looks at hat closely)* It is just an ordinary black hat, much the worse for wear. The lining is discolored, and the initials "H.B." are starting to fade. It's even spotted, although the poor fellow has tried to cover the spots with ink. This hat tells us nothing. *(Hands hat to* HOLMES*)* Or, at least, I can see nothing.

HOLMES: On the contrary, Watson, you see everything. You fail, however, to reason from what you see. First, we know the man is intelligent.

WATSON: Good heavens, Holmes, how could you know that?

HOLMES: A large hat means a large head with a large brain. *(Examining hat)* In addition, the man was once prosperous. This is an expensive hat—note the band of ribbed silk, and the fine lining—but it's in terrible condition now. So obviously the man has lost his wealth.

WATSON *(Thoughtfully):* All excellent deductions, Holmes.

HOLMES: Finally, he seems to be having some trouble with his wife.

WATSON *(Astonished):* Perhaps you're right about the man's former affluence and his brains, Holmes, but how can you tell his marriage is suffering?

HOLMES *(Holding hat up):* This hat has not been brushed for weeks. When a wife allows a man to go out in such a state, I shall fear that he is having domestic problems.

WATSON: He may be a bachelor.

HOLMES: More likely he was bringing home the goose as a peace offering to his wife. Remember the card upon the goose's leg.

WATSON *(Laughing):* You have an answer for everything, but since no crime has been committed, all of this seems rather to be a waste of energy.

HOLMES *(Rising):* Solving a mystery is never a waste of time. *(Door left opens.* COMMISSIONER PETERSON *enters, holding a carbuncle.)*

PETERSON *(Gasping):* The goose, Mr. Holmes. The goose.

HOLMES *(To* WATSON*):* You see, Watson. Our mystery is about to develop. *(To* PETERSON*)* Yes, Commissioner, what about the goose?

PETERSON *(Holding up the stone):* See here. See what my wife found in its crop.

HOLMES *(Taking stone and examining it):* By Jove, Peterson, this is a treasure.

PETERSON: I think it's a diamond. A precious stone. I tested it, and it cut through glass as if it were putty.

HOLMES: It's more than a precious stone. It is *the* precious stone.

WATSON: Not the Countess of Morcar's blue carbuncle?

HOLMES: Precisely. I read in *The Times* that it had disappeared. The Countess has offered a thousand-pound reward, and that's not a twentieth of its market price.

WATSON: It was missing, I recall, from the Countess's room at the Hotel Cosmopolitan.

HOLMES: Precisely. *(Goes quickly to upstage library table and picks up newspaper)* Ah, here it is. I marked the story. *(Crosses downstage, looking at paper)* John Horner, a plumber, has been arrested. Remember that name, Watson.

WATSON: I will, indeed.

PETERSON: I wonder why Horner put the stone in the goose's crop?

HOLMES: Perhaps he didn't, Peterson. *(Looks at paper)* Let's see. . . . It seems that while the Countess was staying at the hotel, some difficulty occurred in the plumbing. A James Ryder, the attendant, called Horner to take care of the problem.

WATSON: Ryder. I'll remember that name, too.

HOLMES: Ryder took Horner to the Countess's room to do his plumbing, and when he returned, Horner was gone, and the Countess's jewelry box, broken and empty, was lying on the bed.

PETERSON: Sounds open-and-shut.

HOLMES: Nothing, my dear Commissioner, is open-and-shut. Ryder and a maid, a Catherine Curack, examined the room. The stone was gone. They called the authorities, who searched, but found nothing.

WATSON: Was Horner apprehended?

HOLMES: He was arrested and taken to jail, protesting his innocence all the time.

PETERSON: He didn't, of course, have the jewel?

HOLMES: They searched him and his rooms. Nothing was found.

WATSON: What do we do now?

HOLMES: Find Henry Baker, the man with the goose.

WATSON: So the problem is still unsolved.

HOLMES: Exactly, and I now have a plan. *(Goes to library table, drops newspaper, picks up pencil and paper)* Watson, I want you to bring this advertisement to *The Times. (Begins to write, speaking aloud as he does)* "Found on the corner of Goodge Street, a goose and a black felt hat. Mr. Henry Baker can have the same by applying at 6:30 this evening at 221B Baker Street." *(Looks up)* That should flush him out. *(Comes downstage and gives paper to* WATSON)

WATSON: Yes, if he sees the ad. *(Takes paper)*

HOLMES: He'll see it. Have it inserted above the Want Ads, which a man in his condition must be reading.

PETERSON: Good thought.

HOLMES: I shall put the stone away for security. *(Looks at stone carefully with magnifying glass)* See how it gleams and sparkles. This jewel is the nucleus and focus of crime. Although it was discovered only twenty years ago, this stone has been responsible for two murders, one suicide, and countless robberies. Who would think that such a pretty toy would be a purveyor to the gallows and the prison? I'll lock it in my strong box and send a message to the Countess.

PETERSON: Then, there's nothing for me to do for the present?

HOLMES (*Looking up*): Yes there is, Peterson. You need to get another goose to replace the one you've eaten.

PETERSON: I will. (*Rubs stomach*) It was a splendid bird. I don't think I'll find another so good. (*Exits*)

HOLMES: Well, Watson, let us await developments. (*Curtain falls.*)

* * * * *

SCENE 2

TIME: *Several hours later.*

SETTING: *The same.*

AT RISE: *Stage is dark. Christmas music is heard. Knock is heard at door; music stops, and lights come up slowly.* HOLMES, *wearing coat, is seen sitting on sofa.*

HOLMES: Come in, Watson. Come in.

WATSON (*Entering, carrying large shopping basket*): Peterson asked me to deliver this goose to you.

HOLMES: Good. Set it on the table.

WATSON (*Setting basket on table*): Tell me, Holmes, how did you know who was knocking on the door just now?

HOLMES: For the trained listener, a knock on the door is like the human voice. No two are alike. Your knock is most distinctive.

WATSON *(Removing hat and coat):* No response to our ad yet, I suppose?

HOLMES: Not yet, but I think we can expect a visitor within minutes. *(Knock at door)*

WATSON: Good heavens, how did you know . . .

HOLMES: I saw two men outside the window, looking at a newspaper. *(Abruptly stands; calls out)* Come in. (HENRY BAKER, *without a hat,* and MR. BRECKINRIDGE, *with a cap, enter.*)

BAKER *(Nervously):* Mr. Sherlock Holmes?

HOLMES *(Rising):* Mr. Baker, I assume.

BAKER: Yes, but how did you know?

HOLMES: You look too intelligent to be out in the cold without a hat, if you had one. *(Picks up hat from table)* Is this your hat, Mr. Baker?

BAKER *(Approaching table, picking up hat, and putting it on):* Yes, sir, this is undoubtedly my hat. *(Adjusting hat on his head)* As you can observe, it fits my head, and *(Sadly)* also my present financial condition.

HOLMES: We have had the hat and the goose for several days. Why didn't you advertise?

BAKER: I don't have shillings to waste. I thought the ruffians who attacked me had taken them. *(Pause)* Oh, I'm sorry. This is my acquaintance *(Indicates* BRECKINRIDGE), Mr. Breckinridge.

HOLMES: A dealer in geese, I assume. You brought him to prove your ownership.

WATSON *(Wryly):* A wise move. He could hardly try on the goose to prove it was his.

BRECKINRIDGE *(Angrily):* The blasted goose. I'm tired of hearing about it.

BAKER *(Looking about):* Where is my goose?

HOLMES: We were compelled to eat the bird. It would have been no use to anyone if we had not done so.

WATSON *(Going to table and handing basket to* BAKER*):*
But we have another for you, about the same weight
and perfectly fresh.

BAKER *(Lifting cloth in basket and looking):* It looks like
a fine bird. *(Smiles)* I am grateful. And my wife will be,
too. She was most annoyed that I had lost our Christmas goose.

HOLMES: Of course, we still have the feathers, the legs,
and *(Takes a long pause)* the *crop* of your bird, if you
should want them.

BAKER *(Laughing):* No, sir, thank you. I don't want any
reminders of my adventure.

BRECKINRIDGE: He got the goose from me, if you need
any proof. But since the goose is gone, I can't identify
it, of course.

HOLMES: Do you handle many geese, Mr. Breckinridge?

BRECKINRIDGE: About a thousand during the season.
(Angrily) But this one has caused me more trouble than
all the others put together. *(To* BAKER*)* Well, Mr. Baker,
if our business here is done, let's be going. I'm losing
business, you know.

HOLMES: A few moments, please. That goose was a fine
bird. I might be in the market for another like it.

BRECKINRIDGE: Then see me tomorrow at my shop.

HOLMES: Would I be presuming if I asked where you got
the goose?

BRECKINRIDGE: Yes, you would. I shan't tell you.

WATSON: Good heavens, man, why not?

HOLMES *(Cautioning* WATSON *with a wave of his hand):*
It's a matter of no importance, but I can't understand
why a simple question should anger you.

BRECKINRIDGE: It may be a matter of no importance to
you, but I have been pestered about the goose for days.
If Mr. Baker weren't an old acquaintance, I wouldn't be

here now. When I pay good money for good articles, that should be the end of the business.

HOLMES: And it wasn't.

BRECKINRIDGE: Every minute it's the same question: "Where are the geese?" and "Who bought the goose?" and "What will you take for the goose?" You would think that was the only goose in the world. Why, just an hour ago a man asked me about it. A little fellow he was, with a little wife, and so nervous it almost made me sweat—cold as it is—just to look at him.

HOLMES: I assure you, sir, I have no connection with any other people making inquiries. *(Pauses and smiles)* I was merely concerned whether it was a city-bred or country-bred goose. As a matter of fact, I would bet it was country-bred.

BRECKINRIDGE: Oh, you would, would you?

BAKER *(Nervously):* Don't you think we should be going? My wife is waiting.

BRECKINRIDGE: Just one minute, Mr. Baker. This man thinks he knows more about birds than I do. Are you willing to bet the bird was country-bred?

HOLMES *(Taking a bill from his pocket):* That's right. I'll bet you a fiver.

BRECKINRIDGE *(Reaching for money):* You lose. It was city-bred.

HOLMES *(Holding money back):* Just one minute, I'd like proof.

BRECKINRIDGE *(Smiling):* And I just happen to have it with me, Mr. Know-it-all. *(Reaches in pocket and brings out paper)* Now, then, Mr. Cocksure, you see this. *(Holds out paper)*

HOLMES: Well? *(Looking at paper)*

BRECKINRIDGE: That's a list of the folks from whom I buy. And that's the list of those to whom I sell. You see:

"Henry Baker." And you see where I got that goose: Mrs. Oakshott, 117 Brixton Road—249. Right here in the city. And the date, December 22. Well, what have you got to say now?

HOLMES *(Feigning irritation):* You win. Here's your money. *(Hands him the bill)*

BRECKINRIDGE: I don't like to take the money. *(Takes it, examines it, and puts it in his pocket)* But geese are my business, and you're my goose today. *(Laughs)*

BAKER *(Insistently):* I really must take my goose and go home now.

BRECKINRIDGE: I'll go along with you. *(To* HOLMES*)* And Mr. Holmes, if you ever want to do any betting again, come and see me. *(Laughs as he exits)*

BAKER: Thank you, Mr. Holmes. You've made this a merry Christmas for me. *(Exits.* HOLMES *moves downstage, deep in thought.)*

WATSON *(Irritated):* That fellow was rude.

HOLMES: That's just what I wanted to happen, Watson. He never would have shown us that list if he hadn't been a betting man—not for ten times what I lost to him.

WATSON: You didn't know it was a city bird.

HOLMES: Of course. I had to know and say otherwise—so I could be sure he would bet. He would not have bet if I had been right.

WATSON: I guess our next stop is Mrs. Oakshott, the one who sold the bird to him.

HOLMES: I don't think that will be necessary. I think our criminal will find us.

WATSON: Good heavens, Holmes, why would he do that?

HOLMES: If he's read the ads, and I am sure he has, he'll come to us for the goose.

WATSON: Holmes, if I were a betting man *(Sudden knock*

at door) . . . I'd lose my bet. (*Goes to door and opens it to* RYDER)

RYDER: Is this the residence of Mr. Sherlock Holmes?

WATSON: It is. Come in. (RYDER *enters. He is a small man.*)

RYDER (*Approaching* WATSON): Are you Sherlock Holmes?

WATSON (*Gesturing toward* HOLMES): No. I'm Dr. Watson. He's Holmes.

RYDER (*Crossing to* HOLMES): Then you're the man that advertised about the lost goose?

HOLMES: And the hat, too. Don't forget the hat.

RYDER: Of course. The hat, too. I've come about them both.

HOLMES: Indeed. And who, sir, are you?

RYDER: I am the owner.

HOLMER: Indeed. And what is your name?

RYDER: Henry. Henry Baker. My name was on the goose.

HOLMES (*Exchanging glances with* WATSON; *to* RYDER): I see you have another hat, Mr. Baker.

RYDER: Yes, yes, of course. In this weather I wouldn't go out without a hat.

HOLMES: That is good, because we seem to have lost your hat. Too bad, too—it looked new.

RYDER: Think nothing of it. It's really the goose I've come about.

HOLMES: The goose, sir?

RYDER: Yes, sir, the goose that you mentioned in your ad. It's the goose I want.

HOLMES (*Slowly*): How interesting that you should want the goose more than the hat.

WATSON: Well, the hat probably didn't fit him well.

RYDER (*Agreeing quickly*): That's true. It didn't fit well.

HOLMES (*Slowly*): Too large.

RYDER *(Suspiciously):* Yes, too large.

HOLMES: Oh?

RYDER: I mean too small. But forget the hat. It's just the goose I want. And may I have it now, please? I'm rather in a hurry. My old mother and father are waiting for me.

WATSON: About the goose, Mr. Baker. I'm afraid . . .

RYDER *(Near panic):* You haven't lost my goose, have you? *(Angrily)* I want my goose. I demand it.

WATSON: Now, see here, Mr. Baker. You're being rude.

HOLMES *(Holding up his hand to stop* WATSON): Now, Watson, let's be fair. Mr. Baker's goose was no ordinary bird. *(Turns to* RYDER *and pauses)* In fact, it proved to be a most remarkable bird.

RYDER: It was? I don't understand you, sir.

HOLMES: It laid an egg after it was dead.

RYDER: An egg?

HOLMES: A remarkable egg. The bonniest, brightest little blue egg that was ever seen. *(Pause)* Are you surprised, Mr. Baker? Or should I say Ryder?

RYDER: My name is . . . *(Shocked; then slowly)* James Ryder.

HOLMES: The attendant at the Hotel Cosmopolitan. And the egg is the missing diamond taken from the Countess.

RYDER: I didn't . . . The maid told me about it. *(Goes to chair and sits)*

HOLMES: The maid. Ah, the old story. The temptation of sudden wealth was too much for you. *(Pauses)* You have the makings of a pretty villain in you. You not only took the stone, but you tried to put the blame on Horner, the plumber. You and your confederate, the maid, rifled the jewel-case and raised the alarm, and had that unfortunate man arrested. You then . . .

RYDER *(Leaping from chair and pleading with* HOLMES):

For heaven's sake, have mercy. Think of my father and
mother. It would break their hearts. I've never done
wrong before, and I'll never do it again. Don't bring me
into court, please.

HOLMES *(Sternly):* Get back in that chair. It's all very well
to beg now, but you thought nothing of putting poor
Horner behind bars for a crime he knew nothing about.
(RYDER *sits.*)

RYDER: Give me a chance, Mr. Holmes. I'll leave the
country and hide. Then they'll release Horner. They'd
need my testimony.

HOLMES: We'll consider that. But first, how did the stone
get into the goose?

RYDER: After Horner had been arrested, I had the stone
on me, but I was worried the police would search me.

WATSON: They should have.

RYDER: I could find no place in the hotel I thought would
be safe, so I went to my sister's house, pretending I was
on an errand to get my Christmas goose from her.

HOLMES: Your sister is Mrs. Oakshott.

RYDER: Yes. She gives me a goose every Christmas. She
lets me pick it out.

HOLMES: So you fed your bird the stone. Clever idea.

RYDER: But there were two exactly alike. I didn't know
that until I got the bird home. When I went back to my
sister, she told me about the two look-alikes.

HOLMES: And the other one had gone to the geese merchant Mr. Breckinridge.

RYDER: Yes. I finally saw him just a few hours ago, and he
told me he had sold it.

WATSON: To Mr. Henry Baker.

RYDER *(Nodding):* I thought I was having such good luck
when I read your ad in the newspaper.

HOLMES: But the real Henry Baker had already seen it

and come a-calling. In fact, he just left with his hat and another goose.

RYDER *(Bitterly):* If only I had seen it first.

WATSON *(In despair):* It wouldn't have helped, Ryder. Your head's too small.

RYDER: I guess I'm not very smart.

HOLMES: No, you're not. But maybe you're smart enough never to try anything like this again. Get out.

RYDER *(Rising from chair):* What, sir?

HOLMES *(Pointing toward door):* Get out.

RYDER *(Jumping up, going to* HOLMES*):* Heaven bless you. I'll never, never . . .

HOLMES *(Pushing him aside):* Not another word. Out. (RYDER *starts to speak, but instead rushes out, leaving door open. Christmas music is heard.* WATSON *closes the door, and music stops.*)

WATSON: Good heavens, Holmes, you let the fellow go.

HOLMES: Well, I wasn't really retained by the police to correct their mistakes. And Horner will be released.

WATSON: But, Holmes!

HOLMES: Besides, it's the Christmas season, a time for forgiveness. Which reminds me, I think it is time to investigate another bird. Let's have dinner. *(Curtain)*

THE END

Little Cosette and Father Christmas

Adapted by Adele Thane

from Victor Hugo's Les Misérables

A memorable episode from a masterpiece . . .

Characters

HENRI THENARDIER
MADAME THENARDIER
PONINE, *10* ⎫
ZELMA, *8* ⎬ *their daughters*
COSETTE
SCHOOLMASTER
PIERRE BOULATRUELLE
GYPSY FORTUNE TELLER
JUGGLER
CLOWN
TWO PEDDLERS
WAGONER

Toy Vendor
Candy Seller
Jean Valjean
Villagers
Children

Scene 1

Time: *Christmas Eve, 1823.*

Setting: *The public room of Thenardier Inn in Montfermeil, France. Up right is a window. A counter, holding small wine cask and bread box, runs along back wall and serves as a bar. At left, there is a fireplace with a pot of soup hanging on crane. Near hearth are stool and water bucket. A table with three chairs is right center; another table with chairs stands left center. Bottles of wine and glasses are on tables.*

At Rise: *Seated at table right center are* Schoolmaster *and* Boulatruelle. Gypsy Fortune Teller *is leaning against wall near window.* Thenardier *is behind bar, serving two* Peddlers. Mme. Thenardier *stands at table left center where* Clown *sits, sipping wine. All watch* Juggler, *who is juggling at center. At fireplace,* Cosette *stirs soup, now and then glancing at* Juggler. Juggler *finishes act to a round of applause.*

Mme. Thenardier (*Pulling out a chair*): Bravo! Now, sit down to your supper. You've earned it.

Thenardier: Not so fast, wife. He should pay for his supper like everyone else.

Schoolmaster: What! On Christmas Eve? Come, Thenardier, make a gift of a bowl of soup to the Juggler for entertaining us.

Thenardier (*Grudgingly*): Oh, very well.

Juggler (*Bowing*): I thank you, monsieur. (*He sits and*

waggles his fingers.) A bowl of hot soup will keep my fingers nimble in the bitter cold outside.

MME. THENARDIER *(Getting soup bowl from under counter):* Do you perform in the square tonight?

JUGGLER: Yes, madame.

THENARDIER: It's good business for the town to have a carnival at Christmas time. (MME. THENARDIER *crosses to fireplace with soup bowl.)*

1ST PEDDLER: You mean, it's good business for your inn.

MME. THENARDIER *(Looking into pot, then, to* COSETTE*):* You careless girl! Can't you see the soup is boiling down? Put some water in the pot!

PONINE *and* ZELMA *(Off left):* Mamma! Mamma! We want you!

MME. THENARDIER: Yes, my pets. I'm coming. *(She sets bowl on mantelpiece and exits.* COSETTE *pours last of water from bucket into pot.* GYPSY *crosses to table right center.)*

GYPSY *(Producing deck of cards):* My cards can tell your future, good gentlemen.

BOULATRUELLE: My future is past, Gypsy. I am an old man. Tell the schoolmaster's future. He is young. (GYPSY *sits opposite* SCHOOLMASTER *and pantomimes telling his fortune.* MME. THENARDIER *re-enters, followed by* PONINE *and* ZELMA. *Girls skip to center of room and sit, playing with rag doll.* MME. THENARDIER *fills* JUGGLER*'s bowl with soup and carries it to table where he is sitting with* CLOWN. *While* COSETTE *sweeps floor, she watches following action with fascination.)*

CLOWN *(Nodding toward* PONINE *and* ZELMA*):* You have two pretty children there, madame. What are their names?

MME. THENARDIER: Ponine is the older, and the little one

is Zelma.

CLOWN *(To girls):* You are very fond of your dolly, aren't you, mamzelles?

PONINE *and* ZELMA: Oh, yes, monsieur.

CLOWN: And you would miss her if she should disappear, wouldn't you?

PONINE *(Puzzled):* Disappear?

CLOWN: Yes—like this! *(He deftly slips doll into a side pocket of his baggy pantaloons.)* There! She's gone!

ZELMA *(Laughing):* No, she isn't. She's in your pocket. *(Girls try to reach into his pocket, and he turns it inside out to show them it is empty.* NOTE: *The trick is to have two pockets set in the pantaloons: one holds doll, the other is pocket that is turned inside out. An identical doll is set inside bread box before play begins.)*

PONINE *(Frowning):* There must be a hole somewhere, and dolly has fallen through. (CLOWN *stretches elastic in ruffle and shakes his leg.)*

CLOWN: You see? Nothing.

ZELMA *(Whimpering):* She really has disappeared.

CLOWN: In that case, there's only one thing to do.

PONINE: What's that?

CLOWN: Collect enough money to buy a new doll.

PONINE: Where will the money come from?

CLOWN: Out of the air. *(He proceeds to pick coins from the air, dropping them into his hat.* NOTE: *This is the usual "palming" trick. He appears to pick a coin off his knee, another from* SCHOOLMASTER's *wine glass, a third from tip of* MME. THENARDIER's *nose, and three more coins from* BOULATRUELLE's *beard.)*

BOULATRUELLE: If I could pick francs out of my beard as easily as that, I'd give up mending roads and retire to Paris.

CLOWN *(Offering his hat to girls):* There you are, mamzelles—money for a new dolly.

PONINE *(Excitedly):* Mamma, is it enough to buy the Princess doll at the carnival?

MME. THENARDIER *(Examining coins):* Bah! That's not real money—it's fake! *(To* CLOWN*)* Give them back their own doll, monsieur.

CLOWN: But I don't have the doll, madame. Your husband has it.

THENARDIER: What!

CLOWN: If monsieur will look in the bread box . . . *(*THENARDIER *raises bread box cover and lifts out rag doll.)*

THENARDIER: I can't believe it! *(There is general laughter, and* CLOWN *returns doll to girls, who follow him over to his table.)*

ZELMA: Show us some more magic, Monsieur Clown. *(He sits and entertains them.* TWO PEDDLERS *exit.* WAGONER *enters right.)*

WAGONER: Madame Thenardier! The watering trough is dry, and my horse needs a drink.

MME. THENARDIER: Cosette, take a bucket of water to this man's horse.

COSETTE: There is no water, ma'am. The cistern is empty.

MME. THENARDIER *(Snatching up bucket and forcing it into* COSETTE*'s hand):* Then go to the spring and get some, you lazy girl! *(She shoves* COSETTE *toward door right.)*

COSETTE: But the spring is almost a mile away—and it's so dark in the woods.

MME. THENARDIER *(Grimly):* Which do you fear most— the dark or the whip? *(She points to whip hanging in corner.)*

COSETTE *(Cringing):* I'll go, ma'am.

MME. THENARDIER: Wait! *(She gets a coin from cash box under counter.)* Here is fifteen sous. Get a loaf of bread at the baker's as you come back. *(*COSETTE *puts coin in* *pocket of her apron.*) Now, be off with you, and don't dawdle along the way. *(She pushes her outside and shuts door with a slam.)* That's the worst girl that ever was! *(Curtain)*

* * * * *

SCENE 2

SETTING: *Main street of village, in front of curtain. Candy booth and toy booth are center. Lighted paper lanterns are strung around booths and across stage. On counter of toy booth stands large china doll, with coronet on its head. Placard reads:* GENUINE PRINCESS DOLL. *Sign pointing off left reads:* TO THE SPRING. *Scene may be played before curtain.*

BEFORE RISE: TOY VENDOR *and* CANDY SELLER *stand at booths. Several* VILLAGERS *and* CHILDREN *stop at booths, looking at various items. Crowd moves off, and* COSETTE, *carrying bucket, enters right. She stops and gazes longingly at china doll.*

TOY VENDOR *(Kindly):* Well, little one, what can I do for you?

COSETTE: Please—may I just *look* at the beautiful Princess?

TOY VENDOR: It costs nothing to look.

COSETTE: I've never had a doll in my life.

TOY VENDER: Where are you going with that bucket, child?

COSETTE: To the spring.

TOY VENDOR: Only a cat could find its way to the spring without a lantern tonight.

COSETTE: Oh, I know the way. Thank you for letting me look at the Princess. (CHILDREN *race onstage and gather in front of toy booth, jostling* COSETTE *rudely aside. She crosses left and peers off fearfully.)* How dark it is in the woods! What if I should meet a wild beast—or a *ghost!* I'll go back and tell Madame Thenardier the water in the spring is frozen. *(She starts back, then hesitates.)* But I'll get a whipping. *(After a pause)* I'll count to ten, and then I'll run through the woods so fast nothing can catch me. One, two, three . . . *(She counts to ten and then dashes off left.* CHILDREN *exit.* SCHOOLMASTER *and* BOULATRUELLE *enter right, deep in conversation.)*

SCHOOLMASTER: Are you sure, Pierre?

BOULATRUELLE: As sure as I am that my name is Pierre Boulatruelle. I saw him go into the woods at this spot. *(Points)* I'd have known him anywhere. He was a convict at Toulon twenty-five years ago when I was there. We were galley slaves on the same chain.

SCHOOLMASTER: What was his crime?

BOULATRUELLE: He stole a loaf of bread to feed his sister and her starving children. He was sentenced to five years in the galleys for that.

SCHOOLMASTER: Incredible!

BOULATRUELLE: He escaped many times, but he was always caught, and his sentence was extended. In the end, it added up to nineteen years. After his release, I heard he became a respected and well-to-do-citizen— though I must say, when I saw him this evening, he was wearing a torn yellow coat and old fur cap.

SCHOOLMASTER: Did you speak to him?

BOULATRUELLE: No. I doubt if he even saw me. He just walked into the woods.

SCHOOLMASTER: What is his name?

BOULATRUELLE: Jean Valjean.

SCHOOLMASTER *(Shaking his head):* Poor unfortunate

man! Nineteen years in the galleys for having taken a
loaf of bread! Well, I must be getting home to my wife.
Won't you come and have supper with us? It must be
lonely in your hut, eating by yourself.

BOULATRUELLE: It is, Schoolmaster—especially on
Christmas Eve.

SCHOOLMASTER (*Taking his arm*): Come with me, my
friend. (*They exit.* COSETTE *enters, struggling with
bucket of water. She takes a few steps and then sets the
bucket down. After a moment, she picks it up and tries
to move ahead, but falls and begins to cry.*)

COSETTE: Oh, I can't go on. (JEAN VALJEAN *enters, carrying knapsack. He stops beside* COSETTE.)

VALJEAN (*Compassionately*): Child, that bucket is too
heavy for you to carry. Let me carry it for you.

COSETTE (*Startled; rising*): Oh, monsieur, thank you.

VALJEAN: Have you far to go?

COSETTE: Not much farther.

VALJEAN: How old are you, and what is your name?

COSETTE: I'm eight years old, monsieur, and I'm called
Cosette.

VALJEAN: Do you have a mother, Cosette?

COSETTE (*Thoughtfully*): I don't know. I don't think so.
(*Sighing*) Everybody else has a mother, but I don't
believe I ever had one.

VALJEAN: Who is it that has sent you out after water at
this time of night?

COSETTE: Madame Thenardier. She's the innkeeper's
wife.

VALJEAN: And is there no servant at the inn—only you?

COSETTE: Yes, monsieur.

VALJEAN: Do you work all day?

COSETTE: Yes, but sometimes, when my work is done, I
amuse myself. I have a little lead sword, no longer than

that. *(She holds up her little finger.)* I wrap it in a cloth and pretend it is a doll. Then I rock it to sleep.

VALJEAN *(Starting toward center):* Well, show me the way to the inn. I'm going to lodge there tonight. *(Points to toy and candy stalls.)* What's all this? Is there a fair in the village?

COSETTE: Oh, no, it's Christmas Eve! Surely you know that! Indeed, I think you must be Father Christmas himself, you've been so kind to me.

VALJEAN: So it's Christmas, is it?

COSETTE *(Excitedly; pointing off right):* See the lanterns and stalls. There are so many beautiful things! But the *most* beautiful is the Princess.

VALJEAN: What Princess?

COSETTE: There—in the toy stall—the Princess doll. Only a queen could afford to have a doll like that.

VALJEAN: Does she cost a good deal?

COSETTE: Oh, yes! No one in the village is rich enough to buy her. Mme. Thenardier's daughters, Ponine and Zelma, have begged and begged their mother to buy the Princess doll for them, but she says the price is too high.

VALJEAN: I suppose you would like to have such a doll for your own, eh, Cosette?

COSETTE *(Sadly):* Oh, monsieur, how would the likes of me ever have such a fine doll? It is enough that I may look at her. *(She touches his arm.)* Please, I'll take the bucket now. If madame sees you carrying it, she will beat me.

VALJEAN *(Giving her the bucket):* Yes, quite so. Go on ahead, Cosette. I have an errand to do. Is the inn close by?

COSETTE *(Pointing off right):* Just past the corner there. Follow the lanterns. *(She exits right.* VALJEAN *goes to toy booth.)*

VALJEAN: How much is the large doll, madame? *(Takes out a purse)*

TOY VENDOR: Fifty francs.

VALJEAN *(Counting out the coins):* There you are. Would you wrap it up, please?

TOY VENDOR: Certainly, monsieur. I have a box all ready. *(She takes box from under counter and puts doll in it.)* Every little girl in the village has wished for this doll. Is it for that poor waif who was with you? *(Shakes her head)* She won't have it long.

VALJEAN: Why won't she?

TOY VENDOR: The innkeeper's wife will give it to her own miserable children. *(She passes box to* VALJEAN.)

VALJEAN: We shall see. Merry Christmas, my good woman.

TOY VENDOR: Thank you, monsieur. Merry Christmas to you! (VALJEAN *exits right.)*

* * * * *

TIME: *An hour later.*

SETTING: *Same as Scene 1.*

AT RISE: WAGONER *is seated at table, left, drinking glass of wine.* MME. THENARDIER *is wiping table right center.* THENARDIER, *behind bar, is polishing glasses, roast lies on a platter on counter.*

WAGONER *(Rising; impatiently):* What is taking that Cosette so long? My horse will die of thirst before she gets back with the water.

MME. THENARDIER: She's a lazy slowpoke, that one, and the only thing that will make her move is the whip. (COSETTE *enters right with bucket, which she sets down wearily.)* Oh, it's you, at last! You've taken your time. Have you been playing?

COSETTE: Oh, no, ma'am. There's a gentleman in a yellow coat who's coming to lodge, and I showed him the way.

MME. THENARDIER: Well, where is he?

COSETTE: He went to do an errand.

MME. THENARDIER (*To* WAGONER): Here is a girl as big as my fist who can tell a lie as big as a house! (*To* COSETTE) There's no lodger, and you know it. You've been to the carnival, you sly wretch, taking in the sights, while this Wagoner's horse can't stand on four legs for want of a drink. Hand me that whip! (VALJEAN *appears in doorway.*)

VALJEAN: Good evening, madame. This little girl directed me here. I should like supper and lodging for the night.

MME. THENARDIER (*Sneering as she takes in his appearance*): So, you are the "gentleman" Cosette has brought here. I'm sorry, but I have no room.

VALJEAN: Put me anywhere—in the attic or the stable. I will pay the same as I would for a bedroom.

MME. THENARDIER: Forty sous. In advance.

WAGONER (*Aghast*): Forty sous! But it's only twenty sous.

MME. THENARDIER: Mind your own affairs, and go out and water your horse! It's forty sous for this man. I don't put up vagabonds for less. It ruins an inn's reputation. (WAGONER *takes water bucket and exits.* VALJEAN *sits at table right center.* MME. THENARDIER *grudgingly brings him a bottle of wine and a glass, which she bangs down on the table. Suddenly she turns to* COSETTE.) Oh! I forgot about the bread! Cosette! Where is the bread I sent you for?

COSETTE (*Terrified*): Please, ma'am, the baker was shut.

MME. THENARDIER: You should have knocked.

COSETTE: I *did* knock—I knocked and knocked, but he didn't open.

MME. THENARDIER: I'll find out tomorrow if you're telling the truth, and if you're not, you'll feel the whip on your back. Give me back the fifteen-sou piece. (Cos-ETTE *searches frantically in her apron pocket for coin.*) Well, where is it? Have you lost it, or do you want to steal it from me? *(She takes down the whip.)*

COSETTE *(Starting to cry):* I must have lost it at the spring. I'll go back and look for it. Just don't beat me! *(She cowers as* MME. THENARDIER *raises the whip.)*

VALJEAN *(Leaping up):* Stop, Madame! I just saw something fall out of Cosette's pocket and roll over there. It may be the money. *(He stoops down with his back to them and searches on floor near fireplace. In clear view of audience, he quickly takes coin from his pocket and pretends to pick it up.)* Yes, here it is—a fifteen-sou piece.

MME. THENARDIER *(Snatching it from him):* Yes, that's it. *(To* COSETTE; *ferociously)* Don't let that happen again! *(She hangs up whip.)* Well, don't stand there idle. Get on with your knitting. You have to work if you expect to eat. I can't feed you for nothing. (COSETTE *sits on stool, takes wool and needle from edge of hearth and begins to knit.)*

VALJEAN *(Kindly):* What are you making, Cosette?

MME. THENARDIER *(Sharply):* Stockings for my little daughters.

VALJEAN *(Looking at* COSETTE's *bare legs):* How long will it take for her to knit that pair of stockings?

MME. THENARDIER: At least three or four days, the lazy thing.

VALJEAN: What will they be worth when they're done?

MME. THENARDIER: At least thirty sous.

VALJEAN: Will you sell them to me for five francs?

MME. THENARDIER *(Shrewdly):* Yes, you can have the stockings for five francs. We never refuse our customers anything . . . *(Holding out her palm)* as long it's paid for in advance.

VALJEAN *(Putting coin in her hand):* I'll buy this pair of stockings. Here's the money for it. *(Turning to* COSETTE*)* Now, Cosette, your time belongs to me. Play, my child. (MME. THENARDIER *glares at* VALJEAN.)

COSETTE *(Timidly):* Is it true, ma'am? May I play a little?

MME. THENARDIER *(Angrily): Play! (She crosses to bar and puts coin on counter. Aside to* THENARDIER*)* Who can that man be?

THENARDIER: He must be one of those millionaires who dress like beggars, so they won't be robbed. *(Meanwhile,* COSETTE *takes box from corner. It contains small sword, which she wraps in a torn kerchief and rocks in her arms.* VALJEAN *smiles down at her tenderly, then returns to table and sits.* MME. THENARDIER *approaches.)*

MME. THENARDIER *(With feigned cordiality):* What will monsieur have to eat?

VALJEAN: Meat and cheese. *(She motions to* THENARDIER, *who goes off to get food, then sits down across from* VALJEAN.)

MME. THENARDIER: Monsieur, I'm very willing that Cosette should play. But, you see, she's poor. She must work.

VALJEAN: Is she related to you in any way?

MME. THENARDIER: I should say not. She's a little pauper that we have taken in out of charity. Worthless child. We do all we can for her, but we're not rich, and we have our own two girls to provide for. *(Laughter is heard off left.)* Ah, here they come now! *(She stands as* PONINE *enters, carrying kitten, followed by* ZELMA, *who carries rag doll.)*

PONINE: Look, Mamma! We have kitty, and we're going

to dress her up in dolly's clothes. Here, Zelma, you hold her while I put the dress on her. (ZELMA *takes dress off doll, tosses doll over near* COSETTE, *and takes kitten.* COSETTE *gazes at doll longingly.* PONINE *stuffs kitten's legs into doll's clothes.*) This kitty doll is more fun than the other.

ZELMA: Let me tie on the bonnet.

PONINE: All right, but I'll pretend she's my little girl. I will be a lady. I'll come to visit you, and you must admire her. When you see her whiskers, you must act surprised. And when you see her ears and tail, you will be even more surprised. (THENARDIER *brings in plate of food, sets it down before* VALJEAN, *then goes behind bar.*)

MME. THENARDIER *(To* VALJEAN*):* Aren't my little girls adorable? *(She joins her husband behind bar, and they begin to count money.* COSETTE *slyly picks up doll and plays with it.*)

ZELMA *(Seeing* COSETTE*):* Mamma, look at Cosette! She's playing with our doll! Make her stop!

MME. THENARDIER *(Furiously):* Cosette! Put that doll down *at once!* (COSETTE *places doll gently on floor, then bursts into tears.*)

VALJEAN *(Rising from table):* What is the matter?

MME. THENARDIER *(Angrily):* That little beggar has dared to *touch* my children's doll.

VALJEAN: And what if she did?

MME. THENARDIER *(Screaming):* With her *horrid, dirty* hands? *(As* COSETTE *cries louder)* Be still, you little wretch! I'll give you something to cry about.

VALJEAN: Just a moment, madame. Calm yourself. *(He opens box on table and takes out Princess doll.* THENARDIERS *all gasp in amazement.* VALJEAN *carries doll over to* COSETTE.*) Here, child, this is for you.

COSETTE *(In awe):* For me? But it's the Princess.

VALJEAN: This is for you, Cosette. The Princess doll is your very own. Take her.

COSETTE *(Tremulously):* May I, ma'am?

MME. THENARDIER *(Impatiently):* How stupid you are! Don't you understand? The gentleman is *giving* you the doll.

COSETTE *(Taking it reverently):* Oh, thank you, monsieur. You're very good to me. I will call her Catherine. Madame, may I put her in a chair?

MME. THENARDIER *(Sullenly, turning away):* I don't care. (COSETTE *puts doll in chair, then sits on floor in front of it, motionless.*)

VALJEAN: Why don't you play?

COSETTE *(Shyly):* Oh, I *am* playing.

ZELMA: Mamma, I want to play with the new doll!

PONINE: Cosette doesn't know how to play with it, Mamma. Give it to me!

MME. THENARDIER: Hush, girls! It's past your bedtime. Run along now, and be sure to set your shoes on the hearth for St. Nicholas to fill.

PONINE *and* ZELMA *(As they run off left):* We will, Mamma! Good night.

MME. THENARDIER: I'll come and tuck you in. *(To* VAL- JEAN, *with cloying sweetness)* You must be very tired, monsieur. My husband will show you to your room.

VALJEAN *(Taking up knapsack):* That won't be necessary. Where is your stable?

MME. THENARDIER: The stable! Mercy, no! You must have the best room in the inn. *(With a little curtsey)* Good night, monsieur. *(She exits left.)*

VALJEAN *(Turning to* THENARDIER, *who is lighting a can- dle):* I assure you, innkeeper, I shall rest as well in the stable.

THENADIER: Impossible! Come this way, please, monsieur. *(He exits left with candle.* VALJEAN *pauses beside* COSETTE, *puts his hand gently on her head.)* Good night, Cosette, my child.

COSETTE *(Looking up at him adoringly):* Good night— Father Christmas. *(He exits.* COSETTE *takes doll out of chair and kisses it.)* Close your eyes, Catherine, and I will sing you to sleep. *(She rocks doll and begins to sing lullaby, as curtain falls.)*

* * * * *

SCENE 3

TIME: *Early next morning, Christmas Day.*

SETTING: *The same.*

AT RISE: THENARDIER *is making out a bill at table right center.* MME. THENARDIER *is in doorway down left, shouting offstage.*

MME. THENARDIER: Cosette! Light the fire in the girls' room, then sweep the front stairs.

COSETTE *(Offstage):* Yes, madame.

MME. THENARDIER *(Crossing to* THENARDIER*):* What are you writing there, Henri?

THENARDIER: The stranger's bill. I've charged him twenty-three francs for his night's lodging.

MME. THENARDIER: Twenty-three francs! Do you think he'll pay it?

THENARDIER: A rich one like that? Of course he'll pay it.

MME. THENARDIER: That doll he gave Cosette must have cost at least fifty francs. After he is gone, I'm going to kick Cosette out of the house for good, and keep the doll for the girls.

THENARDIER: Are you, really?

VALJEAN *(Offstage):* Merry Christmas, Cosette!

THENARDIER: Sh-h! Here he comes!

COSETTE *(Offstage):* Merry Christmas, Monsieur! (VAL-
JEAN *enters with knapsack.)*

MME. THENARDIER: Up so early? Are you leaving us?

VALJEAN: Yes, I must be on my way. What do I owe?

THENARDIER *(Rising):* Here is the bill, monsieur. (VAL-
JEAN *glances at it, then stares hard at Thenardier.)*

VALJEAN: Innkeeper, do you have a good business here?

THENARDIER *(Shrugging):* So-so.

MME. THENARDIER: The times are very hard, and we
have so many expenses. Why, that Cosette eats us out
of house and home.

VALJEAN: Suppose you were relieved of her?

MME. THENARDIER: Why, what do you mean?

VALJEAN: Suppose I take her away with me?

MME. THENARDIER *(Delighted):* Ah, monsieur, you can
take her, keep her, and be blessed for it!

VALJEAN: Very well, call the child.

MME. THENARDIER *(Going to door left):* Cosette!

VALJEAN: In the meantime, I will pay my bill. Twenty-
three francs. *(He gives* THENARDIER *the money.)*

THENARDIER: Thank you, monsieur. Now as to this matter of Cosette. I cannot consent so easily to your taking
her away from us.

MME. THENARDIER *(Turning from door; perplexed);*
What sort of talk is this, Henri?

THENARDIER: I've had her since she was a baby, and I
should miss her. Oh, it's true, she has her faults and
costs us a lot of money, but we must do something for
sweet charity's sake. I love this poor orphan and so
does my wife—though she can be a bit hasty at times.

MME. THENARDIER: Henri, have you lost your wits?

THENARDIER *(Soothingly):* Now, you *know* you love Cosette deep down in your heart. And one does not simply give away a child—(*Snapping his fingers*) like that!—to the first traveler who asks for her. You understand, monsieur?

VALJEAN (*Opening his purse*): I understand.

THENARDIER: Now *supposing*—just *supposing*—that I were to let her go with you. I should want to know where she went. I'd come see her, and she would know I was still watching over her.

VALJEAN (*With a wry smile*): Watching over her?

THENARDIER: I don't even know your name. If you take her away, I must at least see some identification, a passport, something.

VALJEAN (*Firmly*): Monsieur Thenardier, people do not need a passport to come a few miles from Paris. If I take Cosette, I take her, that is all. You will not know my name nor where I live, and it's my intention that Cosette shall never see you again in her life.

THENARDIER: But monsieur—

VALJEAN (*Coldly*): Come to the point, Thenardier. What is your price?

THENARDIER (*Without hesitation*): Fifteen hundred francs.

VALJEAN (*Laying three bank notes on the table*): There it is. Now bring Cosette here.

MME. THENARDIER (*Calling off left*): Cosette! Come here at once!

COSETTE (*Running on, carrying doll*): Yes, ma'am?

MME. THENARDIER: How would you like to go away?

COSETTE (*Puzzled*): Away? But where?

VALJEAN (*Smiling warmly at* COSETTE): With me, child. You are coming with me to be my little girl.

COSETTE (*To doll; delightedly*): Did you hear that, Catherine? We're going away with Father Christmas!

I'm to be his little girl! (VALJEAN *opens door right*.)

VALJEAN: Look, Cosette! It's Christmas morning. Come, take my hand. We will leave this house where you are so mistreated and go to a place where you will be loved and cared for always.

COSETTE: Will I have to sweep and carry water?

VALJEAN: No. You will play all day long and, for the first time in your life, you will know what it is to be happy and have a singing heart. (COSETTE *and* VALJEAN, *hand in hand, exit. Curtain*)

THE END

A Merry Christmas

Adapted from Louisa May Alcott's *Little Women*

by Walter Hackett

Meg, Jo, Beth, and Amy share a simple and loving Christmas in this dramatization from Little Women.

Characters

NARRATOR
JO
MEG
AMY
BETH
MRS. MARCH
HANNAH
MR. KIMBALL
BOY
WOMAN
MR. LAURENCE

NARRATOR: This is a Christmas story from a book that all the world knows and loves. It's about the lives of four young girls, and the name of it is *Little Women*. Our story begins on the day before Christmas in the year 1862. A heavy snow falls quietly, cloaking the little town of Concord, Massachusetts, with an extra layer of whiteness. Set back from the road to Lexington stands the March family house. In the comfortable old parlor are four young ladies. Sprawled on the floor, looking into the fireplace, is tomboy Jo.

JO (*In a complaining voice*): Christmas won't be Christmas without any presents.

NARRATOR: Meg, the eldest and prettiest, looks at her old dress.

MEG (*Sighing*): It's so dreadful to be poor!

NARRATOR: And Amy, the youngest, looks up from her knitting.

AMY: I don't think it's fair for some girls to have plenty of pretty things and other girls nothing at all.

NARRATOR: To this, Beth, the quiet one, adds her comment.

BETH: Never mind. We have Father and Mother and each other.

NARRATOR: The open fire crackles brightly. In the hallway, the old clock laboriously ticks away two minutes. Finally, Meg speaks.

MEG: The reason Mother suggested no presents this Christmas was because it's going to be a hard winter for everyone. She thinks we shouldn't spend money for pleasure when our men are suffering so in the army.

JO: We each have a dollar, and the army wouldn't be much helped by our giving that. I don't expect any presents, but there is a book I'd like so much. What would you like to spend yours on, Beth?

BETH: Some new music.

AMY: I would like a nice box of drawing pencils.

JO: Mother didn't say anything about our money, and I'm sure she doesn't wish us to give up everything.

AMY: What do you mean, Jo?

JO: I say, we should each buy what we want, and have a little fun. I'm sure we work hard enough to earn it.

MEG: I know I do — teaching those tiresome children nearly all day.

JO: You shouldn't complain, Meg. How would you like to be shut up for hours, reading to and waiting on a fussy old lady?

BETH: I hate washing dishes and housework. It makes me cross.

AMY: Suppose you had to go to school with impertinent girls, who laugh at your dresses and label your father if he isn't rich.

JO (*Laughing*): If you mean "libel," say so, and don't talk about labels, as if Papa was a pickle bottle.

MEG: Don't peck at one another. We have enough worries.

JO: Christopher Columbus! We're only making fun of ourselves.

AMY: Jo, don't use such slang expressions. It's not lady-like.

JO: I hate to think I have to grow up and be Miss March and wear long gowns and a prim expression. If I were a boy, I could be in the army with Papa. Instead, I have to stay home and knit, like a poky old woman.

MEG: Jo, you're too wild, and, Amy, you're too prim.

BETH: And what am I, Meg?

MEG: You're a dear, Beth. (*Briskly*) Enough talk, now. Mother will be home in an hour. Amy, get her slippers. Jo, you light the lamp.

AMY: Marmee's slippers are quite worn. She should have a new pair.

BETH: Why don't I get her a pair with my dollar?

AMY: No, you shan't, Beth. I'm going to buy them.

Jo: I'm the man of the family now Papa is away, and *I*
shall provide the slippers.

Amy: And I shall give her — oh, dear, what will I give
her?

Jo: Why don't we each give her something she needs
most? We'll put the gifts on the table and bring her in
to see them tomorrow morning.

Meg: We've forgotten one thing.

Amy: What's that, Meg?

Meg: Tomorrow is Christmas and we haven't bought
a thing.

Amy: But we've just made up our minds to buy presents
for Marmee.

Beth: Oh, and now it's too late.

Jo: Indeed, it's not! I have the solution. We'll put on our
wraps, hurry to Mr. Kimball's store, buy our gifts,
and hurry home before Marmee arrives. On your feet,
everyone. Off we fly.

Narrator: The girls were quickly into their coats and
out of the house, reaching Mr. Kimball's store just as
he was closing for the day.

Kimball (*Heartily*): Well, well! What a surprise! The
March girls! You just caught me in time. I was about
to lock up.

Jo: You can't until we've bought our gifts, Mr. Kimball.

Beth: We're in a dreadful hurry.

Jo: I want to buy a pair of slippers for my mother.

Beth: And I want to get her two linen handkerchiefs.

Amy: I'd like a bottle of cologne — a specially elegant
bottle.

Meg: And have you a warm pair of gloves, Mr. Kimball?

Kimball (*Laughing*): What if I told you I didn't have
these articles?

Amy: Then we'd take our trade elsewhere.

KIMBALL: I can't allow that to happen, not in my store. Step right this way, young ladies.

NARRATOR: The girls quickly made their purchases, and were home before their mother returned. As the clock struck seven, the March family was just finishing their dinner.

HANNAH (*Speaking with a slight brogue*): Will you and the girls be wantin' anything else, Mrs. March?

MRS. MARCH: Thank you, no, Hannah. We've eaten all we should.

AMY: Besides, I'm sure there's nothing else left to eat.

JO: Here, here, enough of that. Hannah, as man of the house, I give you permission to clear the table.

HANNAH: I won't be needin' any permission for that, Miss Jo. It's a duty I have starin' me in the face every night.

MRS. MARCH: If you girls will follow me into the parlor, I have a surprise for you.

AMY (*Eagerly*): What is it, Marmee?

BETH: Is it something we'll like?

JO: Don't spoil it by asking questions.

MEG: Marmee, you sit here by the fire.

MRS. MARCH (*Sighing with relief*): Ah, thank you. Now, where were we?

AMY: Don't tease us.

MRS. MARCH: Here is your surprise.

JO: A letter.

MRS. MARCH: From your father.

JO: Hoorah!

MEG: Nothing wrong, I hope.

MRS. MARCH: He's quite well.

BETH: What does he say?

MRS. MARCH: I'll read you the part that he wrote especially for you girls.

MRS. MARCH: "As for my dear girls, give them all my love and a kiss. Tell them I think of them by day, pray for them by night, and find my best comfort in their affection at all times. A year seems very long to wait before I see them, but remind them that while we wait we may all work, so that these hard days need not be wasted. I know they will remember all I said to them; and I know they will conquer themselves so beautifully that, when I come back to them, I may be fonder and prouder than ever of my little women."

AMY: I *am* a selfish girl, but I'll try to be better.

MEG: We all will. I'm vain of my looks and hate to work hard, but won't any more, if I can help it.

MRS. MARCH: I'm sure you mean that, Meg.

BETH: Poor Papa! Spending Christmas all alone in an army camp.

JO: Never mind! Next Christmas he'll be here with us by the fire.

MRS. MARCH: Do you remember how you used to play Pilgrim's Progress when you were little girls?

MEG: Indeed we do.

JO: You used to tie bags on our backs for burdens and give us hats and sticks and rolls of paper.

MRS. MARCH: You'd travel through the house from the cellar —

BETH: The cellar was the City of Destruction.

MRS. MARCH: And up and up you'd go to the housetop to what you said was the Celestial City.

JO: What fun it was — especially passing through the Valley where the hobgoblins were.

AMY: I don't remember much about it, except that I was afraid of the cellar and the dark entry.

MEG: If I weren't too old for such things, I'd rather like to play it over again.

Mrs. March: We're never too old for this, Meg, because it's a game we are playing all the time in one way or another. The longing for goodness and happiness is the guide that leads us through many troubles and mistakes to the peace which is a true celestial city.

Jo: You mean it's . . . life itself?

Mrs. March: Yes, Jo. So suppose you see how far you can go before your father comes home.

Amy: Where are our bundles?

Mrs. March: Each of you has her burden, except, maybe, Beth.

Beth: I have my burden to carry. Mine is dishes and dusters, and envying girls with nice pianos, and being afraid of people.

Amy: What a peculiar burden to carry. (*The others laugh good-naturedly.*)

Meg: Let's do it. It is only another name for trying to be good.

Jo: We were in the slough of despair tonight, as it says in the book, and Mother came and pulled us out.

Meg: But like the pilgrims in the book, we'll need our roll of directions.

Mrs. March: Perhaps on Christmas morning you'll find your guide books. (*Quickly*) Now, don't ask any questions. It's going to be a quiet Christmas for us, what with no stockings hung from the mantel and no presents.

Amy (*Mysteriously*): Perhaps it won't be so quiet after all.

Mrs. March: What do you mean, Amy?

Jo (*Quickly*): Nothing at all, Marmee.

Mrs. March: Hannah says the four of you went out just before I came home. I hope you haven't been up to any mischief.

Meg: No, Marmee. It was to perform an errand we'd almost forgotten.

MRS. MARCH: It may be a none-too-bright Christmas Eve for us, but at least we're warm and quite happy — happy enough to sing. Beth, do you feel like playing?

AMY: I'll sing soprano.

JO: No, you sing the alto part.

NARRATOR: And so, they all joined in the singing of Christmas carols until it was time to go to bed. Their Christmas Eve slumber was filled with pleasant dreams, and anticipation of the happiness and joy of Christmas.

JO (*Yawning deeply*): Ohhh! Sleepy. Still gray out. It's . . . it's . . . (*Sudden realization*) Why, it's Christmas morning! (*Excitedly*) Meg, wake up. Wake up!

MEG: Hm-m-m! Leave me 'lone.

JO: Merry Christmas, you sleepyhead.

MEG (*Suddenly waking up*): Oh! Merry Christmas, Jo. (*Pause*) Look what's under my pillow! A book!

JO: And there's one under mine.

MEG: Mine's a Bible.

JO: So is mine.

MEG: Look inside of yours. What does it say?

JO: "To Jo — Here is a true guide book for any pilgrim traveling the long journey. Love, Marmee."

MEG: Mine says the same thing.

JO: Marmee gave us a present after all.

MEG: And she has so little money.

AMY: Merry Christmas!

BETH: A very merry Christmas. (*All four ad lib Christmas greetings.*)

AMY: Did you two get Bibles? Beth and I did.

JO: Yes, we did.

MEG. Let's slip downstairs and see if Marmee is there. I'm anxious to see her face when she discovers what we've done.

NARRATOR: Meanwhile, downstairs, Mrs. March and Hannah are looking out at the new-fallen snow.

MRS. MARCH: This is a fine bright day out, Hannah. A real Christmas.

HANNAH: That it is, Mrs. March. Would you like to see what the girls gave me?

MRS. MARCH: A box of sweets! How thoughtful of them.

HANNAH: Indeed it was. (*Sniffing a bit*) I'm so happy I could have myself a good cry. (*Firmly*) But I won't. (*Pause*) Er, Mrs. March, have you looked on the mantel?

MRS. MARCH: No, Hannah.

HANNAH: Then do so at once.

NARRATOR: As Mrs. March goes to look at the mantel, there's a knock on the door.

HANNAH: Now who can that be on Christmas mornin'?

MRS. MARCH: I'll get it.

BOY: Merry Christmas, ma'am.

MRS. MARCH: Merry Christmas to you, little man.

HANNAH: It's one of the lads that lives on the edge of the pine grove.

BOY: My mother asked me to give you this note.

MRS. MARCH: Thank you. Won't you come in?

BOY: No, Mrs. March. I have to go right back home. Bye.

HANNAH: Is it anything bad, Mrs. March?

MRS. MARCH (*Disturbed*): Yes, it is. Poor things. (*Quickly*) Hannah, is the breakfast on?

HANNAH: I'm just about to cook it, Mrs. March.

MRS. MARCH: Well, don't.

HANNAH: What's that, ma'am?

MRS. MARCH: Get the big basket and load it with wood. Hurry, Hannah.

HANNAH: Just as you say, Mrs. March.

NARRATOR: Just then, the girls come running downstairs.

GIRLS (*Ad lib*): Merry Christmas, Marmee. (*Etc.*)

MRS. MARCH: And the same to you, my dears.

BETH: Thank you for our Bibles.

MEG: It was a wonderful surprise.

AMY: I'll always keep mine.

JO: Same with me. Brr! I'm starved. Are we having muffins?

AMY: And buckwheats with maple syrup?

MRS. MARCH: That depends upon all of you.

JO: On us?

MEG: What do you mean, Marmee?

MRS. MARCH: A note was just delivered to me. It's from that poor widow who lives down the road, the one with the six children.

BETH: Her husband was killed in the war, wasn't he?

MRS. MARCH: The same one. They have no wood to burn and nothing to eat. Will you give them your breakfast as a Christmas present?

JO: Christopher Columbus! It won't hurt us to do without breakfast for once in our lives.

MEG: Of course we will.

AMY: May we go with you?

BETH: We can help you carry things.

MRS. MARCH: I knew you wouldn't refuse. We'll make it up at dinner time. After we come back we'll have bread and milk for breakfast, and that'll tide us over.

NARRATOR: They filled a basket with food and firewood for the widow and her family, and set out for their house.

MEG: This is the house, isn't it, Marmee?

MRS. MARCH: Yes, Meg.

JO: Not a bit of smoke from the chimney, and it's so bitter cold out.

BETH: And to think last night we were complaining.

NARRATOR: Mrs. March had to knock several times before the door was opened, and the widow greeted her Christmas morning visitors.

MARCHES (*Together*): Merry Christmas!

MRS. MARCH: We hurried as fast as possible. May we come in?

WOMAN: Do good angels ever need an invitation?

JO: We certainly are peculiar looking angels — dressed in hoods and mittens.

WOMAN: And welcome just the same.

NARRATOR: Mrs. March cooked a fine Christmas breakfast for the poor family, and the girls helped serve them. How thankful the widow and her children were! The March family returned home, tired but filled with the spirit of Christmas.

MRS. MARCH (*Heartily*): Well, that could have been a far worse breakfast.

JO: Bread and milk for breakfast is good enough for anyone.

BETH: Marmee —

MRS. MARCH: Yes, Beth?

BETH: Did you ever see such expressions as those poor children had when you served them those buckwheats and syrup?

MRS. MARCH: The poor dears. I doubt if they've ever had such a fine breakfast.

AMY: How they ate those muffins!

JO: It's just as well you didn't have any, Amy. You're getting too fat.

AMY: I am not.

MRS. MARCH: Jo, I thought you were carrying a burden.

JO: I am, Marmee. Amy, I apologize.

MRS. MARCH: I'm trying to think. It seems to me that just as that boy delivered me the note, Hannah asked me to do something. Now, what was it she said? Something about the mantel . . . looking on the . . . the . . .

Jo (*Teasing her*): The floor.

MRS. MARCH: No. On the —

BETH: Ceiling?

MRS. MARCH: Ah, I remember. She said for me to look on the mantel. Why, I don't know. (*Gasp of surprise*) Now, what is this? Four packages!

Jo: Don't stare at us. Santa Claus must have left them.

MEG: What could they be? Open them, Marmee!

MRS. MARCH: Now, what have we here? (*Pause*) A pair of gloves! Such warm ones, too. Thank you, Meg.

MEG: I hope they fit.

MRS. MARCH: I'll try them on. (*Pause*) They fit perfectly. And what is this? (*Pause*) Two lovely linen handkerchiefs, which I need so badly. How thoughtful of you, Beth.

BETH: I hemmed them last night.

MRS. MARCH: This one looks like a — now, what can it be?

AMY (*Blurting it out*): It's a bottle of real cologne.

MEG: Amy, you spoiled the surprise.

MRS. MARCH: Not really. Thank you, Amy. I'll wear some on Beth's handkerchiefs. (*Pause*) And this last one. Slippers! Aren't they wonderful, Jo!

Jo: Try them on.

MRS. MARCH (*After a pause*): They're a bit large, Jo.

Jo: Jingo! I'll say they are. You can wear them right over your shoes. I'll change them for you, Marmee.

MRS. MARCH: The sentiment is there, just the same. I think I'm a very lucky mother. I have my family around me. Yesterday I had a letter from your father. This morning we helped our neighbor, and ahead of us —

Jo: Ahead of us is practically the whole day.

Mrs. March: For our Christmas dinner we have a pair of fine, plump chickens.

Jo: And tonight . . . tonight. Meg, you announce the news to Mother.

Meg: Tonight will be the first performance of a new play —

Jo: In four acts.

Meg: Titled "The Operatic Tragedy," written by Miss Josephine March. (*Others applaud.*)

Jo: Thank you.

Mrs. March: Have you written another play, Jo?

Jo (*With mock seriousness*): My greatest effort to date. I shall now do part of a scene for you.

Amy: Oh, no. You'll spoil it.

Mrs. March: Go on, Jo.

Jo: This occurs in the second act.

Beth: The third act.

Jo: No, the second. I've changed it. The heroine — that's Amy — is being kidnapped by the villain. She screams (*Dramatically*), "Roderigo! Save me! Save me!" (*She screams.*)

Hannah: Who screamed? What's the matter?

Jo (*Feigning fierceness*): You, Zara, you are a knave. (*The others start to giggle.*)

Hannah: Now, what's the matter, Miss Jo?

Jo: You are a knave. Stand or I shall shoot you. Ah, now I have you, you rogue. Now you shall perish.

Hannah: I haven't done a thing wrong.

Jo: But you have. You are wicked, bad, ill-fated. I arrest you in the name of the law. (*All laugh*)

HANNAH: The excitement of Christmas Day has gone to your head, Miss Jo. I'm going back to my quiet kitchen.

NARRATOR: Hannah backed hastily into the kitchen, and soon after there was a loud crash.

HANNAH: See what you've done now, you and your foolish theatrics, Miss Jo. I've just crashed into the second-best set of chinaware.

NARRATOR: The kitchen mishap was soon forgotten, and the March family enjoyed a wonderful Christmas dinner together. After dinner, the girls performed Jo's play, much to the enjoyment of their mother and Hannah.

JO (*In deep voice*): And so, my children, I give you my blessing. May your lives be happy from this point onward. I clasp your hands.

MEG: We owe our lives to you, Don Pedro.

JO: And so the curtain falls, signifying the end of the play. (MRS. MARCH *and* HANNAH *applaud.*)

MRS. MARCH: A very fine performance. Well-written, well-acted.

HANNAH: Indeed, I enjoyed every minute of it.

MRS. MARCH: Some day, Jo, you'll be a famous writer. Now, Hannah, do you suppose these hungry performers could be rewarded?

JO: I should like something exotic.

AMY: No, let's have something to eat.

MEG: I'm ashamed to say so, but I'm hungry.

BETH: But we did have such a lovely dinner.

JO: There must be some old chicken bones we can gnaw on.

NARRATOR: All of a sudden, there was an insistent rapping on the door.

HANNAH: I'll answer it, ma'am.

MR. LAURENCE (*Sharply*): Well, woman, open the door wide enough so I can get in. Thank you.

MRS. MARCH (*Surprised*): Good evening, Mr. Laurence. Merry Christmas.

MR. LAURENCE: Same to you. What about your girls? Haven't they any tongues? Can't they wish me a Merry Christmas, too?

GIRLS (*Together*): Merry Christmas, Mr. Laurence.

MR. LAURENCE: You, woman, what's your name?

HANNAH: Hannah, sir.

MR. LAURENCE: Well, take these bundles. Put them on the table.

MRS. MARCH: Aren't you making a mistake, Mr. Laurence? We aren't expecting anything.

MR. LAURENCE: I suppose not, but here they are. Hannah, here, told my cook about your breakfast party.

MRS. MARCH: Breakfast party?

MR. LAURENCE: Don't deny it. I heard all about how you gave your breakfast away to that poor family down the road. I thought I should do something to make it up, and I have. Well, good night, and Merry Christmas.

JO: He's a regular nor'wester, I'd say.

MEG: Marmee, what do you suppose is in those packages?

MRS. MARCH: I don't know.

AMY: Mr. Laurence has never before been in our house.

BETH: He's awfully proud, and he hardly ever speaks to anyone.

JO: Well, we may as well open them.

MRS. MARCH: I suppose we may.

NARRATOR: They excitedly opened the many packages their surprise visitor had brought, and were delighted by the contents.

MEG: Ice cream!

AMY: Two kinds — pink and white.

MRS. MARCH: Real French bonbons. And cake.

BETH: Fruit — so many kinds!

JO: What's in this other long package? (*Pause*)

GIRLS (*Gasping; ad lib*): Flowers. Hothouse roses. Beautiful. Such long stems. (*Etc.*)

JO: Christopher Columbus! And we always thought old Mr. Laurence was so proud.

MRS. MARCH: He's an odd old gentleman. He knew my father years ago.

MEG: He won't let his grandson mix with anyone.

JO: From now on we'll see that his grandson gets to know us; and old Mr. Laurence, too, for that matter.

MRS. MARCH: It shows you can't judge people by their exteriors. Tomorrow we'll write a note of thanks to Mr. Laurence, and all sign it.

JO: Hear, hear!

AMY: I'll deliver it.

MEG: Well, we'd better start before the ice cream melts.

AMY: I just want pink.

BETH: I'll eat either kind.

MRS. MARCH: Hannah, get some plates and spoons.

HANNAH: Right away, Mrs. March.

MRS. MARCH: And, Hannah —

HANNAH: Yes, ma'am.

MRS. MARCH: Bring a spoon and plate for yourself.

HANNAH: That I will, thank you.

JO (*Calling*): And get some vases for these flowers. Christopher Columbus! Hasn't this been the best Christmas anyone could ask for? Well, hasn't it?

ALL (*Ad lib*): The very best. Wonderful. We're very lucky. (*Etc.*)

NARRATOR: It was a fitting end to a perfect Christmas Day. Tired from their various holiday activities, the four happy girls went off to bed.

MRS. MARCH: Well, I'll go and see if my girls are tucked in, Hannah. It has been a busy day for you, hasn't it?

HANNAH: A busy day for all of us, ma'am.

MRS. MARCH: But a fine day, Hannah.

HANNAH: Just about the best day we could have wished for.

MRS. MARCH: We helped our neighbor and our neighbor helped us. (*Pause*) Yes, the spirit of Christmas has lived here all day, and I hope it will for many years to come. (*Warmly*) Merry Christmas!

MEG, JO, BETH, AMY (*Calling, as if from a distance*): Merry Christmas!

THE END

Production Notes

RED CARPET CHRISTMAS

Characters: 5 male; 7 female.
Playing Time: 35 minutes.
Costumes: Modern everyday dress. Bessie wears an apron over her clothes. Anita carries a pocketbook.
Properties: Binoculars, newspaper clipping, plate of cookies, packages, strip of red carpet, dress, hanger, glass of punch, handkerchief, folded note.
Setting: The living room of the Hitchcock family. There is a large window at right. The room is furnished with a sofa, coffee table, chairs, television set; other pieces may be added. A rug is on the floor. There is a telephone on one of the tables. Christmas decorations are in evidence.
Lighting: No special effects.

VIDEO CHRISTMAS

Characters: 3 male; 4 female; male and female extras.
Playing Time: 25 minutes.
Costumes: Everyday clothes. In Scene 2, Carsons wear more dressy clothes.
Properties: Packages; handkerchief and package containing corsage

and card; piece of paper; package containing dress.
Setting: Living room. There is a fireplace, right, on which are hung five Christmas stockings. Door, center, leads to front porch; door, left, leads to another room. Christmas tree is on one side. Furnishings include couch, several chairs, table, etc. Telephone is on table.
Lighting: No special effects.
Sound: Christmas carol music (may be a recording).

CHRISTMAS EVE LETTER

Characters: 3 male; 4 female; extras.
Playing Time: 30 minutes.
Costumes: Everyday dress. Norma, Mr. Johnson and Bob add hats and coats.
Properties: Santa Claus ornaments; angels cut out of silver paper; wrapping paper, ribbon, pocket knife; many packages, including one with doll and necklace; newspaper; table covered with brown paper; Christmas cards; plates of sandwiches and cookies.
Setting: The Stevens living room. A large decorated Christmas tree, with stepladder and box of decorations near it; mantel decorated with cards and greens is up center. Diag-

onally up right is sofa, behind which is a small table, piled with presents. Down right is large easy chair and table with telephone. Exit right leads out; exit left to rest of house.

Lighting: No special effects.

A TREE TO TRIM

Characters: 3 male; 3 female.
Playing Time: 25 minutes.
Costumes: Modern everyday dress. Sam wears coveralls.
Properties: Shorthand pad; pen; cardboard file boxes, full of file cards; large book; sheets of a "manuscript"; Christmas tree; yardstick; paper clips; keys; rubber bands; matches; soap bubble pipe; large cardboard box; stool; red Christmas stocking; red Christmas bell; holly wreath; gold stars.
Setting: Mr. Archibald's study. There are two doors—one down left, leading outside; and one down right, leading to other parts of the house. Down right are an easy chair, a footstool, and an end table. At left are a straight chair and a desk, supporting a typewriter, papers, pencils, eraser, and paper clips.
Lighting: No special effects.

CHRISTMAS COAST TO COAST

Characters: 9 male; 4 female; as many extras as feasible.
Playing Time: 25 minutes.
Costumes: Modern business suit, overcoat and scarf for John, work clothes for Peggy, appropriate uniforms for Milkman and Delivery Boys, extravagant, flashy clothes for Mrs. Schultz and Miss George,

Boy Scout uniform with short pants for Mr. Henries, ordinary suit for Jeffrey Lord, sophisticated outfit with mink coat for Dulcie Baker, work clothes for TV technicians. Extras should wear the costumes appropriate for their parts in "The Twelve Days of Christmas."
Properties: Large potted tree with tag attached, overcoat and scarf, briefcase, water pitcher, letter, telephone, covered bird cage, large crate, large box, egg, several yards of cable, microphones, camera and other photographic equipment, small package, lead pipes, drums.
Setting: A living room, conventionally decorated, with easy chair and draperies hung on large curtain rings. Door at one wing should represent front door; back wall should have a closet door.
Lighting: No special effects.
Sound: Doorbell and telephone rings.

A CHRISTMAS PROMISE

Characters: 3 male; 3 female.
Playing Time: 25 minutes
Costumes: Modern, everyday dress for all.
Properties: Tuxedo on hanger, white evening gown and sewing basket, packages in Christmas wrappings, brightly-colored shirt, compact, bracelet, perfume atomizer, and suit box containing Santa Claus outfit.
Setting: The Collins living room, decorated for Christmas with a lighted tree, Christmas cards, wreaths, etc. The room is furnished with a sofa, several easy chairs, and telephone on small table. Exits are left and right, leading to front door and to rest of house. At rise, Mrs. Spencer's coat is on a chair.

Lighting: No special effects.
Sound: Telephone, doorbell, and car horn, as indicated in text.

A STAR IN THE WINDOW

Characters: 4 male; 3 female.
Playing Time: 30 minutes.
Costumes: Modern dress. Otto wears glasses. Alma wears large apron over her dress. Mrs. Flanagan and Mr. Baker are rather shabbily dressed, and Woman and Mr. Jones are well-dressed.
Properties: Book, purse, wallet, money.
Setting: A small neighborhood shop, decorated for Christmas. Door down right leads to street and door at left leads to living quarters in back of store. At left is counter with cash register, telephone, radio, and various items for sale. On right wall is show window, hidden from view by curtain. Upstage wall has shelves filled with books and other merchandise. At right end, on high shelves, are mirrors, one of which is tilted so it slants toward show window. In front of shelves is a table loaded with lights, tinsel, stars, and other Christmas items. Near it is an old rocking chair. Christmas trees are stacked around shop.
Lighting: Ray of light that reflects off mirror.
Music: Recording of chorus singing "The First Noel."

HAPPY CHRISTMAS TO ALL

Characters: 3 male; 3 female.
Playing Time: 20 minutes.

Costumes: Dr. Moore wears long black coat of clerical cut, spectacles, and slippers, which he later changes for shoes, adding a black overcoat and black stovepipe hat, black woolen muffler and gloves. Mrs. Moore wears dark house dress with white apron and white cap. Boys and girl wear warm winter clothes appropriate for 19th century New England. Emily wears smart period dress. Children wear nightgowns in Scene 2.
Properties: Books, quill pen, paper, tall red candle, covered basket, packages with Christmas wrapping, "turkey," black "kitten," newspaper, bowl and spoon.
Setting: The library of Dr. Moore's comfortable home in Chelsea, New York. There is an old-fashioned desk up right, covered with books. Up left is a fireplace with mantel. There is a table center and several comfortable chairs are scattered about the room. There is an armchair near fireplace with a footstool in front of it. Rugs and tables complete the furnishings. Door left leads to rest of house; door up center leads out. There is a window upstage overlooking street.
Lighting: Lights dim, as indicated in text.

WHATEVER HAPPENED TO GOOD OLD EBENEZER SCROOGE?

Characters: 2 male, 2 female; 10 male or female for TV Announcer, Investment Counselor, dwarfs, Mirror.
Playing Time: 25 minutes.
Costumes: TV Announcer and Investment Counselor wear conservative everyday dress. Scrooge wears top hat, long coat and spec-

tacles. Dwarfs wear beards, eccentric clothing, knickers, etc. Snow White, Prince, and Witch wear appropriate fairy tale costumes.
Properties: Hand mirror, papers, pen, etc. for Scrooge's desk, ledger.
Setting: Scene 1: Before Rise, TV studio with table and microphone and two chairs; After Rise, office, with desk and two chairs. Scene 2, factory, with long table and benches at left and desk and chair at right. Scene 3, same as Scene 2.
Lighting: Lights dim, as indicated in text.
Sound: Offstage voice, jingling bells.

SANTA CLAUS IS TWINS

Characters: 4 male; 5 female; optional extra parents and children.
Playing Time: 25 minutes.
Costumes: Modern, everyday dress. Mack wears a turtleneck sweater of a striking design. He and Freddy put on Santa Claus costumes; Freddy's is old and battered-looking. Perkins wears a police uniform.
Properties: Book on desk, appointment book, Polaroid camera with flash bulb, photograph, frame, string of lights, small fir tree, two suitboxes with Santa suits and bells; purse and money for Mrs. Sheldon; box of lollipops.
Setting: The recreation room in Donna's home. The back walls may be covered with curtains. A door right leads outside; door left leads to the rest of the house. A desk, telephone and chair are down left, a sofa with coffee table is at left center; a stepladder stands behind the sofa, a high-backed chair is up right. There is a decorated folding screen at right of sofa. There are

some chairs against wall at extreme left. On the upstage wall is a sign reading TOYS FOR TOTS, and another above it reading OUR CLUB PROJECT. Beside it is a sign reading HAVE YOUR CHILD'S PICTURE TAKEN WITH SANTA CLAUS.
Lighting: No special effects.
Sound: Telephone, as indicated in text.

THE NORTH POLE COMPUTER CAPER

Characters: 2 male; 1 female; 3 male or female for Elves; 1 male or female voice for Kumquat.
Playing Time: 25 minutes.
Costumes: Santa and Elves, traditional costumes; Mrs. Santa, dress and apron; Santa, Jr., sequin-covered western outfit with hat and boots.
Properties: Letters; sewing basket containing tape measure; stamp pad; guitar; roll of adding machine paper; computer on rolling table (may be small portable TV and cardboard mockup of keyboard. Actor playing "Kumquat" may speak his lines offstage, through microphone hooked up to small speaker on computer table); computer disk; big can of wax; 3 fishing poles; red bandanna and cowboy hat; tray of cocoa and brownies; computer printout paper; Santa hat.
Setting: Santa's living room at North Pole. Desk is left of center; armchair and small end table are right of center. A large day-by-day calendar is on upstage wall. Exit up center leads outside. Exit up left, to workshop. Exit up right, to kitchen.
Lighting and Sound: No special effects.

WE INTERRUPT THIS PROGRAM . . .

Characters: 10 male; 3 female; 19 male or female for Cameramen, Scientists, Computer Technician, Assistant, Elves, and Children; as many as desired for Carolers.

Playing Time: 25 minutes.

Costumes: Master of Ceremonies and Pianist wear school clothes. J. Holly Barberry wears suit with green or red tie, spectacles. Ivy Green has on a red and green pants suit or dress. Two Grenadiers, General Revel, and Two Aides wear uniforms (red if possible) and hats with silver or gold plumes. General Revel has gold epaulettes and Two Aides wear green sashes. Three Scientists, Computer Technician and Assistant wear white lab coats, red or green ties (if boys) or red and green scarves (if girls). Bulletin Boy wears shirt, vest, and trousers, and a green eye shade. Two Elves wear red and green motley and pointed shoes. Santa Claus wears traditional costume. Mrs. Santa Claus wears a red gown, with a mobcap, white wig, spectacles, and a white shawl. Carolers wear outdoor winter clothes. Children of the World have appropriate traditional costumes, or wear school clothes. They carry national flags.

Properties: News bulletins, neck microphones, hand microphone, television camera, small Christmas tree, sky charts, red and green telephones, news desk, chairs, banner reading YOUR HOLIDAY STATION—N-O-E-L, signs reading PRIVATE—TOP SECRET AND OPERATION YULE-WATCH, swords, test tube, beaker, earphones, microscope, data sheets, music rack, punch-out cards, bubble gum wrapper, benches, international flags, sack, wrapped gifts, nightcap, shoe tree.

Setting: Scene 1, television station—broadcast news desk, decorated with small Christmas tree and a banner reading YOUR HOLIDAY STATION—N-O-E-L; space laboratories—a computer bank and console up center. Tables and chairs left and right. Sky charts on the walls. Door at left, labeled PRIVATE—TOP SECRET. Scene 2, North Pole—backdrop of Santa's Workshop with northern lights in background. Left and right are tall Christmas trees festooned with snow. There are benches left and right.

Lighting: Flashbulb set off to produce flash of light when rocket lands, as indicated in text.

LONG LIVE CHRISTMAS

Characters: 13 male, 6 female; 13 male or female for Pages and Spirits of Christmas; male and female extras for townspeople.

Playing Time: 25 minutes.

Costumes: Grandfather Lorenz, Peter, and Barbara wear modern clothes. People of Camerovia wear simple peasant costumes. Bert wears sandwich board, which reads STEW BEEF on one side, and CHRISTMAS TURKEYS on the other. Pages, Chamberlain, and King wear court costumes; King is dressed in lavish robe and wears crown. Christmas Fairy wears white costume and carries wand. Fun is dressed as a jester and carries jester's stick and bells; Childhood carries large colored ball; other spirits are colorfully dressed and carry wands. Each spirit wears ribbon with his name on it.

Properties: Large scrolls wound on sticks reading THIS IS THE KING-

DOM OF CAMEROVIA and CHRIST-
MAS EVE IN CAMEROVIA; Christmas
wreathes and decorations; small
package and large pile of brightly
wrapped packages; long list; trumpets; small tray; scroll; mop, pail,
bulky brown packages; newspaper.
Setting: A public square. Stage is
bare, except for an arch up center
and benches at left and far right.
Lighting: Spotlight, stage lights fad-
ing as indicated in text.
Sound: Christmas music as indicated
in text; sound of trumpets.

RANDY THE RED-HORNED
RAINMOOSE

Characters: 18 male or female.
Playing Time: 20 minutes.
Costumes: Randy wears moose costume. His bright red antlers are
covered with green felt (or similar
material resembling moss) until the
end of play—actor playing Randy
must be able to remove material
quickly and easily. Hustle, Bustle,
Fred, and Tissue Elf wear brown
tights, green jerkins with wide
belts, and elf caps. Weather Elf has
three costumes: bright Hawaiian
shirt, shorts, sandals, and straw
hat, with beach towel draped over
his shoulder and bottle of suntan
lotion in his pocket; raincoat, rain
hat, galoshes, and umbrella; ski
jacket, ski cap, snow boots, mittens, and earmuffs. Santa wears
traditional costume. Rudolph and
the reindeer wear reindeer suits
with antlers and brown face
makeup. Rudolph has red nose.
Properties: Broom, two clipboards,
long sheets of computer paper,
wagon with small garbage can in it,
several boxes of tissue, can of soda.
Setting: Santa's workshop. There is a
workbench covered with tools,

boxes, and wrapping paper. Large
can reading SLEIGH WAX and tool
chest holding screwdriver, flashlight, pliers, large battery, and jar
labeled MOMMA ELF'S MAGICAL,
MULTI-PURPOSE OVEN CLEANER
AND REINDEER FLYING ELIXIR are
at rear. Sheet, three white smocks,
and three sets of white gloves are
hidden under workbench.
Lighting and Sound: No Special
effects.

CHRISTMAS AT THE CRATCHITS

Characters: 4 male; 4 female.
Playing Time: 15 minutes.
Costumes: Suggestions for costumes
can be found in any illustrated edi-
tion of *A Christmas Carol.* Bob
Cratchit should have a long white
scarf. The female characters should
wear dark, plain dresses decorated
with colored bows. Martha has a
shawl.
Properties: Long fork, plates, knives
and forks, saucepan containing
"goose and potatoes," crutch for
Tiny Tim, platter, dishes of food,
pudding, glasses and cup, jug.
Setting: The Cratchit home. On the
upstage wall at center is a large fireplace. In the fireplace is a saucepan, and on the mantel above the
fireplace are some glasses and a
jug. At center is a long table with
eight chairs, one chair at either end
and the rest of the chairs lined up
on the side near the fireplace. (A
circular table may be used.) On one
side of the fireplace is a large window, on the other, a screen. A few
Christmas decorations may be
placed around the room.
Lighting: No special effects.

SANTA'S MAGIC HAT

Puppets: 9 hand puppets. Play may
also be performed by actors, if desired.

Playing Time: 15 minutes.
Costumes: Traditional costume for Santa. Elf wears pointed hat, colorful outfit. Wizard wears decorated robe. Snow Fairy wears white, carries wand. Others wear appropriate costumes. Snow Elf and Snow Boy are dressed in white.
Properties: Christmas wrappings, box, cookie boxes, powder, sign reading CLOSED FOR THE HOLIDAYS. Santa's hat is in two parts, lightly taped together so that it comes apart easily.
Setting: Scene 1: backdrop showing living room. Scene 2: backdrop of sky with snowflakes. Scene 3: backdrop showing village square with Christmas decorations.
Lighting: No special effects.

THE CHRISTMAS DOUBTERS

Characters: 5 male; 4 female.
Playing Time: 20 minutes.
Costumes: Karen, Cheryl, and Helen wear robes. Jake, nightshirt and cap. Nick and elves, modern clothing in green and red. Harry Smithers, Santa suit and beard.
Properties: Wrapped gifts; rope; handkerchief; candy plums.
Setting: Living room, traditionally furnished and decorated for Christmas. Christmas tree with lights is left; large brick fireplace center; door right leads outside, and staircase down right leads upstairs.
Sound: Bells; Christmas music.

A CHRISTMAS CAROL

Characters: 12 male; 7 female; 5 male or female for Ghost of Christmas Past, Ghost of Christmas Present, Ghost of Christmas Yet to Come,

Fiddler and Collector; as many male and female extras as desired for Carolers.
Playing Time: 30 minutes.
Costumes: Nineteenth-century dress. Cratchits' clothing is plain and threadbare. Marley's Ghost is haggard and sickly, wrapped in chains that drag behind him; cash boxes, keys, and ledgers hang from chains. Ghost of Christmas Past is youthful, white tunic with gold belt, shining crown and carries holly branch. Ghost of Christmas Present is dressed in simple, deep green robe, with antique scabbard around waist, and holly wreath with icicles hanging from it, carries horn of plenty torch. Ghost of Christmas Yet to Come wears black robe that hides his face.
Properties: Ledgers, ruler, 2 pen-and-ink stands, 2 candles, metal cash box containing coins and roll of bank notes; coal hod and shovel; notebook; calling card; pocket watch; chains weighted with cash boxes, keys, padlocks and ledgers; branch of holly; small Christmas tree on stand; holly wreath; fiddle and bow; ring; torch shaped like horn of plenty, holding glitter; plates, cutlery, mugs and glasses, goose on platter, carving knife, covered vegetable dishes; mantel clock; crutch; punch bowl and ladle; sewing basket and sewing; book.
Setting: Scene 1: The business office of Scrooge and Marley, in London. In right wall is door that opens to the street. Upstage of the door there is a clothes tree, holding two hats, muffler, and greatcoat. At center is flat-topped desk for Scrooge, with a stool behind it. Bob Cratchit's high clerk's desk and stool are set against the left wall. Each desk has pen and ink-stand, ledger, and lighted candle on it, and

Scrooge's desk also has metal cash box with money in it, and ruler. A casement window is downstage of clerk's desk, and pot-bellied stove is upstage between two desks. Coal hod and shovel are beside stove. Scene 2: This scene is played before the curtain. School desk and bench are center, representing schoolroom, then moved to right stage, to represent Fezziwig's warehouse. Scene 3: The kitchen of the Cratchit home. Setting is the same as Scene 1, except that office window frame down left has been removed to make an exit. Fireplace is left stage. At center is large table covered with red-checked tablecloth, plates, glasses, etc. Chairs and stools for eight are placed around the table. Scenes 4 and 5, same as Scene 1.
Lighting: Candle flickers; spotlights dim down and come up; blackout, as indicated in text.
Sound: Bell striking; whistling of wind; live or recorded fiddle music; church bells; live or recorded Christmas carols.

SHERLOCK HOLMES' CHRISTMAS GOOSE

Characters: 6 male.
Playing Time: 25 minutes.
Costumes: Typical 19th century English dress. Watson wears overcoat and hat when he first enters; Peterson, Baker, Breckinridge and Ryder are dressed for winter.
Properties: Large blue stone; large shopping basket; money; paper.
Setting: Study/living room. Up center is large sofa. Up right of it is library table covered with papers and books. Down right and left of sofa are chairs. Down left is small

table on which sit a large magnifying glass and large hat. Exits down right and left.
Lighting: Lights come up in Scene 2.
Sound: Christmas music.

LITTLE COSETTE AND FATHER CHRISTMAS

Characters: 9 male; 7 female; male and female extras for Villagers and Children.
Playing Time: 30 minutes.
Costumes: Cosette wears thin, ragged dress, wooden shoes, and apron. Henri and Madame Thenardier, Boulatruelle, Two Peddlers, Wagoner, Villagers, and Children wear ordinary work clothes appropriate to the period. Ponine and Zelma wear bright, ruffled dresses. Schoolmaster has a worn, dark suit; Gypsy Fortune Teller, Juggler, Toy Vendor, and Candy Seller wear gaily-colored costumes. Clown has ruffled top and pantaloons; pantaloons have two pockets on one side, as indicated in text. Valjean wears torn yellow coat and old fur cap, and carries a knapsack.
Properties: Colored balls, bowl, deck of cards, rag doll, coins, water bucket, small coin purse and coins for Valjean, glasses, bottle, knitting needles and yarn, lead sword and kerchief, stuffed kitten, Princess doll, box, bank notes.
Setting: Public room of Thenardier Inn. Up right is a window. Counter, holding small wine cask and bread box, runs along back wall and serves as bar. Upstage of door down left is fireplace with leg of mutton roasting over fire on a spit. Pot of soup is hanging on crane. Near the hearth are stool and a

water bucket. Table with three chairs is right center, another table with chairs is up left center. Bottles of wine and glasses are on table. Scene 2, Before Rise: Main street of the village. Two open-air stalls are at right: a candy booth, and a toy booth. Lighted paper lanterns are strung overhead. Large doll with coronet on its head stands on counter of toy booth. A placard reads: GENUINE PRINCESS DOLL. Signpost at left, pointing off, reads: TO THE SPRING.

CHRISTMAS BOOK

© THE BAKER & TAYLOR CO.